"To govern democratically requ[...]
interests. Throgmorton deftly br[...]
balances that must be negotiated so that cities can be effectively and justly governed. *Co-Crafting the Just City* is an impressive capstone to a career spent exploring the many pathways to the practices of progressive and democratic change."

Robert A. Beauregard, *Professor Emeritus,*
Columbia University, USA

"This insightful and complex account reveals how Jim Throgmorton struggled with class and economic inequalities, and with racial and cultural politics too, to craft a more inclusive, resilient and just city."

John Forester, *Professor,*
Cornell University, USA

"This book provides a much needed insiders' view in political decision-making in a relatively small American city. The fine-grained story illustrates how a mayor with a planning background was instrumental in crafting the city's future for the benefit of ordinary citizens."

Louis Albrechts, *Emeritus Professor of Planning,*
University of Leuven, Belgium

"This is a really valuable record, not just of the life of a Councillor and Mayor, but of the mechanics and dynamics of small town city government in the US. Throgmorton shows through his experience how cities are constructed through multiple webs of relations, and highlights the importance of building relationships and networks if new ideas and ways of working are to become established practices."

Patsy Healey, *Emeritus Professor of Planning,*
Newcastle University, UK

CO-CRAFTING THE JUST CITY

The 2016 election in Iowa City would provide an opportunity that planning faculty have long desired: the opportunity for one of their own to serve as mayor.

In this new book, former Iowa City Mayor and Professor Emeritus James A. Throgmorton provides readers a sense of what democratically elected city council members and mayors in the United States do and what it feels like to occupy and enact those roles. He does so by telling a set of "practice stories" focusing primarily, but not exclusively, on what he, a retired planning professor at the University of Iowa, experienced and learned as a council member from 2012 through 2019 and, simultaneously, as mayor from 2016 through 2019. The book proposes a practical, action-oriented theory about how city futures are being (and can be) shaped, showing that storytelling of various kinds plays a very important but poorly understood role in the co-crafting process, and demonstrating that skillful use of ethically sound persuasive storytelling (especially by mayors) can improve our collective capacity to create better places. The book documents efforts to alleviate race-related inequities, increase the supply of affordable housing, adopt an ambitious climate action plan, improve relationships between city government and diverse marginalized communities, pursue more inclusive and sustainable land development codes/policies, and more.

It will be of great interest to urban planning faculty and students and elected officials looking to collaboratively craft better cities for the future.

James A. Throgmorton is Emeritus Professor, School of Planning and Public Affairs, The University of Iowa. He served on the Iowa City Council from 2012 through 2019 and was elected Mayor in 2016.

CO-CRAFTING THE JUST CITY

Tales from the Field by a Planning Scholar Turned Mayor

James A. Throgmorton

Mary,
I have been deeply
inspired for years watching
you pour your heart and
intellect into improving state
policy for the people of Iowa.
Bless you! Thank you!

Jim

Routledge
Taylor & Francis Group

NEW YORK AND LONDON

Cover image: Jack Brooks

First published 2022
by Routledge
605 Third Avenue, New York, NY 10158

and by Routledge
4 Park Square, Milton Park, Abingdon, Oxon OX14 4RN

Routledge is an imprint of the Taylor & Francis Group, an informa business

© 2022 James A. Throgmorton

Library of Congress Cataloging-in-Publication Data
A catalog record for this title has been requested

ISBN: 978-0-367-75105-0 (hbk)
ISBN: 978-0-367-75104-3 (pbk)
ISBN: 978-1-003-16099-1 (ebk)

DOI: 10.4324/9781003160991

Typeset in Bembo
by codeMantra

CONTENTS

FIGURES

ACKNOWLEDGMENTS

This book is the product of years of dialogue and engagement with a large number of people. Some of those people are scholars. Others are professionals of one kind or another. But most are people I have been living with for almost four decades. So, let me begin by thanking the people of Iowa City. Without their support, I would never have had the opportunity to serve as a city council member for slightly over 10 years and as mayor during the last 4 of those years. Among them are particular individuals whose timely support, advice, or assistance proved especially valuable. At the risk of omitting dozens of other people, those individuals include Donald Baxter, Dick Dorzweiler, Charlie Eastham, Mary Gravitt, Henri Harper, Diana Harris, Marcela Hurtado, Eric Johnson, Feather Lacy, Dan Lechay, Derek Maurer, Jean-Paul Mugamuzi, Harry Olmstead, Royceann Porter, Misty Rebik, Fatima Saeed, Sally Scott, Libby Shannon, Min Dong Throgmorton, and Orville Townsend. Friday afternoon conversations with a group of friends I think of as "the philosophers" also proved invaluable. Their camaraderie nurtured my soul when political conflicts became too intense. So, cheers to Scott Samuelson, David Depew, Rob Ketterer, David Hingstman, and all the other philosophers.

Likewise, I want to thank city council members, key staff, and other employees in Iowa City government. As the council members know well, serving as an elected official in the present context can feel very difficult and stressful. Probably the hardest part of the job is engaging people whose values, knowledge, and opinions differ from one's own. Consequently, working with my fellow council members taught me that resolving conflicts and crafting better cities require democratic governance which is both skillful and compassionate; one must treat the people with whom one conflicts as adversaries and not as enemies. Working with city staff also enabled me to see more clearly how crafting better cities requires good governance that extends all the way down to the street level.

Straying beyond the boundaries of Iowa City government, I want to direct my thanks to a diverse mix of scholars. Special thanks go to Professors Louis Albrechts, Robert Beauregard, John Forester, Patsy Healey, Lucie Laurian, and Scott Samuelson, and to former city council member Karen Kubby for reading drafts of the manuscript and providing important suggestions about how to improve it. Their constructive comments enabled this book to be far better than it would otherwise have been. Likewise, I thank David Depew and Wes Grooms for providing constructive feedback on very early partial drafts of the manuscript. Thanks go as well to Professor Bish Sanyal and visiting Fulbright scholars at the Massachusetts Institute of Technology and, separately, to Professor Lisa Björkman at the University of Louisville's Department of Urban and Public Affairs for inviting me to present my preliminary thoughts about what I had learned by serving as a council member and mayor. Thanks also go to Miriam Gilbert and other emeriti faculty at the University of Iowa for engaging me in a Zoom dialogue about what I had learned. Another special thank you goes to Professor Raine Mantysalo and his colleagues at Aalto University who invited me to make a keynote presentation to faculty, students, and practitioners in Helsinki, Finland. Thanks go as well to scholars who attended my presentations during the 2015 and 2017 conferences of the Association of European Schools of Planning and during the 2019 conference of the Association of Collegiate Schools of Planning. Additional thanks also go to Professor Barbara Buchenau, Jens Martin, Maria Sulimma, and other scholars affiliated with the "Scripts for Postindustrial Urban Futures" research group at University of Duisburg-Essen, and to faculty and students in Iowa State University's Interdisciplinary Program in Sustainable Environments. I also appreciate the timely and helpful editorial advice Kathryn Schell and Sean Speers at Routledge Press provided as I was preparing the book for publication. And I give a special thanks to my wife and colleague, Barbara Eckstein, for being a constructive interlocutor and critic, not to mention for being a calm sounding board when I returned home ranting after one of my many late-night city council meetings. Last, I want to dedicate this book to my sons, Patrick and Paul Throgmorton, and especially to my step-daughter, Zoë Eckstein, and my two granddaughters, Madeline Jade and Isabel Helena Throgmorton. The quality of their futures depends in large part of on the quality of our actions in the present.

Portions of this book (especially Chapter 4) draw extensively from the following article: Throgmorton, J. A. (2020), "Storytelling and city crafting in a contested age: One mayor's practice story" in Albrechts, L. (ed.), *Planners in Politics: Do They Make a Difference?* Edward Elgar, Cheltenham (UK), pp. 174–197. © Louis Albrechts 2020. The material is adapted with permission of the Licensor through PLSclear Reference Number 47515.

This book is derived, in part, from an article published in *Planning Theory & Practice*, 22:3, 495–502. © Taylor & Francis, available online at: www.tandfonline.com/doi10.1080/14649357.1921972

1

INTRODUCTION

City Crafting in a Contested Age

This book is about crafting city futures in a contested age. It conveys a former mayor's story about how the residents and elected leaders of one city in the Midwest of the United States tried, from 2012 through 2019, to craft their city's future while being immersed in a complex, emotionally charged, and politically contentious flow of action. And it seeks to stimulate creative thought, research, and action about how the crafting of city futures can be improved.

At least since the horrific events of September 11, 2001, those of us who live in the U.S. have found ourselves living in an increasingly turbulent and contested age. As one disaster has followed another, we have grown increasingly conflicted over immigration, abortion and same-sex marriage, racial justice and police–community relations, global climate change and the threat of species extinction, economic globalization coupled with extreme inequality in income and wealth, and, in the deep background, techno-biological threats associated with computerization, biotechnology, robotics, and nanotechnology.[1]

Conflicts over these issues have both contributed to and been caused by growing distrust of government, skepticism about scientific expertise, distrust of mainstream news media, manipulation of social media, and more. The familiar world seems to be collapsing all around us, and it is not at all clear whether contemporary politics and practices of governance are capable of responding successfully.

In light of these conflicts, we U.S. Americans have found ourselves increasingly divided by at least three divergent visions for our country's future. One argues we should live in a country guided by neoliberal globalism and marked by multiculturalism and free trade. Another imagines a country based on social-conservative morality and libertarian economics in the service of ethno-nationalism. And a third envisions people living in a socially progressive

DOI: 10.4324/9781003160991-1

and environmentally sustainable country guided by democratic governance. As this book will show, the first empowers the few, marginalizes the many, and thereby undermines democracy. The second explicitly seeks to replace democracy with a more authoritarian style of governance. The third requires and nurtures a democratic form of governance which is skillful but also inclusive and compassionate.

While the public typically focuses on how those polarized conflicts and divergent visions affect national politics, cities are key sites in which the conflicts are enacted. The future of our country and the future of our cities are deeply intertwined. Roughly 82 percent of Americans live in urbanized areas, and at least 39 percent live in cities with populations of 50,000 or more residents (Toukabri and Medina, 2021). The cities in which they live are places where local governments and their elected leaders have to produce real solutions to real problems. But cities are also places in which polarized conflicts and wicked problems become manifest on the ground and have to be addressed in local government meetings, often in ways that are more direct and democratic than is possible at the national level.[2] We need new ideas about how to guide the transformation, or what I will call the unfolding, of American cities and about how to create better places for all their residents in the face of the profoundly difficult problems and conflicts we face.

However, public understanding of what cities are, how city governments work, what local elected officials can do, and what might happen when constituents and their elected representatives try to change the policies of their city governments is surprisingly thin. Real flesh-and-blood people, whether residents or elected officials, need help in order to create better places. This leads me to pose a question which lies at the heart of this book: *how can the real flesh-and-blood residents and elected leaders of a city, using democratic processes of governance, craft their city's future while being immersed in a complex, emotionally charged, and often politically contentious flow of action?*

With this question in mind, this book tells a story about how people in one relatively small Midwestern American city tried to guide the future unfolding of their place. I narrate this story as a retired professor of urban planning who served as a city council member from 2012 through 2019 and, simultaneously, as mayor from 2016 through 2019. By providing a fine-grained tale about what happened in one city during those years, I offer readers a ringside seat from which they can (1) gain a better understanding of the kinds of problems we U.S. city residents face and (2) learn what cities and local elected officials can and cannot do to address those problems in a democracy. I hope as well to help readers discover ways by which, using democratic processes of governance—which include conflict, persuasion, negotiation, compromise, inclusion, and transparency—we can imagine and enact better ways of (1) addressing those problems, (2) guiding the transformation of American cities, and (3) creating better places for all city residents.

Insofar as this book focuses on the transformation, unfolding, and future of cities, urban planners have a critical role to play. They often serve quite ably in local governments, but they (and the scholars who study and theorize what planners do) rarely govern. Consequently, planners and scholars of planning often acknowledge but do not understand the critical role that elected officials play in crafting their cities' futures. I hope in this book to enhance planners' understanding of what elected officials actually do and thereby enhance their mutual ability to guide the step-by-step unfolding of their cities.

Aims of the Book

I have four specific aims. *First, this book intends to give readers a sense of what democratically elected city council members and mayors in the United States do and what it feels like to occupy and enact those roles.* The book does so by telling a set of "practice stories" (Forester, 1999) focusing primarily, but not exclusively, on what I experienced and learned as a council member from 2012 through 2019 and, simultaneously, as mayor from 2016 through 2019 in Iowa City, Iowa. I narrate these practice stories from a first-person singular point of view, which necessarily focuses attention on what I witnessed, thought, felt, and did.[3]

Second, this book seeks to document what happened when council allies and I tried, during my term as mayor from 2016 through 2019, to lead our relatively small Midwestern city toward becoming a more inclusive, just, and sustainable place.[4] My sense is that there is a big difference between being a mayor who wants to keep her or his city on its current path versus mayors who seek to alter the direction of their cities' step-by-step unfolding. When I was mayor in Iowa City, the vision of fostering a more inclusive, just, and sustainable city acted as my "north star," and, to move in that direction, we took actions to reduce race-related inequities, increase the supply of affordable housing, adopt an ambitious climate action plan, improve relationships between city government and diverse marginalized communities, pursue more inclusive and sustainable land development codes/policies, and more. These efforts involved engaging in, and sometimes ameliorating, conflicts with (1) members of the local/regional "growth machine";[5] (2) libertarians, white supremacists, Christian fundamentalists, and ethno-nationalists allied, at that time, with the president of the United States; and (3) progressive allies of ours who demanded immediate action on their priorities while displaying little concern about legal constraints or spillover effects on related issues.

Third, this book endeavors to help readers understand what it feels like to be an urban planning scholar serving as a council member and mayor, and to share lessons I learned with other scholars, especially those who focus on planning theory. Inevitably, all local elected officials draw upon their own unique background and experiences when serving as a council member or mayor; however, it is relatively rare for professors to serve in those positions. Even more rarely does one find urban planning scholars occupying them.[6]

Fourth, the book offers a practical, action-oriented set of ideas about how city futures are being (and can be) shaped. These ideas emerged primarily during the first 4 years of my council term and guided much of how I performed the role of mayor during the subsequent 4 years. The set of ideas begins with a simple premise: to get to the future city, one has to continually start from the here and now.[7] And it presumes that action (what really gets done) is more important than formal plans about what should be done. As is discussed in slightly greater detail near the end of this introduction, my initial thoughts about cities, the key issues pertaining to them, and how their futures can and should be crafted were based on decades of research, writing, traveling, and conversing with urban planning scholars around the world. That background shaped what I was thinking when I joined my city's council in 2012. From that point on, I encountered novel situations and challenges, learned through experience, and refined my thinking about how cities change and the ways in which elected officials can guide the direction of that change. Although reading the work of planning scholars had to take a back seat while I was in office, I see now that some of my ideas share many similarities with recent scholarly literature pertaining to urban theory and the complexity of urban governance, such as Gerald Frug and David Barron's (2011) *City Bound*, Bruce Katz and Jeremy Nowak's (2017) *The New Localism*, Richard Schragger's (2016) *City Power*, and Michael Batty's (2018) *Inventing Future Cities*. I discuss the relationship between their work and mine in the concluding chapter. For now, I simply want to briefly outline the set of ideas that initially guided my work as mayor.

Cities and City Crafting

According to the editors of *Encyclopedia of the City*, "the term 'city' means anything and everything," and a city "is indeed a complex organism" (Caves, 2005, p. xxviii). If you are an economist, for example, you might characterize it as a large, complex, input–output device. But, if you are a sociologist, you might understand the city to be a state of mind, a body of customs, and traditions, a theater of social action, and so on. If you are a legal scholar or a practicing elected official, you would be more inclined to define the city as a territorially bounded municipal corporation that has the legal right to undertake a variety of actions on behalf of the residents of the city (Frug, 1999; Frug and Barron, 2011). It typically has a chief executive (usually called "mayor"), a legislative body consisting of elected representatives of the citizens (usually called a "council" or "board of aldermen"), and other officers having special functions.

But cities are more than territorially bounded municipal corporations.[8] In what follows, I will frequently refer to them as what urbanist Jane Jacobs (1961) called "problems in organized complexity"; that is, as "organisms that are replete with unexamined but obviously intricately interconnected, and surely understandable, relationships" (pp. 438–439).[9] In addition to being extraordinarily complex internally, individual cities are typically embedded in regions consisting of multiple (sometimes hundreds or more) overlapping governmental jurisdictions. Moreover, cities draw various networks (e.g., electric power) and flows (e.g., water) together into specific buildings, neighborhoods, and the city, with the networks and flows extending far beyond the legal territorial limits of the city. In this sense, cities can be thought of as nodes in a *global-scale web*, a web that consists of a fluid and constantly changing set of relationships. These relationships can in turn be defined as links between nodes, as paths through which people, goods, services, energy, capital, information, and other social exchanges flow (Throgmorton, 2005a).

No two cities are alike; they vary considerably in history, size, population, landscape, economy, and many other important ways. Some are very large, whereas the rest are considerably smaller. Some have been declining economically; others have been booming. Some have relatively homogeneous populations, whereas others are quite diverse. Some are severely threatened by specific environmental risks and hazards that are irrelevant to other places. Some are "blue" (Democratic) cities in "blue" states, whereas others are "red" (Republican) in "red," and still other are either red in blue or blue in red. And so on. Located in the middle of the United States and in the east-central part of Iowa, Iowa City has about 76,000 residents. The city has been growing fairly rapidly, has become increasingly diverse demographically, is a "blue" city in a "red" state, and has experienced two very costly floods in the past 20 years.[10] Although it is relatively small, Iowa City is the sixth largest city in Iowa, the second largest city in the Cedar Rapids–Iowa City region, and the home of the University of Iowa.[11] Two smaller but rapidly growing cities and several smaller towns are located immediately nearby (see Figure 1.1). Most of those smaller cities and towns are, like Iowa City, located in Johnson County and within the Iowa City Community School District, which serves kindergarten through 12th grade students throughout most, but not all, of the city region.

Cities also differ in terms of institutional structure, regulatory codes, and practices. In the United States, they vary in institutional structure primarily because they derive all their powers from the individual state. In some states, local governments can do only that which states explicitly permit them to do. In other states, some cities are granted "Home Rule" authority; that is, they can govern themselves within constraints established by their state governments. Home rule status notwithstanding, states can "preempt" local governments' authority to act on particular issues. Moreover, in the U.S., the role of the mayor varies from city to city. Some cities have a "strong mayor" form of government in which the mayor pretty much runs the show. Such a mayor typically has the power to appoint and replace key department heads and to veto ordinances passed by a majority of the city's legislative body. Other cities, Iowa City included, have a "council/manager" form of government.

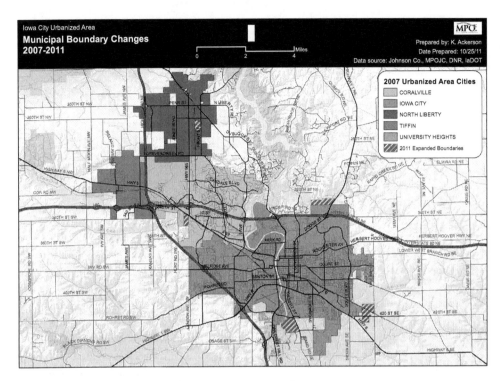

FIGURE 1.1 Map of key governmental jurisdictions in the Iowa City area.
Source: Metropolitan Planning Organization of Johnson County, 2012, p. 27.

In Iowa City's case, candidates for city council seek election on a nonpartisan basis (that is, they do not publicly campaign as members of any political party). The elected council formally sets policy, makes authoritative decisions for the City, and appoints a city manager, the city clerk, and the city attorney.[12] The city manager appoints department heads and, through the technical staff, executes the council's policies, plans, and codes, while also recommending possible actions to the council. In brief, the city manager runs the day-to-day operations. Iowa City's Charter stipulates that the seven-member council elect from its members a mayor for a 2-year term. The Charter also specifies that the mayor runs the meetings, but also votes as one of the seven members of the council and does not have veto power. The council is divided into three geographically based district seats and four "at-large" seats representing the city as a whole.

Given the variability among cities, mayors differ in what they value and how willing they are to promote fundamental changes in their city's structure, policies, and practices. To the extent I could (given constraints on the powers of a mayor in my city), I tried to lead my city toward becoming more inclusive, just, and sustainable. But such efforts raise a crucial question: is it possible to guide the direction in which such "problems in organized complexity" will change over time?

One answer comes from my own discipline of urban and regional planning. As John Friedmann's (1987) magisterial *Planning in the Public Domain* amply documents, urban planning grew out of the presumption that experts can and should guide the transformation of entire cities, regions, and national economies. From its earliest days, therefore, the profession of urban planning has had a normative mission: to improve the quality of cities and the lives of people who live within them. Consequently, people trained as urban planners have always sought to imagine better futures, convey their visions in persuasive ways, and help bring those imagined futures to life. This normative mission sets urban planning apart from most other academic disciplines. Like scholars in other disciplines, we seek to advance the state of knowledge within our discipline, but, for us, producing new knowledge is not sufficient. We must somehow translate that knowledge into action.

Consequently, scholars at schools of urban planning and policy also have a practical and immediate task: they must teach graduate students how to become effective practitioners. Those practitioners work on a wide range of topics (such as transportation, housing, economic development, environmental health, and more) for a wide range of public, private, and non-profit organizations at scales ranging from the neighborhood to the city, the region, the state, the nation, and beyond. For these urban planners, converting knowledge into action requires having a detailed understanding of the contexts in which their knowledge might be applied.

This has engendered a subfield within planning that we scholars call "planning theory." Research by these planning theorists has amply documented that planning requires high-quality research and analysis. But it has also documented that planning practitioners must not only have substantive *knowledge* and expertise, but also, at least within viable democracies, be able to *engage* with diverse publics, *prescribe* what should be done, and *influence* those who must act in order for the planners' plans and recommendations to be implemented (Beauregard, 2020). Oddly missing from this body of research, however, is inquiry into how elected officials in specific locations affect the conditions within which planners work and thereby help guide the transformation of their cities over time. Consequently, very few planning scholars know what it is like to be a local elected official.

As one who served as an elected council member in the mid-1990s, I did have a pretty good idea of what local elected officials do. And I put that knowledge to use when I returned to Iowa City's city council in 2012. But, as an elected official, especially as mayor, I wanted to use my position to ensure planning was being used to help our city make a turn in what I thought was the right direction—that is, toward becoming a more inclusive, just, and sustainable city. But there was still much for me to learn. As a scholar of urban planning, I was especially interested in developing a better understanding of the relationships between local elected officials, professional planners of various kinds, and everyone else who has a hand in shaping how cities change. Based on my prior experience, I strongly believed that urban planning scholars had much to learn by taking a close look at how particular elected officials, especially mayors, use their positions and skills to influence the directions in which their cities change over time. I also wanted to identify the constraints and limitations under which elected officials and professional planners operate. What else influences the direction a city unfolds?

As Chapter 2 documents, I began thinking, during my first 4-year term as a council member, that human and non-human forces *co-craft the step-by-step unfolding of cities*.[13] By co-crafting, I mean interactions that cause a city to "unfold" (Alexander, 2002–2004; Pierson, 2004)—that is, to produce real outcomes in physical design and social relationships at the street level.[14] In this context, multiple actors (elected officials, professional staff, business people, nongovernmental organizations, and others) interact on a complexly interwoven mix of topics that cut across institutional, professional, and disciplinary boundaries. Planning of various types is part of this co-crafting process. *However, plans mean very little until people act.* Like political philosopher Hannah Arendt (1958), I believe that a meaningful life is found by acting in the plurality of the public realm. Such actions unfold step-by-step in an ever-shifting context, with each step changing the context for subsequent actions by other actors who respond in terms of their own interests, values, and stories. Specific actors use stories and storytelling to influence the actions of others, with some storytellers getting prime-time attention and others being marginalized, trivialized, or worse. All of these actions produce effects that bleed across territorial and functional boundaries, escape the control of the initiating actors, and ultimately cause the city itself to unfold. Hurricanes, tornadoes, floods, droughts, pandemics, derechos, earthquakes, fires, famines, and other non-human forces also play crucial roles in shaping this unfolding.[15]

The Role of Storytelling in City Crafting

As is true for any storyteller, I have had to decide where to begin and end my tale. While I have opted to focus on the 8 years of my council term, one should not assume that the story literally began in the middle of 2011 and ended on the last day of December in 2019. The story I tell emerged from past actions and will continue to unfold.[16]

I try to configure events and ideas into a coherent and consequential whole. But the plot of this story is not something I simply dreamed up; rather, it emerged from the actions and conflicts that occurred during the 8-year period. I am acutely aware that one cannot tell everything that happened with regard to the overall story. Like any storyteller, I have had to be selective when choosing what to emphasize and what to omit. As Kidder and Todd (2013, p. 40) write,

> The fundamental elements of a story's structure are proportion and order. Managing proportion is the art of making some things big and other things little: of creating foreground and background; of making readers feel the relative importance of characters, events, ideas. Often this means upsetting normal expectations by finding a superficially trivial detail or moment that, on closer examination, resonates with meaning.

Unavoidably, the choices I have made reflect my values. Also, although I wrote large portions of the book well after the events transpired, I have written each of the chapters as I understood and felt the unfolding of action at the time. In other words, none of the real-life characters in the book knew what would happen next. I have tried to convey that *sense of not knowing the future* throughout the book.

When narrating this story, I have done so from a point of view: the tales I narrate highlight what I saw, heard, did, and experienced.[17] This has non-trivial consequences. Drawing upon recent research in psychological and brain sciences, writer Will Storr (2019) argues that "the world we experience 'out there' is actually a *reconstruction* of reality that is built *inside* our heads" (p. 21). Consequently, each of us has a partial, and therefore flawed, perception of ourselves and our surroundings. This, in turn, affects our behavior and memory and produces "a coherent tale that tells us who we are, why we're doing what we're doing and feeling what we're feeling" (p. 109). It also leaves us blind to our flaws and our limited perceptions of the world. Given this, I cannot claim my practice stories contain no factual errors; however, I do claim my stories are *truthful* in the context of the purposes for which this book was written. Other actors in this tale surely have their own stories to tell and their own interpretations of mine.

Characters and setting also matter. I have tried to bring this story's characters to life in the readers' imagination. Because one cannot report everything one knows about another character, I have tried to provide "telling details" that grab the readers' attention (Kidder and Todd, 2013, p. 30). My sense is that the result is far from perfect, for all of the real flesh-and-blood individuals mentioned in the book are far more interesting in real life than I have been able to convey. Getting the details right without burying readers in the excruciating details of real life has been one of the biggest challenges I have faced in writing this tale.

Characters do not free-float in the ether; they need settings in which they can come to life. "Above all," Kidder and Todd (2013) advise, "a setting tells what is at issue—what a character is trying to do, what a character fears or is trying to hide, hopes to gain or stands to lose, what a character is up against" (p. 34). Readers will quickly see that most of the action and conflicts in this book take place in the city council's chambers, Emma J. Harvat Hall. It is a clean, brightly lit place in which council members (along with the city manager, city attorney, city clerk, and assistant city manager) sit in a semi-circle, slightly above and removed from, yet facing, the public audience (see Figure 1.2). A glass-and-metal railing provides a degree of separation between the council and the public, with a speaker's podium at the center facing the council. It is in this room that elected council members, technical experts, residents, business people, property owners, developers, students, and the City's critics focused their attention on matters of public concern and sought to influence the direction in which the city would unfold.

Based on my prior experience as an elected official, I knew that these and other characters would come to the council to share important facts with us; to express their concerns, desires, hopes, and anger; to make claims about what the council should do. I knew that many of them would communicate their thoughts to us by telling stories rooted in their personal experiences, and I anticipated that I would encounter characters who expressed views consistent with what Ruth Finnegan (1998) has termed "common urban narratives."[18] What I did not know was which specific kinds of stories we would hear, how deeply they would be grounded in Iowa City, how they would interact with one another on particular matters of concern, and how they would affect decisions the council made and actions the City government took.

FIGURE 1.2 Audience waiting for a council meeting to begin.
Source: Photo by the author, April 23, 2019.

Based on my prior research and experience, I also knew that the meaning of a story lies not just in the teller's intent or the written, oral, or cinematic version of the tale. It lies also in what the various audiences bring to the story. The meaning of a story is, in other words, contestable and negotiated between the teller and its many audiences.[19] Moreover, stories circulate through webs of relationships. These webs involve both face-to-face interactions (which are influenced by the spatial distribution of people by race, class, and other key socio-economic markers) and virtual interactions via communication technologies and media. Often, these stories circulate in very condensed forms as canned plot lines or repeatable formulas—for example, President Obama's "socialist" health care policy will force us to "pull the plug on Grandma." Because they are told, interpreted, and contested as they circulate through these webs, stories can stimulate a chain reaction in which each part becomes the cause of new processes with unpredictable consequences. The meaning of the story will, in other words, go well beyond the control of the original teller.

I also knew from prior research that individuals and organizations can craft stories that are intended to persuade. My sense was that persuasive storytelling can be *naïve* (that is, guileless or innocent), *intentionally manipulative*, or *ethically sound*. In the case of naïve storytelling, tellers have no real sense of how their diverse audiences might respond to the tellers' stories. If only people knew "our story," they say, people would see things the way we do and then support us and what we are doing. The second couples the emotional power of stories (Davis, 2002) with a casual disregard for facts to manipulate audiences into believing what the tellers want them to believe. And the third recognizes that the meaning of a story depends not just on the text or the author's intentions, but also on how diverse audiences interpret and respond to it (Eckstein, 2003). For tellers of ethically sound, persuasive stories, therefore, the key question becomes: *persuasive to whom and for what purposes?* Once again, I did not know how these forms of persuasive storytelling would affect actions in Iowa City.

Intended Audiences

Readers located in and around Iowa City are likely to take an interest in the book, especially those who took part in the stories I tell. I have considerable respect for all the key actors mentioned in the following chapters, especially those who served as mayors and council members. Regardless of our various disagreements, I recognize that being a council member is a demanding job, and I know they all performed their roles in ways they thought would be good for Iowa City. Likewise, I have great respect for the two people who served as city manager and the one person who served as city attorney during this 8-year period. The jobs they occupy are extremely demanding, and all three individuals performed their roles with considerable expertise and skill.

In light of my own disciplinary background, I would expect urban planning faculty and students to be one of the book's key audiences. Scholars and doctoral students who focus on planning theory would likely be interested in the ways I connect planning theorists' knowledge to the practical requirements of being a council member and mayor. Beyond urban planning, scholars and students who focus on the politics of local governments would also likely find this book to be of value. These would include scholars in urban politics and governance, urban studies, public administration and management, American politics, cultural studies, urban sociology, environmental studies, and other related disciplines. Likewise, scholars in the humanities who want to make their work more relevant to contemporary public debates might also be drawn to the book.

I hope planning professionals, mayors, council members, city managers, and other professional staff in cities would benefit from reading this book, especially if they work in cities that are comparable to Iowa City in size and governmental structure. Local elected officials who seek to alter the direction of their city's step-by-step unfolding might find the book to be especially valuable. And I hope that members of the general public who are interested in urban life, want to enhance the quality of life in cities, and are committed to democratic governance will benefit from reading the book. Among these would be anyone who is thinking about the possibility of running for elected office at the local level.

I should emphasize that this book is not a case study driven by social-scientific theory and hypotheses. It is a story which seeks to convey what it feels like to act without knowing what the future will bring. With this in mind, I invite readers to imagine that they are witnessing this unfolding from a ringside seat, being privy to what I was thinking as I participated in the action, and engaging in dialogue with me as the action proceeds. Being engaged in dialogue, readers will probably find themselves wanting to ask many questions—for example: How did your background as a planning scholar influence the actions you took? Did your fellow council members and the City staff value your technical knowledge, your analytical or design skills, your theoretical insights into the importance of how problems are defined? When you disagreed with other council members, did you try to negotiate with them? Upon reflection, knowing what you know now, would you have acted differently? And readers might ask: What would I (the reader) have done if I had been in the council person's/mayor's shoes? Many such questions will arise. I ask readers to be patient and be friendly but constructive interlocutors as the story unfolds, for they are likely to find many of their questions being answered at the end of each chapter or in the conclusion to the book as a whole.

The Point of View from Which I Write[20]

In their outstanding advice to would-be authors of creative non-fiction, Kidder and Todd (2013) write, "Many selves compete inside. … Finding the 'I' that can represent the pack of you is the first challenge of the memoirist" (p. 51). So, who is the "I" that writes this book? Much like the poet Walt Whitman, and much like the United States of America as a whole, I contain multitudes. I am a middle-class, 76-year-old, white man who descends, on my father's side, from a long line of English settlers who moved to western Tennessee and Kentucky early in the 1800s and, on my mother's side, from Irish and Welsh mining families who immigrated to the U.S. in the mid-1800s.[21] I have been a day laborer in construction work, a union member engaged in hard physical labor, a garbage collector, a rather mediocre undergraduate student who majored in history,[22] a company commander in a tank battalion based in Germany, a young man trying to discover himself by traversing western states, a counterman in a restaurant, a chief of air-quality monitoring in a highly polluted city, a diligent Master's student,[23] an environmental consultant for city and state governments,[24] a successful doctoral student,[25] a management scientist for a national energy laboratory,[26] a professor of urban and regional planning at a major research university, an author of many dozens of scholarly journal articles and conference papers,[27] an author or co-editor of two scholarly books,[28] an organizer or co-organizer of three scholarly symposia, an eager traveler to cities throughout Europe and the U.S., a guide for student trips to several cities in the Midwest of the U.S., a pilgrim to Santiago (Spain), a writer of dozens of guest opinions in newspapers,[29] an elected city councilman, and a mayor. I am also a husband, a father, a son, a brother, a loyal friend, a cousin to a small and dispersed brood of relatives, a stepfather to a young Chinese woman, a father-in-law to a Chinese-American woman, a grandfather to two beautiful Chinese-American girls, a former Catholic who wonders at the mystery of life and sees great value in building spiritual connections within faith-based communities, and much more.

As a professor of urban and regional planning at the University of Iowa for 24 years, I focused my teaching on the history of urban and regional planning, theories of (and in) urban planning, environmental policy and planning, sustainability, and conflict resolution. As a scholar, I initially focused my attention on the uses of rhetoric with regard to electric power planning. Gradually, this emphasis on rhetoric transformed into a claim that planning can be thought of as a form of persuasive and constitutive storytelling about the future which occurs within a web of relationships and partial truths. I understood my turn to rhetoric and persuasive storytelling to be part of a larger post-modernist or post-structuralist turn in planning and other disciplines, and I drew heavily upon the work of scholars in the humanities.[30] Although I continued my emphasis on planning as persuasive storytelling, I shifted my focus away from the electric power industry and toward planning as practiced in cities, the "New Urbanism," and the topic of sustainability.[31] In the early 2000s, my focus on cities took a "spatial turn," which led me to explore other cities, to conduct a "Storytelling and Sustainability" symposium with Barbara Eckstein,[32] and to connect my claim about persuasive storytelling to contemporary scholarship by geographers and urban theorists about global cities, the network society, transnational city regions, and the production of space (e.g., Lefevbre, 1991; Castells, 1996; Smith, 2001; Graham and Marvin, 2001; Massey, 2005). From that point on, the spatial turn in my thinking about cities, storytelling, and sustainability was deeply affected by a series of unanticipated events that began with the September 11, 2001 attack on the World Trade Center. That horrific attack was soon followed by our nation's invasion of Afghanistan in 2001 and Iraq in 2003,[33] by the virtual destruction of New Orleans in the aftermath of Hurricane Katrina in 2005, by a "500-year" flood of the Iowa and Cedar Rivers in 2008, by the financial crisis of 2007–2008 and the subsequent "Great Recession," by rising public antagonism toward "illegal aliens" in the U.S. and Europe, by British Petroleum's massive 2010 "Deepwater Horizon" oil spill in the Gulf of Mexico,[34] and by many other calamitous events, all mediated by new web-based social media such as Facebook and Twitter. In some ways, it seemed as if the whole world had been turned upside down.

Other scholars have been far more productive and influential than I, so I am very leery of claiming too much. At best, I would describe myself as a moderately productive scholar who was not afraid of stepping out of the mainstream of my discipline and inventing and applying new ways of thinking about urban planning. I consider myself very fortunate to have had an opportunity to engage in dialogue with brilliant and accomplished scholars around the world while also engaging in a different kind of dialogue with the diverse people of Iowa City.

For the purposes of this book, the most important features of this brief autobiography have to do with my continuing effort to be a fruitful scholar while also being practically engaged in the public world. When I was working for the Air Pollution Control District in Louisville, Kentucky, for example, I was also completing a Master's degree in community development and pursuing a Master's in political science. While working for an environmental consulting firm in Kansas City, Missouri, I took graduate courses in urban planning.[35] Likewise, while pursuing a doctoral degree at UCLA, I worked part time for an environmental consulting firm and, later, an architecture and urban planning firm.

While teaching urban planning at the University of Iowa, I gradually became engaged in practical action at the local level. At first, this involved serving as a city council member in the mid-1990s, but, in the 2000s, it also involved writing guest opinions for local newspapers, guiding students on a study abroad tour of several European cities, and guiding graduate students in urban planning on field trips to Minneapolis–St. Paul, Louisville, Kansas City, New Orleans, and Milwaukee. In 2007, I organized a "Planning for a Better Region" summit for policymakers in the Cedar Rapids–Iowa City region. And, early in 2010, I also co-organized and co-directed a "Media, Space, and Race" series of public rhetoric seminars responding to the increasingly racist overtones of harsh public controversy concerning Iowa City's African-American population. My opportunity to serve as a city council member in the mid-1990s exemplifies this effort to blend my scholarly work with practical action. This service, from late 1993 through 1995, while teaching full-time was intense work, which I wrote about in a 2000 article that appeared in the *Journal of the American Planning Association*. In that article, I argued that planning practice can be understood as *action in the flow of persuasive argumentation*, and that planners can best be understood not as heroic experts, but as *skilled-voices-in-the-flow*.[36]

In the middle of 2010, shortly after conducting the public rhetoric seminars, I retired from the university as an emeritus professor. Done with participating in faculty meetings! Done with teaching! And done writing scholarly articles! I was not sure what to do next. But the unfolding of history does have a way of influencing one's life, does it not? As I was trying to discover how to live as a retiree, the deteriorating political situation in the United States was sending an answer my way.

In the fall of 2010, I found myself responding to yet another dramatic event: the rise of the "Tea Party" and its successful effort to shift the national political landscape toward the far (a.k.a. "Populist") Right. This led me to write an article (Throgmorton, 2013) entitled "What Can Planning Theory Be Now?" How, this paper asked, should proponents of "interactive-communicative planning theory" respond to the rise of the Tea Party in the United States?[37] This paper began answering this question by briefly reviewing the communicative turn in planning, paying particular attention to John Forester's (1999) treatment of planning as "attention-shaping, communicative action." It then synthesized much of my own past work. This synthesis concluded that four factors of governance (the extraordinary complexity of national policy implementation, the variety of rhetorics practitioners use, the ubiquity and power of storytelling, and the increasing complexity of places and place connection) had, by the late 2000s, left many Americans feeling bewildered and outraged, wanting to blame someone for the "Great Recession" of 2007–2008. The paper then narrated a story about the Tea Party's sudden emergence in 2009–2010, highlighting five key features of the story. The final section of the paper explicitly interpreted the Tea Party's rise in relation to interactive-communicative planning theory. Consistent with Forester, this section observed that the Tea Party emerged in response to a messy, problematic situation that needed to be converted into a problem that made sense and could be acted upon. But, consistent with my own work, this section also observed that conservative organizations (which articulated and enacted a story rooted in a quasi-mythical "Founders Tale" of the United States) played a crucial role in making that conversion. Their version of this tale sought to define and control the spatial boundaries of places (at every scale, from the nation to the neighborhood) and the composition and identity of the community of people who live within them. Instead of engaging in public dialogue with people who held different views, Tea Party fundamentalists condemned efforts to promote dialogue and inclusiveness with people they considered illegitimate and lacking any right to be in America or be considered "true Americans." In my view, the way this story was being used to shape attention and define the problem revealed the political core of planning, and it suggested that planning theorists needed to articulate a coherent and persuasive *political* rationale for rejecting essentialist conceptions while also providing democratic space for both essentialist and multicultural ideas to be articulated. This political rationale would have to be articulated not just to fellow scholars in journals, but to a wide range of people in the public arena. And it would have to include a process for answering the two key questions posed by the Tea Party movement: first, who should be included within or excluded from this community, and, second, whose stories should be told, be heard, and influence the construction of the place? In other words, planning theorists needed to devise a viable process for facilitating democratic deliberation about who we (U.S. Americans) are and who we want to become.

For me, the context revealed by these events and changes also demanded an answer to a very personal question: what should I—a retired professor who had a lot of time on his hands, a great deal of practical and relevant knowledge, and a modest amount of political experience—do in response? In the spring of 2011, I began thinking very seriously about becoming a candidate for Iowa City's city council in November of that year.

Notes

1 For radically contrasting assessments of these techno-biological transformations, see Kurzweil (2005) and Wilson (2014).
2 The concept of "wicked problems" comes from Rittel and Weber (1973). A wicked problem is a social or cultural problem that is difficult or impossible to solve definitively for at least four reasons: there is no consensus on the definition of the problem to be solved or goals to be achieved, no correct answer, no objective way to determine what would be a good decision, and no stopping rule because of the interconnections among problems.
3 To a degree, this book is a memoir like former Minneapolis Mayor R. T. Rybak's (2016) *Pothole Confidential*, former Philadelphia Mayor Michael Nutter's (2017) *Mayor*, former Detroit Mayor Dennis Archer's (2017) *Let the Future Begin*, former South Bend, Indiana, Mayor Pete Buttigieg's (2019) *Shortest Way Home*, and others. But, narrated by an urban planning scholar who also served as council member in addition to being a mayor, the book also has similarities to autobiographical essays, such as those which appear in Haselsberger (2017). And, to the extent that my practice stories are narrated by a person with practical experience as a city planner, it is similar to Ken Greenberg's (2011) *Walking Home*.
4 Almost 40 years ago, urban planning scholar John Friedmann (1987) distinguished between planning oriented toward *system maintenance* and planning oriented toward *system transformation*. The distinction remains relevant today.
5 First introduced by sociologist Harvey Molotch (1976), growth machine theory maintains that growth is the essence of local politics, and that those who directly

benefit from development—landowners, developers, bankers, construction companies, etc.—are generally able to manipulate local planning processes to foster growth and increase land use intensities. They legitimate their actions by claiming that everyone benefits from growth. For details, see Molotch and Logan (1996), Logan and Molotch (1987/2007), and Jonas and Wilson (1999).

6 An important set of exceptions can be found in Louis Albrechts' (2020) edited volume, *Planners in Politics*. In it, ten executive politicians (myself included) with backgrounds in planning from around the world dissect their own political careers.

7 To succeed, mayors implicitly follow philosopher Stephen Toulmin's (1990) advice: to act wisely, we must "start *from where we are, at the time we are there*" (p. 179). For Toulmin, that means paying attention to "the oral, the particular, the local, and the timely" (p. 186). Moreover, Toulmin says, "[s]ound rhetoric demands that we speak to the condition of an audience; honest human understanding requires us to listen to their condition with equal care" (p. 199).

8 In my experience, City officials often talk about "the City" when they are actually referring to City government. This has non-trivial consequences: City officials might act as if what is good for City government is good for the city as a whole. In this book I try to distinguish between the two meanings by capitalizing City when referring to City government.

9 This characterization has important similarities with social theorist Bruno Latour's "assemblage." As urban planning scholar Robert Beauregard (2015) describes it, an assemblage exists when a network of actors (human and non-human things) have come together around a matter of common concern.

10 Between 2000 and 2010, the percentage of the city's population that was Hispanic or non-Hispanic Asian, black, or other grew from slightly over 14 to just over 20 percent (City of Iowa City, 2013).

11 The University of Iowa is a prominent public university which, in the fall of 2014, had roughly 31,000 undergraduate, professional, and graduate students. Roughly two-thirds were undergraduates. With just under 30,000 employees, the university (including its hospital and clinics) is by far the largest employer in Iowa City. For historical background about the city, see Mannsheim (1989).

12 The city clerk's diverse responsibilities orient around record-keeping. For example, the clerk's office publishes public notices, agendas for council meetings, ordinances, and minutes as required by law. The City attorney acts as chief legal counsel to the city council, city manager, and other units within or affiliated with the City.

13 My use of "crafting" derives from Sennett's (2008) *The Craftsman*. It implies that elected officials need to apply their knowledge and skills at each step in transforming new priorities into new plans and then into incentives, regulations, and investments. This blend of knowledge and skill is roughly analogous to a carpenter's skill at turning a blueprint into an addition on a house. "Co-crafting" presumes that multiple individuals and organizations affect outcomes and is, therefore, similar to related terms such as co-producing and co-creating.

14 Planning theorists will recognize some similarity between Alexander's concept of unfolding and Charles Lindblom's (1959) idea of "incrementalism" and the market's "invisible hand." However, Alexander's unfolding is guided by the pursuit of wholeness and a desire to bring greater life to the world, whereas incrementalism is mere drift, with the direction of change being the resultant of contending interests, and the "invisible hand" is narrowly focused on economic self-interest.

15 Bruno Latour labels these and other forces "actants." According to him, an actant is anything, human or not, that causes another thing to respond (Beauregard, 2020, p. 61).

16 My thinking about how to craft and tell good stories derives primarily from Burroway (1987), Davis (2002), Kidder and Todd (2013), Simons (2006), Storr (2019),

and many others, plus a large number of outstanding novels—e.g., Coetzee (1980). With regard to the uses of stories and storytelling in the social sciences and urban planning, I have been influenced by Ameel (2020), Benton (2019), Bulkens (2015), Cameron (2012), Childs (2008), Czarniawska (2004), Finnegan (1998), Flyvbjerg (1997), Forester (1999), Ivory (2013), Keskin et al. (2016), MacIntyre (1981), Mandelbaum (1991), Marris (1997), Riessman (2008), Sandercock (2003), Stoetzler and Yuval-Davis (2002), Tilly (2002), Tucker (2017), and Van Hulst (2012). My thinking about the relationship between storytelling and cities in general has also been influenced by many histories and "biographies" of cities, including: Alexander (2017), Benvenisti (1996), Burns and Sanders (1999), Freely (1998), Goldstein (2017), Gurda (1999), Hughes (1993), Jones (2006), Mannsheim (1989), Marozzi (2014), Mazower (2004), Millett (1996), Molesky (2015), Montefiore (2011), Moynahan (2013), Norwich (1989), Pamuk (2006), and Richie (1998).

17 Political psychology scholar Molly Andrews (2014) claims that imagining future possibilities emanates from a location in the present, a location which is not only temporal but also spatial. She uses the term "situated imagination" to express this idea and she stresses that, "[w]hat can be imagined from a particular location is integrally tied to what can be known" (p. 7).

18 For Finnegan, these are tales "we use to shape our understanding and our experience of urban life" (p. 1). They include academic urban theories, stories told by professional planners, and personal narratives based on life in particular locales.

19 My thinking about how audiences/readers interpret and respond to stories derives primarily from Arendt (1958), Andrews (2014), Eagleton (2013), Eckstein (2003), Tompkins (1980), White (1984), and many others.

20 This section also responds to a question posed by literary scholar Barbara Eckstein (2003), namely: what authorizes the author?

21 As a young boy, I learned my country's foundational national myth about English settlers moving west, bringing civilization to the "virgin land," and pushing "Indians" farther west. But I had no idea how my parents, their ancestors, and I fit into that myth. Early in the 2010s, I discovered that one of my father's great-grandfathers had settled upon his western Kentucky farm in 1831 after the Chickasaw had been compelled to leave. One of my father's great-great-grandfathers had settled in western Tennessee around 1808 and owned three slaves. Two of that man's grandsons (my grandmother's uncles) died fighting for the Confederate Army during the Civil War after their father had voted against having Tennessee secede from the union. Likewise, I learned that one of my mother's grandfathers, a Welsh coal miner, had played a role in the 1885 massacre of Chinese coal miners in Rock Springs, Wyoming (Sorti, 1991).

22 In 1966, I completed a senior thesis about the mid-1930s "Popular Front" in France under the guidance of Professor David L. Lewis, who later became a Pulitzer Prize-winning author.

23 I earned an M.S. in Community Development at the University of Louisville in 1972. A few years later, I completed all but a thesis toward an M.A. in Political Science. My draft thesis focused on political power and decision-making in relationship to a planned Riverport Industrial Park in Louisville, Kentucky.

24 In the mid-1970s, I worked for two separate environmental consulting firms and one architecture and urban planning firm. Among the many reports I authored or co-authored were Throgmorton and Axetell (1978), Throgmorton (1979), and Wachs et al. (1982).

25 I received a Ph.D. in Urban and Regional Planning at the University of California, Los Angeles, in 1983. My dissertation (Throgmorton, 1983) analyzed the implementation of a new national energy policy which had profound implications for the long-term transformation of the electric power industry. The dissertation's focus on policy implementation was deeply influenced by emerging scholarly literature on

the topic, especially Bardach (1977) and Lipsky (1980). Substantively, my focus on renewable sources of energy was largely inspired by Lovins (1979). While at UCLA, I had the opportunity to learn from an impressive cluster of scholars, including John Friedmann, Peter Marris, and Martin Wachs.

26 While working at Argonne National Laboratory, I managed an energy policy project assessing the impact of national energy policies and programs on minority populations for the U. S. Department of Energy. I also completed one scholarly paper derived from my dissertation (1987) and two others pertaining to the Argonne project (Throgmorton and Barnard, 1986; Throgmorton, 1988).

27 These have included Throgmorton (1990, 1991, 1992, 1993, 2000, 2003, 2005a, 2005b, 2007a, 2007b, 2008, 2010, 2012, 2013, 2020), Throgmorton and Fisher (1993), and others.

28 Throgmorton (1996) and Eckstein and Throgmorton (2003).

29 These guest columns can be found (along with summaries of most of my scholarly and practical work) on my "Storytelling and Cities" blog site at: https://persuasivestorytelling.wordpress.com/

30 These scholars included Bernstein (1983), Rorty (1979), MacIntyre (1981), Habermas (1979, 1987), Burroway (1987), Nussbaum (1990), White (1984), and many others. I was also influenced by colleagues at the University of Iowa's Project on Rhetoric of Inquiry (POROI) (e.g., McCloskey, 1985; Nelson, Megill, and McCloskey, 1987), as well by planning and public policy scholars at other universities, including Hoch (1984), Forester (1989), Fischer and Forester (1993), Rein and Schön (1993), Schön (1993), Innes (1995), Healey (1997), and many others who are identified later in this book.

31 The work of the World Commission on Environment and Development (1987) combined with my own prior work outside academia and my research about conservation, preservation, natural resource economics, ecosocialism, deep ecology, bioregionalism, ecofeminism, social ecology, environmental planning, and the natural environmental features of eastern Iowa to inspire my interest in sustainability (e.g., Leopold, 1948; Carson, 1962; Tietenberg, 1984). With regard to the New Urbanism, I was especially influenced by Calthorpe (1993), Duany and Plater-Zyberk (1992), Kuntsler (1993), and Katz (1994).

32 My contribution to the book that came out of this symposium (Throgmorton, 2003) explored the complexities associated with envisioning and creating sustainable places. It concluded that, to care skillfully for our shared world in a context of "tentacular radiations" (Buell, 2001), remoteness (Plumwood, 1998), "environmental unconscious" (Buell, 2001), and unpriced "negative externalities," we have to make space for stories which draw attention to: (1) the place's "ecological footprint" (Wackernagel and Rees, 1996), (2) "Factor-10 economy" ways of increasing the efficiency of the "value chains" that produce that footprint (Hawken, Lovins, and Lovins, 1999), and (3) developing a shared sense of moral purpose in a "Regional City" (Calthorpe and Fulton, 2001). I also found sociologist Lyn Lofland's (1998) work on the public realm to be quite relevant.

33 I was persuaded by James Crosswhite's (1996) argument that audiences, not timeless and universal logical principles and rules, provide the proper standard for assessing the worth of arguments. But I thought it would be wrong-headed to interpret a story (such as the one the U.S. government used to justify its invasion of Iraq in 2003) purely on rational grounds. Although that story was factually flawed in many important respects, I discerned an "emotional truth" within it. Oral historian Alessandro Portelli (1991) argues that stories often contain "telling errors"—that is, factual mistakes that, by being repeated, reveal the "emotional truth" of the storyteller's story. Consequently, to discern the emotional truth of a story, one has to attend carefully to ways in which people misremember past events and tell a story to serve their purposes.

34 By the mid-2000s, I was being influenced by the literature pertaining to environmental justice. See Agyeman (2005), Bullard (2004), Corburn (2005), and others.

35 One of the courses focused on planning theory. It was in this course that I first learned about "rational planning" (Banfield, 1959), "incrementalism" (Lindblom, 1959), and "advocacy planning" (Davidoff, 1965).

36 This means the City's professional staff must: (1) be very knowledgeable about the flow of decisions directly pertaining to specific topics at hand, (2) use their professional expertise to frame topics and recommend actions, and (3) know how to present information and recommendations persuasively to their primary audience (the council) in public and private settings.

37 For an overview and critique of the communicative turn, see Healey (2012).

References

Agyeman, J. (2005), *Sustainable Communities and the Challenge of Environmental Justice*, NYU Press, New York (NY).

Albrechts, L. (Ed.). (2020), *Planners in Politics: Do They Make a Difference?* Edward Elgar, Cheltenham (UK).

Alexander, B. (2017), *Glass House: The 1% Economy and the Shattering of the All-American Town*, Picador, New York (NY).

Alexander, C. (2002–2004), *The Nature of Order.* Center for Environmental Structure, Berkeley (CA).

Ameel, L. (2020), *The Narrative Turn in Urban Planning: Plotting the Helsinki Waterfront*, Routledge, London.

Andrews, M. (2014), *Narrative Imagination and Everyday Life*, Oxford University Press, New York.

Archer, D. W. (2017), *Let the Future Begin*, Atkins & Greenspan Writing, Gross Pointe Farms (MI).

Arendt, H. (1958), *The Human Condition: A Study of the Central Dilemmas Facing Modern Man*, Doubleday Anchor, Garden City (NY).

Banfield, E. (1959), "Ends and means in planning", *International Social Science Journal*, v. 11, n. 3, pp. 361–368.

Bardach, E. (1977), *The Implementation Game*, MIT Press, Cambridge (MA).

Batty, M. (2018), *Inventing Future Cities*, MIT Press, Cambridge (MA).

Beauregard, R. A. (2015), *Planning Matter: Acting with Things*, University of Chicago Press, Chicago (IL).

Beauregard, R. A. (2020), *Advanced Introduction to Planning Theory*, Edward Elgar, Cheltenham (UK).

Benton, M. C. (2019), "The glorious future never came: An interpretive narrative analysis of the 1947 St. Louis city plan", *Journal of Planning Education and Research*, v. 21, n. 3, pp. 254–66.

Benvenisti, M. (1996), *City of Stone: The Hidden History of Jerusalem*, University of California Press, Berkeley (CA).

Bernstein, R. (1983), *Beyond Objectivism and Relativism: Science, Hermeneutics, and Praxis*, University of Pennsylvania Press, Philadelphia (PA).

Buell, L. (2001), *Writing for an Endangered World: Literature, Culture, and Environment in the U.S. and Beyond*, Belknap Press, Cambridge (MA).

Bulkens, M. (2015), "Storytelling as method in spatial planning", *European Planning Studies*, v. 23, n. 11, pp. 2310–2026.

Bullard, R. D. (2004), "Making environmental justice a reality in the 21st century", *Sustain*, v. 10, Spring/Summer, pp. 5–12.

Burns, R. and Sanders, J. (with Ades, L.) (1999), *New York: An Illustrated History*, Alfred A. Knopf, New York.

Burroway, J. (1987), *Writing Fiction. A Guide to Narrative Craft* (2nd ed.), Scott, Foresman, Glenview (IL).

Buttigieg, P. (2019), *Shortest Way Home*, Liveright, New York.

Calthorpe, P. (1993), *The Next American Metropolis: Ecology, Community, and the American Dream*, Princeton Architectural Press, Princeton (NJ).

Calthorpe, P. and Fulton, W. (2001). *The Regional City: Planning for the End of Sprawl*, Island Press, Washington (DC).

Cameron, E. (2012), "New geographies of story and storytelling", *Progress in Human Geography*, v. 36, n. 5, pp. 573–592.

Carson, R. (1962), *Silent Spring*, Houghton Mifflin, Boston (MA).

Castells, M. (1996), *The Rise of the Network Society*, Blackwell, Oxford.

Caves, R. W. (Ed.), (2005), *Encyclopedia of the City*, Routledge, New York.

Childs, M. C. (2008), "Storytelling and urban design", *Journal of Urbanism: International Research on Placemaking and Urban Sustainability*, v. 1, n. 2, pp. 173–186.

City of Iowa City (2013), *Sustainability Assessment*, Iowa City (IA).

Coetzee, J. M. (1980), *Waiting for the Barbarians*, Penguin Books, New York.

Corburn, J. (2005), *Street Science: Community Knowledge and Environmental Health Justice*, MIT Press, Cambridge (MA).

Crosswhite, J. (1996), *The Rhetoric of Reason: Writing and the Attractions of Argument*, University of Wisconsin Press, Madison (WI).

Czarniawska, B. (2004), *Narratives in Social Research*, Sage, London.

Davidoff, P. (1965), "Advocacy and pluralism in planning", *Journal of the American Institute of Planners*, v. 31, n. 4, pp. 331–338.

Davis, J. E. (Ed.), (2002), *Stories of Change: Narrative and Social Movements*, SUNY Press, Albany (NY).

Duany, A. and Plater-Zyberk, E. (1992), "The second coming of the American small town", *The Wilson Quarterly*, v. 16, n. 1, pp. 19–48.

Eagleton, T. (2013), *How to Read Literature*, Yale University Press, New Haven (CT).

Eckstein, B. (2003), "Making space: Stories in the practice of planning", in B. Eckstein and J. A. Throgmorton (Eds.), *Story and Sustainability: Planning, Practice and Possibility for American Cities*, MIT Press, Cambridge (MA), pp. 13–36.

Eckstein, B. and Throgmorton, J. A. (Eds.), (2003), *Story and Sustainability: Planning, Practice, and Possibility for American Cities*, MIT Press, Cambridge (MA).

Finnegan, R. (1998), *Tales of the City: A Study of Narrative and Urban Life*, Cambridge University Press, Cambridge (UK).

Fischer, F. and Forester, J. (Eds.), (1993), *The Argumentative Turn in Planning and Policy Analysis*, Duke University Press, Durham (NC).

Flyvbjerg, B. (1997), *Rationality and Power: Democracy in Practice* (tr. by S. Sampson), University of Chicago Press, Chicago (IL).

Forester, J. (1989), *Planning in the Face of Power*, University of California Press, Berkeley (CA).

Forester, J. (1999), *The Deliberative Practitioner: Encouraging Participatory Planning Processes*, MIT Press, Cambridge (MA).

Freely, J. (1998), *Istanbul: The Imperial City*, Penguin Books, New York (NY).

Friedmann, J. (1987), *Planning in the Public Domain: From Knowledge to Action*, Princeton University Press, Princeton (NJ).

Frug, G. E. (1999), *City Making: Building Communities without Building Walls*, Princeton University Press, Princeton (NJ).

Frug, G. E. and Barron, D. J. (2011), *City Bound: How States Stifle Urban Innovation*, Cornell University Press, Ithaca (NY).

Goldstein, A. (2017), *Janesville: An American Story*, Simon & Schuster, New York.

Graham, S. and Marvin, S. (2001), *Splintering Urbanism: Networked Infrastructures, Technological Mobilities and the Urban Condition*, Routledge, New York.

Greenberg, K. (2011), *Walking Home: The Life and Lessons of a City Builder*, Random House, Toronto, Canada.

Gurda, J. (1999), *The Making of Milwaukee*, Milwaukee County Historical Society, Milwaukee (WI).

Habermas, J. (1979), *Communication and the Evolution of Society* (tr. by T. McCarthy), Beacon Press, Boston (MA).

Habermas, J. (1987), *The Philosophical Discourse of Modernity* (tr. by E. Lawrence), MIT Press, Cambridge (MA).

Haselsberger, B. (Ed.), (2017), *Encounters in Planning Thought: 16 Autobiographical Essays from Key Thinkers in Spatial Planning*, Routledge, New York.

Hawken, P., Lovins, A., and Hunter Lovins, L. (1999). *Natural Capitalism: Creating the Next Industrial Revolution*, Little, Brown, Boston (MA).

Healey, P. (1997), *Collaborative Planning: Shaping Places in Fragmented Societies*, Macmillan, London.

Healey, P. (2012), "Communicative planning: practices, concepts and rhetorics", in B. Sanyal, L. Vale, and C. Rosan (Eds.), *Planning Ideas That Matter: Livability, Territoriality, Governance, and Reflective Practice*, MIT Press, Cambridge (MA), pp. 333–357.

Hoch, C. (1984), "Doing good and being right: The pragmatic connection in planning theory", *Journal of the American Planning Association*, v. 50, n. 3, pp. 335–345.

Hughes, R. (1993), *Barcelona*, Vintage Books, New York.

Innes, J. E. (1995), "Planning theory's emerging paradigm", *Journal of Planning Education and Research*, v. 14, n. 3, pp. 183–189.

Ivory, C. (2013), "The role of the imagined user in planning and design narratives", *Planning Theory*, v. 12, n. 4, pp. 425–441.

Jacobs, J. (1961), *The Death and Life of Great American Cities*, Vintage, New York.

Jonas, A. E. G. and Wilson, D. (Eds.), (1999), *The Urban Growth Machine: Critical Perspectives Two Decades Later*, SUNY Press, Albany (NY).

Jones, C. (2006), *Paris: The Biography of a City*, Penguin Books, New York.

Katz, B. and Nowak, J. (2017), *The New Localism: How Cities Can Thrive in the Age of Populism*, Bookings Institution Press, Washington (DC).

Katz, P. (Ed.), (1994), *The New Urbanism: Toward an Architecture of Community*, McGraw-Hill, New York.

Keskin, H., Akgun, A. E., Zehir, C., and Ayar, H. (2016), "Tales of cities: City branding through storytelling", *Journal of Global Strategic Management*, v. 10, n. 1, pp. 31–41.

Kidder, T. and Todd R. (2013), *Good Prose: The Art of Nonfiction*, Random House, New York.

Kunstler, J. H. (1993), *The Geography of Nowhere: The Rise and Decline of America's Man-Made Landscape*, Simon & Schuster, New York.

Kurzweil, R. (2005), *The Singularity Is Near: When Humans Transcend Biology*, Viking, New York.

Lefevbre, H. (1991), *The Production of Space*. (tr. by D. Nicholson-Smith), Blackwell, Oxford.

Leopold, A. (1948), *A Sand County Almanac, Oxford University Press*, Oxford.

Lindblom, C. (1959), "The science of 'muddling through'", *Public Administration Review*, v. 19, n. 2, pp. 79–88.

Lipsky, M. (1980), *Street Level Bureaucracy: Dilemmas of the Individual in Social Services*, Russell Sage Foundation, New York.

Lofland, L. (1998), *The Public Realm: Exploring the City's Quintessential Social Territory*, Aldine De Gruyter, New York.

Logan, J. R. and Molotch, H. L. (1987/2007), *Urban Fortunes: The Political Economy of Place*, University of California Press, Berkeley (CA).

Lovins, A. (1979), *Soft Energy Paths: Towards a Durable Peace*, HarperCollins, New York.

MacIntyre, A. (1981), *After Virtue: A Study in Moral Theory*, University of Notre Dame Press, South Bend (IN).

Mandelbaum, S. (1991), "Telling Stories", *Journal of Planning Education and Research*, v. 10, n. 3, pp. 209–214.

Mannsheim, G. (1989), *Iowa City: An Illustrated History*, Donning Company, Norfolk (VA).

Marozzi, J. (2014), *Baghdad: City of Peace, City of Blood*, Da Capo Press, Boston (MA).

Marris, P. (1997), *Witnesses, Engineers, or Storytellers*, University of Maryland at College Park Urban Studies and Planning Program, College Park (MD).

Massey, D. (2005), *For Space*, Sage, Los Angeles (CA).

Mazower, M. (2004), *Salonica: City of Ghosts Christians, Muslims and Jews 1430–1950*, Vintage Books, New York.

Metropolitan Planning Organization of Johnson County (2012), *Long Range Transportation Plan 2012–2040*, Iowa City (IA).

McCloskey, D. N. (1985), *The Rhetoric of Economics*, University of Wisconsin Press, Madison (WI).

Millett, L. (1996), *Twin Cities Then and Now*, Minnesota Historical Society, St. Paul (MN).

Molesky, M. (2015), *This Gulf of Fire: The Great Lisbon Earthquake or Apocalypse in the Age of Science and Reason*, Vintage Books, New York.

Molotch, H. (1976), "The city as a growth machine: Toward a political economy of place", *American Journal of Sociology*, v. 82, n. 2, pp. 309–332.

Molotch, H. and Logan, J. (1996), "The theory of the growth machine", in S. S. Fainstein and S. Campbell (Eds.), *Readings in Urban Theory*, Blackwell, Oxford, pp. 291–337.

Montefiore, S. S. (2011), *Jerusalem: The Biography*, Alfred A. Knopf, New York.

Moynahan, B. (2013), *Leningrad: Siege and Symphony*, Grove Press, New York.

Nelson, J. S., Megill, A., and McCloskey, D. N. (Eds.), (1987), *The Rhetoric of the Human Sciences*, University of Wisconsin Press, Madison (WI).

Norwich, J. J. (1989), *A History of Venice*, Vintage Books, New York.

Nutter, M. A. (2017), *Mayor*, University of Pennsylvania Press, Philadelphia (PA).

Nussbaum, M. (1990), *Love's Knowledge: Essays on Philosophy and Literature*, Oxford University Press, Oxford.

Pamuk, O. (2006), *Istanbul: Memories and the City*, Vintage Books, New York.

Pierson P. (2004), *Politics in Time: History, Institutions, and Social Analysis*, Princeton University Press, Princeton (NJ).

Plumwood, V. (1998), *Environmental Culture: The Ecological Crisis of Reason*, Routledge, New York.

Portelli, A. (1991), *The Death of Luigi Trastulli and Other Stories: Form and Meaning in Oral History*, SUNY Press, Albany (NY).

Rein, M. and Schön, D. (1993), "Reframing policy discourse", in F. Fischer and J. Forester (Eds.), *The Argumentative Turn in Planning and Policy Analysis*, Duke University Press, Durham (NC), pp. 145–166.

Richie, A. (1998), *Faust's Metropolis: A History of Berlin*, Carroll & Graf, New York.

Riessman, C. J. (2008), *Narrative Methods for the Human Sciences*, Sage, Thousand Oaks (CA).

Rittel, H. and Webber, M. (1973), "Dilemmas in a general theory of planning", *Policy Sciences*, v. 4, n. 2, pp. 155–169.

Rorty, R. (1979), *Philosophy and the Mirror of Nature*, Princeton University Press, Princeton (NJ).

Rybak, R. T. (2016), *Pothole Confidential. My Life as Mayor of Minneapolis*, University of Minnesota Press, Minneapolis (MN).

Sandercock, L. (2003), *Cosmopolis II: Mongrel Cities in the 21st Century*, Continuum, New York.

Schön, D. A. (1983), *The Reflective Practitioner: How Professionals Think in Action*, Basic Books, New York.

Schragger, R. (2016), *City Power: Urban Governance in a Global Age*, Oxford University Press, New York.

Sennett, R. (2008), *The Craftsman*, Yale University Press, New Haven (CT).

Simons, A. (2006), *The Story Factor* (2nd ed. Rev.), Basic Books, New York.

Smith, M. P. (2001), *Transnational Urbanism: Locating Globalization*, Blackwell, Cambridge.

Sorti, C. (1991), *Incident at Bitter Creek: The Story of the Rock Springs Chinese Massacre*, Iowa State University Press, Ames (IA).

Stoetzler, M. and Yuval-Davis N. (2002), "Standpoint theory, situated knowledge— and the situated imagination", *Feminist Theory*, v. 3, n. 3, pp. 315–334.

Storr, W. (2019), *The Science of Storytelling: Why Stories Make Us Human and How to Tell Them Better*, William Collins, London.

Throgmorton, J. A. (1979), *Technical Assistance in Developing Nonattainment Plans for Selected Areas in California*, EPA 909/9–79-003, U.S. Environmental Protection Agency, Research Triangle Park (NC).

Throgmorton, J. A. (1983), *A Bridge to a Distant Shore: Implementing Section 210 of the Public Utility Regulatory Policies Act of 1978*, Ph.D. diss., Graduate School of Architecture and Urban Planning, University of California, Los Angeles.

Throgmorton, J. A. (1987), "Community energy planning: Winds of change from the San Gorgonio Pass", *Journal of the American Planning Association*, v. 53, n. 3, pp. 358–367.

Throgmorton, J. A. (1988), "Synthesizing politics, rationality, and advocacy: Energy policy analysis for minority groups", *Review of Policy Research*, v. 8, n. 2, pp. 300–321.

Throgmorton, J. A. (1990), Passion, reason, and power: Electric power planning in Chicago", *Journal of Architectural and Planning Research*, v. 7, n. 4, pp. 330–350.

Throgmorton, J. A. (1991), "The rhetorics of policy analysis", *Policy Sciences*, v. 24, n. 2, pp. 153–179.

Throgmorton, J. A. (1992), "Planning as persuasive storytelling about the future", *Journal of Planning Education and Research*, v. 12, n. 1, pp. 17–31.

Throgmorton, J. A. (1993), "Planning as a rhetorical activity: Survey research as a trope in arguments about electric power planning in Chicago", *Journal of the American Planning Association*, v. 59, n. 3, pp. 334–346.

Throgmorton, J. A. (1996), *Planning as Persuasive Storytelling: The Rhetorical Construction of Chicago's Electric Future*, University of Chicago Press, Chicago (IL).

Throgmorton, J. A. (2000), "On the virtues of skillful meandering: Acting as a skilled-voice-in-the-flow of persuasive argumentation", *Journal of the American Planning Association*, v. 66, n. 4, pp. 367–383.

Throgmorton, J. A. (2003), "Imagining sustainable places", in B. Eckstein and J. A. Throgmorton (Eds.), *Story and Sustainability: Planning, Practice, and Possibility for American Cities*, MIT Press, Cambridge (MA), pp. 39–61.

Throgmorton, J. A. (2005a), "Planning as persuasive storytelling in the context of 'the network society'", in L. Albrecht and S. J. Mandelbaum (Eds.), *The Network Society: A New Context for Planning?* Routledge, London, pp. 125–145.

Throgmorton, J. A. (2005b), "The magistrate's position: Planners in the empire's story." Paper presented at the 45th annual meeting of the Association of European Schools of Planning, Vienna, Austria (July 13–17).

Throgmorton, J. A. (2007a), "Inventing 'the Greatest': Constructing Louisville's future out of story and clay", *Planning Theory*, v. 6, n. 3, pp. 237–262.

Throgmorton, J. A. (2007b), "Transforming 'Rubbertown': The rhetorical construction of environmental justice and sustainability in Louisville." Presented as part of "Toxic Talk: A Semester-long Cross-Disciplinary Conversation about Environmental Justice and Sustainability", University of Iowa, Iowa City (IA) (September 7).

Throgmorton, J. A. (2008), "The bridge to Gretna: Three faces of a case", *Planning Theory & Practice*, v. 9, n. 2, pp. 187–208.

Throgmorton, J. A. (2010), "Why storytelling matters: Three stories from the heart of America." Invited presentation at the Department of Urban Studies and Planning, Massachusetts Institute of Technology, Cambridge (MA) (December 1).

Throgmorton, J. A. (2012), "Pork, place, and planning", *Poroi*, v. 8, n. 1. https://ir.uiowa.edu/poroi/vol8/iss1/3/ (last accessed on January 6, 2021).

Throgmorton, J. A. (2013), "What can planning theory be now? Storytelling and community identity in a Tea Party moment", in G. Young and D. Stevenson (Eds.), *The Ashgate Research Companion to Planning and Culture*, Ashgate, Farnham (UK), pp. 105–120.

Throgmorton, J. A. (2020), "Storytelling and city crafting in a contested age: One mayor's practice story", in L. Albrechts (Ed.), *Planners in Politics: Do They Make a Difference?* Edward Elgar, Cheltenham (UK), pp. 174–197.

Throgmorton, J. A. and Axetell, K. (1978), *Digest of Ambient Particulate Analysis and Assessment Methods*, EPA-450/3–78–113, U.S. Environmental Protection Agency, Research Triangle Park (NC).

Throgmorton, J. A. and Bernard III, M. (1986), "Minorities and energy: A review of recent findings and a guide to future research", *Proceedings of the American Council for an Energy-Efficient Economy's 1986 Summer Study on Energy Efficiency in Buildings Vol. VII*, American Council for an Energy-Efficient Economy, Washington (DC), pp. 260–280.

Throgmorton, J. A. and Fisher, P. S. (1993), "Institutional change and electric power in the city of Chicago", *Journal of Economic Issues*, v. 27, n. 1, pp. 117–153.

Tietenberg, T. (1984), *Environmental and Natural Resource Economics*, Scott, Foresman, Glenview (IL).

Tilly, C. (2002), *Stories, Identities, and Political Change*, Rowman & Littlefield, New York.

Tompkins, J. P. (1980), *Reader-Response Criticism from Formalism to Post-Structuralism*, Johns Hopkins University Press, Baltimore (MD).

Toukabri, A. and Medina, L. (2021), "America: A nation of small towns" (May 21), available at: www.census.gov/library/stories/2020/05/america-a-nation-of-small-towns.html (last accessed May 7, 2021).

Toulmin, S. E. (1990), *Cosmopolis: The Hidden Agenda of Modernity*, University of Chicago Press, Chicago (IL).

Tucker, J. (2017), "City-stories: Narrative as diagnostic and strategic resource in Ciudad del Este, Paraguay", *Planning Theory*, v. 16, n. 1, pp. 74–98.

Van Hulst, M. (2012), "Storytelling, a model *of* and a model *for* planning", *Planning Theory*, v. 11, n. 3, pp. 299–318.

Wachs, M. J., Throgmorton, J. A., Findley, L., and Schlesinger, G. (1982), *A Bridge to the Nineties: Transportation Proposals for Downtown Los Angeles*, Final report prepared for the Los Angeles Central City Association and Chamber of Commerce, Urban Innovations Group, Los Angeles.

Wackernagel, M. and Rees, W. (1996), *Our Ecological Footprint: Reducing Human Impact on the Earth*, New Society, Gabriola Island (BC).

White, J. B. (1984), *When Words Lose Their Meanings: Constitutions and Reconstitutions of Language, Character, and Community*, University of Chicago Press, Chicago (IL).

Wilson, E. O. (2014), *The Meaning of Human Existence*, Liveright, New York.

World Commission on Environment and Development (1987), *Our Common Future*, Oxford University Press, Oxford (UK).

2

TRYING TO BE A TEAM PLAYER, 2012–2013

Roughly 15 years after my first term as a council member ended and less than a year after retiring from the university, I decided to seek election once again. I knew the basics of what the job entailed, knew the city and its people, and had been writing regular guest opinions for the local newspaper. I was also in excellent health for a person of my age (66).

But those factors would not by themselves persuade the people of Iowa City to vote for me. Much had changed since the mid-1990s, myself included. Iowa City had become more diverse demographically, two neighboring cities had emerged as significant economic competitors to Iowa City, the leadership of key governmental entities and other major organizations had almost completely turned over, the city and region had experienced an extremely costly flood, and national politics had become far more polarized. To campaign effectively, I had to build on my existing base of knowledge and relationships, connect with the new leaders, and construct a political campaign that took all those changes into account.

I spent a great deal of time talking with elected officials and heads of major organizations to establish new relationships and learn what they thought were the major challenges and opportunities facing Iowa City. As for challenges, they emphasized state-level policy decisions to reduce local property taxes along with our neighboring city Coralville's very aggressive and controversial use of tax increment financing (TIF) to lure businesses out of Iowa City.[1] In their view, the biggest opportunities had to do with Iowa City's downtown and the emerging "Riverfront Crossings District" located immediately to its south.[2] A proposed Amtrak rail line could stimulate private investment in that district, as would likely investments by the university. I also attended meetings of several local groups, including a race and poverty group which gradually

DOI: 10.4324/9781003160991-2

became known as the Coalition for Racial Justice (CRJ); FasTrac, which had been formed by a leader in the local black community; and a climate advocacy group that several parishioners at Trinity Episcopal Church had organized. The conversations with these groups led me to think that, in important respects, the leaders I had initially spoken with were out of touch with important clusters of people in the city.

My ambitions as a candidate were quite modest, bland even. In brief, I hoped to contribute my knowledge, experience, and skills as a good member of the council team while also giving greater voice to marginalized or disadvantaged populations and concerns. As an early-June press release announcing my candidacy for the District C seat said,

> We are lucky to be living in a lovely city, but we will be facing some significant challenges over the coming years. I believe my combination of experience, knowledge, skills and vision can help us respond in a way that enables us to make it an even better place.

After issuing this press release, I started doing all the things candidates typically do: preparing a campaign photo and brochure, constructing an informal campaign advisory committee, knocking on doors, collecting signatures for a nomination petition, going to diverse events, talking with residents and business owners, soliciting around $1,000 in campaign contributions, ordering and installing yard signs, preparing position papers, and the like. The campaign brochure highlighted three specific themes: (1) ensuring good jobs and a strong tax base, (2) keeping Iowa City a safe and welcoming place for all, and (3) promoting long-term sustainability.[3] I also stressed my ability to resolve conflicts skillfully, which I thought might help the council in this time of political polarization.[4]

As I spoke with residents while campaigning, I sensed that the mood of the local electorate had changed substantially since I first ran for election in 1993. The playful joy of 1993 was gone, and I sensed the public's trust in democratic governance had declined significantly. In part this was owing to widespread nationwide disappointment about how President Obama had responded to the Great Recession of 2007–2008. Many people were angry that banks had been bailed out while ordinary people saw their jobs, and often their homes, go away.[5]

In August, just 3 months before the election, my wife, daughter, and I took a 10-day trip to the United Kingdom. I felt a bit awkward about going just as serious campaigning would normally begin, but I had paid for the trip prior to deciding to seek election. Moreover, many private conversations led me to think I would not be facing an opponent in November. So, off we went. It proved to be a wonderful trip in every respect except one. While we were there, riots broke out on the streets of London at several locations; there were reports about criminality, fires, and gratuitous violence; and there was a call from the prime minister for "zero tolerance" of criminals. It appeared as though global capitalism might be on the verge of collapse, and yet no progressive agent of change seemed capable of responding to it effectively. I thought it was far more likely that a new authoritarian strongman rather than an effective democratic leader like Franklin Roosevelt would arise.

We also saw great beauty on our trip: York Minster, the ruins of Whitby Abbey, the countryside of southwest England, the western tip of the Gower Peninsula, and the core of London. Always inspired by beauty, part of me wanted to be an advocate for great architecture and great public places, but, as London had just demonstrated, high-quality urban design by itself is not sufficient: it must be accompanied by action to promote social justice.[6] Over the preceding 12–18 months, I had also read or reread a great deal of work by Jane Jacobs and Christopher Alexander and had been very influenced by both of them, especially Jacobs's thinking about cities as "problems in organized complexity," Alexander's ideas about "unfolding," and their ideas about good urban design and planning.[7] I began engaging in routine conversations with a retired local landscape architect (John T.) who had been playing a major role in designing renovations of a key park in the city's Northside neighborhood and who also had been influenced by their work.

No one challenged me for the District C seat. My sense was that I had defused concerns among mainstream business people, and that my friends in the progressive community had discouraged people from running against me. However, by late August, seven candidates had filed for two at-large positions, and two had filed for the District A seat. This meant that a primary election would have to be held early in October for the two at-large seats. One of the at-large candidates was a young partner in a downtown law firm, Matt H., who was just completing his first term as mayor. Another was an operations supervisor for the MidAmerican Energy Company (Michelle P.), and a third was an Indian-American student at the university (Raj P.). On October 11, the mayor finished first by being named on 64 percent of the ballots, and Michelle P. narrowly defeated Raj P. for second. Even though I would be running unopposed in the general election, I still put up some campaign signs, participated in candidate forums, had a campaign poster printed, filmed an interview, arranged to have a temporary website built, and constructed a social media presence on Twitter and Facebook.

On November 6, roughly 7,000 registered voters (13.5 percent of the total) cast their ballots in the general election. Mayor Matt H. led for the two at-large positions by being named on 65 percent of the ballots, whereas Michelle P. finished second at 42 percent. A male clinical physician at the University of Iowa, Rick D., won the District A seat by 65 to 33 percent over a right-wing radio talk show host. And I was elected to the District C seat after being named on almost as many ballots as the mayor.

Trying to Be a Team Player

Serving on the council while otherwise being retired was a novel experience for me. At first, I simply wanted to test the waters and develop a better understanding of my fellow council members and what they cared about. Likewise, I needed to familiarize myself with the city manager. He, Tom M., was an experienced professional who had come to Iowa City from Birmingham, Michigan, late in 2010. In general, I hoped to contribute my knowledge, experience, and skills as a good member of the team. As I said to the mayor, "I want this city to become even better, and that means I want to help you succeed."

The council had recently decided to establish a strategic planning process as a way of setting short-term priorities for City government.[8] Late in 2011, we three newly elected council members met twice with the returning council members, the three departing ones, and key City staff to, with the assistance of a trained facilitator, identify and prioritize the City's overall goals and objectives for the next 2 years. Joining Mayor Matt H. as returnees were two other downtown business owners, Connie C. and Terry D. I had submitted a lengthy set of suggestions, which were based on my campaign themes. I suggested, for example, that we needed to invent better ways of making newcomers feel they are a part of the Iowa City community, while also ensuring that all residents feel safe in their homes and neighborhoods. I also suggested that our economic development efforts needed to be integrated with our efforts to mitigate and adapt to long-term environmental threats, especially global climate change. In the end, however, the council identified five priorities which I found less than inspiring: economic and community development, development of the downtown and near downtown areas, neighborhood stabilization, a strong and sustainable financial foundation, and coordinated communication and customer service orientation.

Early in January, we held an organizational meeting in which we unanimously re-elected the young lawyer as mayor and, as mayor pro tem, a female financial advisor and former school board member, Susan M., who was entering her third year on the council. When council members were being assigned to committees, the mayor assigned me to four: East Central Iowa Council of Governments' Board of Directors, the Iowa City UNESCO City of Literature Board, the Chief Executive Board of the Regional Workforce Investment Board, and, along with five other council members, the Metropolitan Planning Organization of Johnson County's (MPOJC's) Urbanized Area Policy Board. As were all council members, I was also expected to participate in quarterly "Joint Cities" meetings and annual budget meetings of the Iowa City Conference Board, which concerned the City's assessor and assessments of property values for taxing purposes.[9]

From that point on, I found myself becoming immersed in the standard rhythm of the city council's work. With occasional exceptions, we met in City

Hall every other Tuesday night for work sessions, which typically began at 5 p.m. and ran until 6:30 p.m., and formal meetings, which began at 7 p.m. and continued until the agenda had been completed. The formal meetings were televised live and rebroadcast on the City's cable TV channel. Work sessions were not. To help us prepare for these meetings, the city clerk would distribute (often very long) formal meeting packets and information packets on the Thursday afternoon prior to our meeting dates. For the first few meetings, I chose not to prepare written notes about the topics to be discussed, but, within just a few months I realized I was asking too much of my memory. I started preparing comprehensive notes.

I took council work very seriously. And, having retired a little more than a year before taking office, I had the time and energy to do it. This meant spending every other weekend reading the council packet, establishing or strengthening relationships with key city staff and other council members, attending public events, and meeting with people throughout the city.

It didn't take long for me to recall what it feels like to have a flood of topics and issues flowing one's way, week after week. Many, perhaps most, of what we encountered in this torrent of topics on our formal meeting agendas were routine administrative matters that required little thought from council members. Other topics were more complicated, and the number and variety of such topics proved to be quite daunting. Some of them popped up in response to specific requests from segments of the public—for example, to permit chickens in the backyards of homes, ban the use of plastic bags in grocery stores, prohibit new payday lenders from locating in the city, and ban the smoking of e-cigarettes in City-owned parks. Other topics came from the staff, including: considering major changes in the City-owned senior center, building a new animal care and adoption facility to replace one that had been flooded in 2008, possibly using traffic cameras to catch traffic violations at intersections, and, most important, approving draft annual budgets and 3-year capital improvement plans. Still other topics required coordination with other local governmental entities, such as a very difficult 2013 decision about whether to eliminate Sunday service and half-price fares for paratransit users. Appointing members to the City's boards and commissions also demanded time and sometimes proved controversial. And there was a seemingly endless flow of requests to rezone property and thereby permit new residential developments, most of which were on the outer periphery of the city.

Some of the staff's topics arrived with little or no advance notice and often concerned matters that we council members, regardless of background and experience, knew little or nothing about. For example, in 2013, the staff presented us with a very complicated proposal to transfer many of the City's landfill operations to a private firm, which would use a technological process to separate solid wastes and then transform some of the residual waste into ethanol.

The deluge of diverse topics was relentless. As I had learned in my previous council term, one must learn to distinguish the mundane from the important and, as much as possible, to focus one's attention on what really matters. To do this, one has to know (and sometimes discover) what one values. Even so, I became so immersed in the day-by-day processing of issues that I found it very difficult to find time, week by week, to reflect on where the council's decisions were leading the city and on how well my decisions matched my values and campaign themes.

Of all the topics and issues that came our way in 2012 and 2013, I want to draw attention to four. One set of topics involved City government's efforts to recover from the 2008 flood and to mitigate damages from future floods. It highlights how complex decisions on specific topics can be. A second set concerned the interaction of Iowa City and the School District concerning the district's facilities planning and diversity policy and the City's land development policies. It draws attention to ways in which issues can cut across jurisdictional and topical boundaries. The third, which consumed enormous amounts of our time, concerned projects and plans pertaining to economic development and densification of the downtown. It highlights the role of conflict as a necessary part of democratic governance. And the fourth concerned the City's responses to demands for racial equity in relation to Johnson County's planning for a new "justice center." It emphasizes ways in which people normally excluded from governmental processes can induce changes in those processes. We also encountered at least two major unexpected events, including a large fire in the City's landfill and a major water main break, which flooded the basements of many buildings downtown. Luckily for us council members, those events could only be dealt with by our technical staff.

Four Major Topics/Issues

Space does not permit me to go into great detail about each of these four topics/ issues, or about the diverse perspectives that helped shape action (or inaction) on each of them. What I will do instead is provide a fairly high-level overview of how actions unfolded in each case, how I tried to influence those actions, what the council ultimately decided to do, and how the processes and outcomes affected my own subsequent actions and my thinking about the complexity of cities and the role of elected officials in guiding their transformation. Each story about these cases ends with some uncertainty about what would happen in 2014 and whether post-election changes in council membership would have any significant effect on the council's actions.

Mitigating against Damage from Future Floods

The Iowa River runs north to south through the middle of Iowa City. Late in the spring of 2008, Iowa City (along with other cities in east-central Iowa) were struck with a flood that caused enormous damage to buildings and infrastructure. In Iowa City, the University of Iowa's campus, especially its Arts campus on the west side of the river, was hit especially hard.[10] The flood also rendered a major entryway to Iowa City (Dubuque Street) impassable for many weeks and partially inundated five other parts of the city. These other areas included two residential neighborhoods located along the river (Parkview Terrace and Idyllwild Condominiums), the City's North Wastewater Treatment Plant located south of downtown, and two other areas south of the treatment plant.

In the 3 years following the flood, the City had diligently pursued a range of flood recovery and mitigation projects, and the City staff briefed us about those efforts in a late-2012 work session. A memo from the director of public works informed us that the City had identified 17 flood mitigation projects totaling almost $160 million.[11] It was an impressive list, which indicated that considerable progress had been made using a mix of federal, state, and local funding sources including a 4-year local option sales tax. Iowa City voters had narrowly approved the tax in 2009, and it was expected to generate roughly $33 million over its 4-year life span. These funds enabled the City to purchase flood-damaged homes, build new homes to replace ones removed in the buyout, and build new rental homes on the southeastern side of the city. City staff told us that four major flood projects remained: the Taft Speedway Levee/Floodwall, the Gateway project on Dubuque Street, the Eastside and Westside levees, and demolishing the North Wastewater Treatment Plant and moving its sewage treatment capacity to the South Wastewater Treatment Plant. The first and second of these demanded the council's immediate attention.

For 3 years after the 2008 flood, the council and staff had explored what could be done to protect the Idyllwild neighborhood from future floods. The neighborhood consisted of 92 condominiums in the Idyllwild complex, nine single-family houses located right next to the river, and a church. In November 2011, a consulting firm had submitted a preliminary study of ten alternatives.

Several months later, in October 2012, our council discussed the possibility of authorizing construction of a levee or floodwall along Taft Speedway to protect the neighborhood. The information packet for the meeting was long, and the material about the levee was, from a council member's point of view, extremely complicated. It included a consulting firm's preliminary estimated costs of seven flood mitigation alternatives. It was a careful and helpful assessment; however, all but one of the alternatives involved building a floodwall or a levee which would provide flood protection for the Idyllwild condominiums but leave nine homes on the river side of the levee. The remaining alternative simply involved elevating a road on the northern edge of the neighborhood. This alternative would not protect Idyllwild or the church, but it would ensure access to the Peninsula neighborhood—which is a New Urbanism-inspired development on an upland above the Iowa River—during flood events.[12] The levee/floodwall was estimated to cost between $8 million and $13 million, and federal Community Development Block Grant funds would provide $8 million of the total. The City staff recommended construction of an $8 million levee that would provide protection against a 0.01 probability flood plus 3 feet.

This was a complex issue legally, technically, and politically. This complexity led to further debates in late November and early December. On the evening of November 27, we held a public hearing concerning a resolution that would authorize construction of the staff's recommended alternative. In the end, we decided 5:2 to reject the staff's recommendation, with only the mayor and council member Terry D. supporting the resolution. I made a lengthy statement explaining my reasoning.[13]

In this statement, I acknowledged that Idyllwild residents and Parkview Church had experienced considerable physical loss, financial harm, and emotional trauma as a result of the 2008 flood. The best response would have been to remove those buildings from the floodplain through buyouts, but Idyllwild condominium owners were, for complex legal reasons, not eligible for a buyout using federal funds. I thought developers should never have proposed a condominium complex in the floodplain 20 years ago, the city council should not have approved it, and people who bought condominiums there prior to 2008 should have understood they were risking that their property would be damaged by flooding and, hence, should have purchased flood insurance.[14] I also thought it would be unfair to build a levee that would leave nine Taft Speedway homes on the river side of the levee, and that using public funds to protect Idyllwild and Parkview Church with a floodwall or levee would privatize benefits while socializing costs: assuming that 92 condo owners would equally benefit from the $8 million levee recommended by the staff, each would be receiving a subsidy of $88,000. Also, almost half of the condos had been purchased after the 2008 flood at highly discounted prices. People who purchased these condos were not, therefore, "flood victims" who deserved the public's help.

Instead of building a floodwall or levee, I suggested an alternative, which would involve a modest subsidy to help condo owners purchase flood insurance. Regardless of my reasoning and my effort to propose an alternative that might provide residents with some support, I doubt that I made any new friends in Idyllwild that night. Two weeks later, the council discussed my additional recommendations and, following the staff's advice, concluded they should not be adopted.

Roughly 9 months after deciding not to construct the Taft Speedway levee, we turned to the Gateway project, which focused on Dubuque Street and the Park Road Bridge. Dubuque Street was, and still is, one of the most important and surely the most scenic of entryways into Iowa City and the University of Iowa. Owing to its low elevation, however, Dubuque Street had a history of flooding. In 1993, floodwaters had inundated Dubuque Street for 54 days, and flooding in 2008 had covered the street again for a month. In that same year, the Park Road Bridge had also been overtopped and closed.

Dubuque Street's scenic value derives partly from the fact that it runs parallel to a major portion of the Iowa River and partly from the wooded bluffs on the east side of the street. Dubuque also carried more than 25,000 vehicles a day between Interstate 80 and the downtown and the University of Iowa's campus. Park Road and its bridge have long served as a critical east–west transportation link within the city. And the University's Arts campus had been located on the west side of the river just south of Park Road until the 2008 flood forced the demolition of some of its key buildings, including its iconic Hancher Auditorium. The university was planning to replace that structure with a new auditorium located close to Park Road and the bridge, but at a higher elevation than its pre-2008 level.

City government had already completed a substantial amount of preparatory work before Rick D., Michelle P., and I joined the council. Most importantly, the prior council had authorized initiation of the Gateway project. This project sought to: (1) reduce closures of Dubuque Street and the Park Road bridge due to river flood events and localized flash floods; (2) minimize backwater flood impacts created by the existing bridge; (3) better serve transit, pedestrians, and bicyclists; and (4) preserve and enhance the natural entry to Iowa City from I-80. Fulfilling these purposes required completing a National Environmental Policy Act (NEPA) planning process, completing detailed design and engineering work, and building the project as designed. Reasonable alternatives had been identified and evaluated, two public meetings had been held, and the federally required planning document had been prepared. We council members were called upon to review and approve the detailed design elements.

We grappled with the proposed project early in the fall of 2013 and continued working our way through details during our first meeting in October. This very important $52 million project would involve elevating Dubuque Street, building a new Park Road bridge, and installing new water and sewer infrastructure under the elevated roadway. The public works staff told us that, as part of the NEPA evaluation process, the City had developed a "Purpose and Need" statement to guide the development of alternative solutions.

Our discussion was guided by a very detailed memo we had received from the City engineer. We could choose any elevation between a "500-year flood + 1 foot" and a "100-year flood + 1 foot" and we should consider flood protection, grading effects, and construction and constructability of each alternative.[15] The staff and consultant had considered three flood protection elevations: "100 + 1," "Year 2008 flood + 1," and "500 + 1." According to the memo, Dubuque Street had been closed as a result of flood events for approximately 150 days over the preceding 20 years, plus an unknown amount of time for clean-up after very localized heavy rains. Although it was not possible to predict the severity of heavy rainfall, flood events, or road closures in the future, there had been a steady increase in rainfall amounts and severe weather events since the 1950s.[16] The memo further indicated that the elevation level for the roadway depended on the mitigation level chosen for the bridge. Moreover, the roadway elevation would not protect a university residence hall or other structures on the east side of Dubuque (they would have to protect themselves), but the elevations would ensure continued access to those buildings during flood conditions. As for construction, the City engineer reported that each of the three roadway flood protection elevations could be built in two construction seasons, traffic flows would be maintained, and unavoidable road closures would be as brief as possible and take place when the university was on break. The memo also provided considerable detail for five bridge options, focusing especially on their effects on backwater heights, height of the Dubuque–Park Road intersection, grading impacts, cost, and potential to catch debris floating down the river.

I cannot speak for other council members, but my head was spinning from all the detail our public works staff had provided. Knowing the city very well, and having talked at length with people who lived on the east side of Dubuque Street, my sense was that our challenge was to mitigate against future flood damage without compromising the aesthetic/historic integrity of the Dubuque Street entryway, and to do so in as cost-effective a manner as possible. Moreover, I thought the design for the Gateway project should, as our recently updated Comprehensive Plan stated, "protect and promote the character and integrity of existing neighborhoods" (City of Iowa City, 2013a, p. 23). As far as the Gateway project was concerned, I understood this to mean that the roadway should fit well into its context and enhance the unique character of this major entryway to Iowa City. I was quite worried that the City staff would recommend an alternative that would cause excessive damage to the wooded bluff, would damage a historic residential structure at the northern end of the project, and would produce a high-speed, suburban-style divided highway that would undermine the quality of the entryway to the city.

During a work session at the start of October, the public works staff recommended that we adopt the 2008 flood + 1 roadway elevation and approve either a "through arch" or "deck girder" bridge, with an elevation of "200 + 1" for steel components at the bottom of the bridge.[17] The director of public works also recommended that design details about the project's footprint should be left to a later design phase. He indicated that the 100 + 1 level would be 39 inches below the flood level reached in 2008 and would have resulted in the closure of Dubuque Street for 6 days in the past 20 years; the 200 + 1 would be 11 inches below the 2008 level and would have closed Dubuque Street for 4 days; the 2008 + 1 elevation would be above the 2008 level and would not have forced closure of Dubuque Street for any days over the past 20 years. The 200 + 1 through arch bridge coupled with a 2008 + 1 roadway would reduce backwater at Idyllwild and Taft Speedway by 4.9 inches and cost $38 million, whereas the deck girder bridge would reduce it by 6.1 inches at a cost of $35 million. I advocated the through arch, primarily because its design would be more compatible with the planned design of the university's new auditorium.

As the year ended, it was not clear whether the council would accept or modify the staff's recommendations about the roadway and bridge elevations. It looked like we would be focusing a work session on that topic sometime in January 2014. We were also waiting to learn whether the U.S. Federal Highway Administration would approve a "Finding of No Significant Impact," as required by the National Environmental Policy Act. By that time, there would be one new council member, and none of us knew how that new person might affect our decision.

Schools and Affordable Housing

The second major topic concerned the interaction of Iowa City and the Iowa City Community School District with regard to the district's facilities planning and diversity policy and the City's land development policies. To understand what that interaction entailed, one has to know a few basic facts.

Iowa City and the Iowa City Community School District have different missions and geographical boundaries. Whereas the district focuses on public education, Iowa City government has a more generalized mission, and the district encompasses an area which includes Iowa City and its two rapidly growing neighboring cities (Coralville and North Liberty), plus other parts of Johnson County. Consequently, the political constituencies of the two entities differ, and neither of the entities has formal authority over the other. And yet, the fates of the two entities are intertwined. Most of the district's older schools are located in Iowa City, and a majority of its property tax base is found there as well, but much of the demand for new schools is generated by new residential construction in the neighboring cities. The cities' land-use decisions have major consequences for the district's school siting and investment decisions, and vice versa.

In 2012 and 2013, a great deal of public attention focused on whether the district should build more new schools and, if it should, where those buildings should be located and how they would be paid for. The district's decisions would have major effects on the social and economic health of our city and its neighborhoods, as well as on the pocketbooks of Iowa City property taxpayers. Moreover, its decisions were tightly connected to questions pertaining to the spatial distribution of lower-income housing and to the changing demographic composition of the district's student body. Consequently, during this 2-year period, the School Board initiated several actions, which stimulated our council to look more carefully at the City's own actions pertaining to affordable housing and zoning, and to begin considering whether the City should take steps to help the district achieve its diversity objectives.

At that moment, I knew next to nothing about the district's budgetary system. So, I had to learn. According to state law, the School District had the option to spend its share of a penny sales tax fund (better known as SAVE) on building and infrastructure projects, but only if its voters first approved a revenue purpose statement (RPS), which would identify the purposes for which the funds could be spent. The district's existing RPS would expire in 2017. Without an RPS, the district could build the desired projects only by issuing general obligation (GO) bonds, each of which would have to be approved by 60 percent of the voters in a referendum. If the RPS passed, the School Board could fund at least some of the desired construction projects by borrowing against future sales tax revenues. Doing so would require only a majority vote from the board, not a 60 percent majority from the voters.

Interest in adopting a new RPS grew throughout 2012 until the School Board decided to schedule a referendum for early in February 2013. Our mayor had taken great interest in how the School Board's decisions might affect Iowa City's schools. He was especially worried that past construction of new schools in the "North Corridor" had been helping our two neighboring cities grow quite rapidly at the expense of Iowa City, and that construction of a new high school in the North Corridor would only worsen the situation. He also worried that the percentage of students in Iowa City's schools who were lower-income and minorities had been increasing. In August 2012, he expressed the council's views in a letter to the board. Having studied how urban development, racial animosity, and poverty had caused metropolitan areas in other parts of the U.S. to become increasingly segregated by race and class, I shared the mayor's concerns. By late August 2012, our council had also received many letters and emails drawing our attention to the School District's lack of investment in Iowa City's schools. No new schools had been built in Iowa City since around 1990, at least one elementary school had been closed, and several older schools were continually threatened with closure. Many Iowa City residents wanted the older schools in the city to be upgraded and better maintained, and possibly to have one or more new elementary schools be built. Residents in the two largest adjacent cities, which had been growing rapidly, wanted the district to build additional elementary schools and a new junior high school in their area to alleviate overcrowding. And they wanted the district to build a new high school in their area to supplement the two existing high schools, which were located on the east and west sides of Iowa City. In December 2012, our council adopted a resolution recommending a shared vision for the future planning and development of the School District and the City of Iowa City.

At our meeting in late January 2013, we adopted a resolution endorsing the proposed RPS. I fully supported this resolution, but I also asked that we explicitly address how we could achieve better socio-economic balance among Iowa City's neighborhoods, as well as among neighborhoods throughout the School District. Ideally, this would be done in collaboration with neighboring cities in the district. Achieving better balance would require more than changing where new subsidized rental housing could be located. It would also require ensuring that neighborhoods throughout the city, both new and old, included housing affordable to lower-income households, especially in locations that were accessible via public transit.

In making this recommendation, I was challenging an "affordable housing location model" the council had adopted in 2011 in response to the prior council's concerns about increasing concentrations of lower-income people in certain parts of the city. Based on what I learned while co-conducting the "Media, Space, and Race" public rhetoric seminar prior to retiring from the university, my sense was that these concerns were implicitly about lower-income black people becoming more concentrated in the southeastern part of the city. The model prevented additional assisted rental housing from being built in areas that exceeded certain criteria and, thereby, also indicated in which parts of the city new assisted rental housing could be built. But most of the eligible parts of the city were already developed and zoned RS-5 (residential single-family, five units per acre), which greatly constrained where new rental housing could be built. And the model did not provide developers with incentives to build affordable units elsewhere (Hawkinson and Garza, circa 2016).

The referendum about the School District's proposed RPS was held on February 5, 2013. With about 6,000 people voting, slightly less than 56 percent voted to recertify the district's RPS until 2029. Voter approval of the referendum meant that the School District could begin building or renovating some schools. But it would need to plan which buildings would be constructed or renovated, as well as when and where. And, ultimately, the district's voters would have to approve a referendum authorizing the district to issue bonds to pay for the remaining construction costs.

With the RPS recertified, the School District turned its attention to devising a facilities master plan (FMP) for the whole district. The School District created an FMP steering committee early in the spring of 2013, and our mayor appointed Michelle P., the council woman who worked for MidAmerican Energy, as Iowa City's representative on it. I anticipated that the district's school-siting criteria were likely to be suburban in character and, hence, be incompatible with, and undermine, our older neighborhood schools. Consequently, I thought we needed to give Michelle P. some guidance with regard to the siting criteria.

On the same night that the referendum passed, the School Board approved a new diversity policy by a 4:3 vote (Hennigan, 2013a). This new policy sought to achieve better socio-economic balance among the district's schools and thereby help ensure that every student received a high-quality education. Achieving better socio-economic balance among the district's schools was intimately connected with the diversity, or lack thereof, within the School District's neighborhoods. Put simply, housing costs varied dramatically from neighborhood to neighborhood, and so elementary schools varied dramatically in terms of the percentage of students who were eligible for Free and Reduced Lunch (FRL), which the district used as a surrogate measure for poverty.[18] It also meant that the elementary schools varied dramatically in terms of their percentages of minority and ELL (English language learner) students. Therefore, the district's diversity policy raised a key question for Iowa City: what could we do to ensure that housing low-to-moderate-income households can afford is distributed fairly across the city and, ideally, across the district?

This question set into motion a series of council discussions. City staff reported on 2007 and 2009 studies, which had documented there was a large unmet need for rental housing that households with incomes at or below 80 percent of area-wide median income could afford. The staff also informed us about a range of City programs related to affordable housing, including the federally funded Section 8 housing voucher, public housing programs managed by the Iowa City Housing Authority, and a variety of other, much smaller programs. With regard to influencing the distribution of lower-cost housing throughout the metropolitan area, the staff suggested that the MPOJC's Urbanized Area Policy Board could invite the Johnson County Housing Trust Fund to devise—in collaboration with cities and other stakeholders—a regional housing strategy.

Although the staff report was informative, I thought the staff had deflected attention away from what Iowa City could be doing, regardless of what nearby cities did. In my view, the staff had implicitly suggested that, instead of leading the way, we should do no more than what our nearby competitor cities were doing. I thought we should creatively explore ways in which Iowa City could support the development of more affordable housing while also pursuing the environmental sustainability ambitions expressed in the 2030 update to the Comprehensive Plan we had recently adopted. This led me to begin circulating a short paper I had written about increasing socio-economic diversity in housing at the regional scale in order to achieve a better balance among the district's schools.[19]

While we were starting to have these discussions, the School District was deep into the process of developing its FMP. The effort included assistance from a consultant, a large amount of public engagement, and tremendous effort on the part of the School Board members and administrative staff. In May 2013, I was one of roughly 400 people who attended an intense meeting about school facilities investment scenarios. Disagreements about what should be included in the FMP abounded. In the end, the School District was able to devise a plan that called for construction of a new high school and a new junior high school in the North Corridor, construction of two new elementary schools in Iowa City and two more in the North Corridor, and renovations and/or additions to almost of the district's older schools, including two in my council district. The School Board approved its 10-year FMP on December 10, 2013.[20] The question remained, however: would voters in the district approve a referendum authorizing the district to issue bonds for the remaining construction costs? At this point, it looked as though the School Board would schedule a referendum for some time in 2014 or 2015.

As the School Board was approving the FMP, our council considered two proposals to approve voluntary annexations and to rezone land that would accommodate the two new elementary schools in Iowa City. The good news was that the district would use SAVE funds to build those schools. Much to my disappointment, however, the board decided to build both of those schools on "greenfield" sites on the southern and eastern edges of town.[21] Having no control over their decision, I decided to vote for both of the annexations while also noting that I thought the City's planning staff, our Planning and Zoning (P&Z) Commission, and the council should be taking a much more active role in shaping the design of the new neighborhoods surrounding those new schools. The area surrounding the site of the new school on the southeastern edge of town appeared especially promising. We had a clear choice: we could simply replicate the suburban model that had guided development over the past couple of decades, or we could rethink how these new neighborhoods should be designed and facilitate achievement of the sustainability goals articulated in our Comprehensive Plan. With this in mind, I successfully urged the council to direct the staff to prepare and present two alternative development scenarios for the area around the new school: a conventional suburban neighborhood and one based on New Urbanist principles of mixed uses and mixed housing types.

Economic Development and Densification of the Downtown

As noted previously, the city council adopted a new strategic plan early in January 2012. Two of its five priorities were (1) economic and community development and (2) densifying the downtown and near downtown areas. Early in that same month, we also held two lengthy meetings concerning the draft budget for the fiscal year (FY) 2012–2013 and proposed Capital Improvements Plan (CIP) for 2013–2015. The draft budget was a very complicated document that manifested the Strategic Plan's economic development priorities. Probably like other new council members, I found it very difficult to process the proposed budget and CIP after only being on the council for a few days.

We soon encountered three private projects that revealed what densifying the downtown and adjacent areas would entail. Residents disagreed (often intensely) about the merits of each of the projects, and the way the council handled those conflicts raised troubling questions for me.

We council members learned about the first project during the public comment period of our first formal meeting in 2012. Upset members of the public poured out their anger and grief about a local developer's surprise plans to demolish a cluster of older residential buildings located near City Hall and a food co-op that had long been the heart of the local progressive political community. Do something to stop it, they demanded. But, from the council's point of view, there was nothing we could do: the developer owned the property and had a legal right to demolish the buildings. The building he proposed as a replacement complied with the site's existing zoning; an effort to downzone the area had failed just a few years earlier. The older buildings were soon demolished. This action left a bitter taste. The size, scale, and design of the four-story, half-block-long structure that was ultimately built did not help. Many Iowa Citians thought it was ugly and out of scale with its surroundings.[22]

Three months later, we approved a development agreement and $2 million TIF for a proposed 14-story modernist building on the Pedestrian Mall downtown. The first two floors of the $10 million building would provide retail space, the next three would provide "Class A" office space, and the remaining ten would include luxury condos and apartments. The development team was led by Marc M., a man who had, in the late 1990s, built a very large and controversial but very successful 14-story building downtown. I supported the TIF, but I also thought the building could turn out to be an albatross around the city's neck if it was not designed well. During the council meeting, I said if there was anything I could change about the project it would be to chop off the top two stories of luxury residential units. But the developer had not proposed an 11-story building or one that would conform with my ideals of good architecture or urban design. I also saw a worrisome flaw in the council's process: we had not provided the public with sufficient time to consider and express what they thought about the proposed project and subsidy prior to our decision. At home after the vote, I tossed and turned in bed, thinking the building should be two or three stories lower.

None of my political friends liked the building or the TIF, and some of them began circulating a petition asking the council to submit the subsidy to the voters at a special election. In light of these objections, I felt compelled to explain in a late-June *Iowa City Press-Citizen* guest opinion why I had supported it (Throgmorton, 2012): I voted for the TIF because the building would: (1) attract quality jobs to the downtown; (2) provide high-quality housing for people who work in the downtown area; (3) enhance the vitality and health of the downtown both day and night; (4) strengthen surrounding residential neighborhoods; (5) increase property tax revenues almost tenfold over the existing building; and (6) counter a common (if greatly exaggerated) perception that our downtown had become a dirty and dangerous place full of student-oriented bars, scruffy-looking panhandlers, and dangerous teenagers. (Rarely stated overtly, these concerns about teenagers often had racial connotations.) But I also stated that I would not support any future proposal involving a significant TIF unless we provided a minimum of 2 weeks between the time the staff proposed a TIF-based project and the date we would hold a public hearing and vote on it. In the end, the council decided in mid-July to bypass the petition calling for a public vote on the funding by using revenue bonds instead of GO bonds. Mayor Pro Tem Susan M. voiced the views of several council members (though not mine) when she said, "I don't believe economic development can be done by the public-vote process" (Hennigan, 2012a, n.p.).

The third project concerned a City-initiated proposal to redevelop a mostly empty City-owned site located immediately east of downtown at the northeast corner of the College and Gilbert Street intersection. This project proved to be much larger, more important, and more controversial than the first two, and the council's decision process pertaining to it had a lasting effect on my thinking and actions.

Six weeks after the vote on the Ped Mall building, the City staff issued a request for proposals (RFP) for redevelopment of that site. I do not recall being shown the RFP prior to it being issued. City staff received ten proposals in response to the RFP. A review committee (which included two council members—Rick D. and Susan M.) had narrowed the list to five finalists. I do not recall being asked to serve on that committee or even knowing the committee existed until those five finalists presented their proposals at a council work session in late November. The five proposals varied significantly in terms of height (from 5 to 20 stories), mass, architectural design, mix of uses, cost (ranging from $29 million to $54 million), and degree of commitment to sustainability and low-carbon-based-energy use. All five requested public subsidies, especially in the form of TIF, ranging from about $4 million to $13 million.

A week later, we held a lengthy public hearing pertaining to the site's redevelopment. During this public hearing, as well as in the large number of emails and letters we received, many people expressed strong support for selecting any one of the four proposals that included the food co-op (which needed space to expand). Conversely, many other people strongly supported the one proposal (the Chauncey) that included two theaters to be managed by a relatively new entity named FilmScene. This proposal came from the same developer, Marc M., who had recently received TIF support to build the controversial 14-story building in the downtown core. In addition to FilmScene's two theaters, the Chauncey would contain two bowling alleys, a boutique hotel, a few floors of Class A office space, and several floors of luxury condos. Beyond the large number of FilmScene advocates, the Chauncey's supporters primarily included the major economic development organizations. Conversely, opposition to the Chauncey came from neighbors who lived in the residential area to the east of the site, people who simply did not like the developer, and parishioners at Trinity Episcopal Church, located directly west of the proposed site. The church dated back to 1870, was a historic landmark, and had a lovely sanctuary with many stained-glass windows, which any tall new building would shadow. Some commentators strongly supported a second project that highlighted its "net zero" carbon emission features. Many people advocated synthesizing the best features of each of the proposals.

The staff initially recommended that we identify a preferred development (and possibly our second and third preferences) at a meeting 2 weeks later. To help us evaluate the competing proposals, the staff provided us with six evaluation criteria (which had been part of the original RFP). These criteria basically favored proposals that would increase the taxable valuation of property and transform downtown by attracting more office workers, visitors, and residents drawn from a variety of age groups and income levels. Other factors could also be considered.

Although we were scheduled to select the preferred developer during our mid-December formal meeting, I did not want us to vote that night. I argued that we should either identify three applicants and ask them to revise and resubmit or else defer for 2 weeks. Because our decision would send a very strong signal to the public and to private developers about the kind of future we envisioned and wanted for Iowa City and its downtown, I thought it would be very important for us to proceed thoughtfully, at a pace that demonstrated we had sufficiently considered the public's hopes and concerns. The council decided to narrow the list to three proposals (4Zero4, Chauncey Gardens, and the Chauncey) and to instruct the city staff to prepare a matrix that would help us choose among them.

During this meeting, I articulated my views as clearly as I could. First, to choose wisely, we needed to keep *the baseline alternative* in mind. If the City simply sold the land to a private developer for redevelopment consistent with CB-5 zoning, the developer would probably construct a four- or five-story building, with commercial space on the first floor and student housing on the top three or four floors.[23] If we kept this baseline alternative in mind, we would be better able to answer the most important question we faced: would the preferred project really add value to the baseline alternative and would the added value justify the requested subsidy? And, second, we had to think carefully about what we really valued. The staff's criteria emphasized economic consequences and omitted other factors that many Iowa Citians considered important.

I elaborated on this point about value during the work session that night and subsequently in a statement I posted on my Storytelling and Cities Word-Press site.[24] I argued that it was especially important that the successful building's design be compatible with and enhance our downtown's unique sense of place, and that its scale (height and mass) be appropriate for a transitional zone between downtown and the residential neighborhood to its east.[25] Regardless of the building's height or location, the developers needed to consider the relationship between the building and other nearby structures and public spaces. Trinity Church, which my wife and I attended, was the building that was most susceptible to adverse shadowing. I also argued that the successful building should help transform a City-owned park (located immediately north of the development site) into a gem that would strengthen community ties in the city. Accordingly, the developers' proposals should explicitly demonstrate how they would enhance the park, and how their planned rooftop gardens and terraces would be integrated with it. Third, I argued that we had a great opportunity to make a strong statement about the City government's commitment to a sustainable future. We should, therefore, require the revised proposals to achieve at least LEED Gold certification plus a specified degree of energy efficiency (perhaps using 60 percent less energy than currently required by code).[26] Fourth, I supported the idea of subsidizing "workforce housing" at the site, but I was not willing to subsidize construction of luxury penthouses and other condos which the vast majority of the city's residents could not afford. Moreover, I thought a specified percentage of the units should be affordable to lower-income workforce households (60 percent of median household income) and/or elderly or disabled people on fixed incomes. Fifth, I was attracted to the possibility of including one or two small film theaters into the chosen project, but I saw no merit in subsidizing construction of a boutique hotel. Nor was I persuaded that we should subsidize a few bowling lanes, which were part of the Chauncey's proposal. Last, I saw very good reasons to support projects that would generate substantial property tax revenues for the city and, hence, pay for the public services that Iowa Citians expect, but it was not at all clear that the *promise* of additional revenues 15 or more years in the future could— unless the non-monetary benefits were very large—justify deflecting property taxes away from the County and the School District and committing such a large amount of GO bonds in the present. On this point, I also claimed that— according to data provided by the staff—at the end of Year 15, the three surviving proposals would have generated roughly $2–6 million *less* in property taxes than the "baseline" alternative. Whichever development we selected, I argued, it should be one that would symbolize and manifest our city's commitment to a sustainable future, a future that displayed continuity with the past while also responding creatively to the challenges of the future. If the revised proposals did not demonstrate substantial monetary and non-monetary benefits *that we valued highly*, I believed we would be better off selling the property to a private developer with conditions, but without any public subsidy.

We were scheduled to assess the three proposals on January 8, 2013. The City's urban planning staff had put substantial effort into preparing a decision matrix to help us make the decision. The matrix included five "criteria/factors" which could be scored and which the staff had assigned weights to reflect their respective importance: (1) financial considerations (30 percent), which included information about each alternative's request for TIF support and 30-year present value estimates of property tax revenues; (2) each alternative's proposed mix of uses within the building (25 percent); (3) design elements incorporated into each alternative, including evidence of sustainable design (20 percent); (4) the mass and scale of the proposed building (15 percent); and (5) each developer's statement summarizing its experience, passion, and vision (10 percent).

The staff proposed to walk us through each criterion and solicit our rank order scores. They would then average our scores. As we entered our scores, weighted average scores would be generated for each project, and the scores would be displayed on a screen visible to both us and the public. This would be done during the work session, with council members considering the matrix, public comment, developer information, and other factors. If consensus already existed, the staff said, there would be no need to use the matrix. The council's preferred development choice would be ratified during the formal meeting. The staff also indicated that they would be returning to us later in the year with a request that we rezone the parcel of land from P-1 and CB-5 to CB-10.

Having read the decision matrix and accompanying material quite closely, I thought we needed to discuss the matrix and the criteria thoroughly to make sure we understood them. I also thought we should consider whether we wanted to add/delete any criteria, and consider whether we thought the criteria were weighted appropriately. In my view, each council member should be free to assign her/his own weights to them. I also thought we should calculate scores for the baseline alternative, especially because the staff had just told us it would be recommending rezoning the land to CB-10.

My concerns and intentions proved completely irrelevant, for a majority of the council quickly decided to set the decision matrix aside. Long-serving council member Connie C. seemed to express the feelings of other council members when she said, "I don't need the matrix to make up my mind … and I really don't want to go through it with numbers."[27] "Let's find out where people are," the mayor said. Council member Susan M. said,

> I went through and did the matrix and it … confirmed…what my gut and my perception and all the public input had told me, … and so…we … may be wasting our time going through and giving staff all of these numbers and having it all calculated.

Rick D. agreed, as did Connie C., who said, "I don't … want to play the numbers game" and "I really do love that project [the Chauncey]." Terry D. did not disagree, and Mayor Matt H. said, "I scored it myself … and frankly confirmed … where I'm already leaning." Feeling silenced and seeing no reason to ask my questions, I could say little more than, "I think it's a mistake." Suddenly it became clear that a 5:1 majority of council members supported the Chauncey (Hennigan, 2013b)[28] (see Figure 2.1).

What? I was stunned, almost speechless. There was a pretty large crowd of people present in the council chambers when this work session took place. Looking out at the audience, I could see a look of shock on their faces too. Expecting a thorough and thoughtful discussion comparing the merits of the three projects, what they witnessed instead was a sudden decision. "What just happened?" one of them asked me immediately after the work session ended. Many friends of mine were furious to say the least; they thought the shocking speed of the decision implied it had already been made, and the meeting was just for show.

All that remained was to ratify this decision during the formal meeting. Each council member commented on why he or she had chosen the

The Chauncey

The Chauncey L.L.C.
A Development Proposal for the City of Iowa City
26 November 2012

FIGURE 2.1 Rendering of "the Chauncey" as viewed from the northwest.
Source: City of Iowa City, 2012.

Chauncey. Having had virtually no opportunity to share my own thoughts during the work session, I expressed my views more forthrightly during the formal meeting. I thanked the development teams and the public and then described what I thought of each proposal. After reviewing each of them, I said I respected the will of the majority, congratulated the winning project team, and would do what I could to make sure it succeeds. But, I said, this decision was a mistake.[29]

In my judgment, the council had made a serious error, primarily because it had used a bad deliberative process during the work session. I thought we had collectively embarrassed ourselves and insulted the staff, the losing developers, and the public by not explicitly engaging the issues the developers and the public had raised. Surely the other development teams thought, damn, did we waste our time and money? I had a very frank conversation with the mayor a week or so later about the dreadful decision process. Several days later, I had a similar discussion with the city manager.

The council's decision that night—a decision about the biggest building yet to be constructed in Iowa City outside the university—proved to be enormously controversial. By mid-January, we had received lots of letters/emails expressing anger, disappointment, outrage, and so on over our selection of the Chauncey and only one communication expressing support.

Still, further steps needed to be taken to bring the Chauncey to life. The staff began negotiating the details of the project and development agreement with the developer. This began with a staff report early in 2013 recommending rezoning the site from CB-5 to CB-10. However, a complication arose in late February when a community group (Iowa Coalition against the Shadow) co-led by a young lawyer (Rockne C.) applied to have the site rezoned to CB-5 instead. In early April, the P&Z Commission held two public hearings about the coalition's application. The commission voted 5:2 against the proposed rezoning to CB-5, even though several members expressed many misgivings about the proposed 20-story building.

The proposed rezoning to CB-5 came before the council on May 14.[30] During the public hearing, the applicants for the rezoning stressed the importance of "providing proper transitions" and critiqued the council for having made its "rash, unpredictable, and unforeseen decision" to select the Chauncey as the preferred developer. An engineer affiliated with Trinity Church presented a shadow analysis that was far more accurate and revealing than the City staff's analysis had been. Another supporter of the proposed rezoning presented some very compelling photos of the poor transition provided by the new building that had provoked so much controversy early in 2012. And another used Legos to create a very funny scale model of the 20-story building and its surroundings. Representatives of the Chamber of Commerce, the Convention and Visitors Bureau, realtors, downtown businesses, and others argued against the rezoning because they thought the Chauncey would be a great addition to Iowa City's downtown.

I supported the proposed rezoning to CB-5 but indicated I might be willing to support a later rezoning to CB-10 if the proponents of the project significantly modified their project to take opponents' views and values into account. During discussion, City staff displayed on a large screen in the council's chamber a photo I had provided of the scale model of the Chauncey. Referring to the photo, I made four specific points, many of which directly pertained to inadequacies in the overall planning process. First, as demonstrated during the public hearings, public opinion was overwhelmingly opposed to extending downtown eastwards at the density contemplated when the council selected the Chauncey. Of 55 people who had spoken during the P&Z Commission's two public hearings, 44 supported the rezoning, and only 11 opposed it. Most of the 11 opponents had expressed support for the Chauncey and the economic benefits they associated with it, but they had not made a strong case that this site was an appropriate location for such a building. Second, all five of the P&Z commissioners who voted against the rezoning to CB-5 agreed that a 20-story building would be inappropriate on the site, and a majority appeared inclined to favor CB-5. Third, the proponents of rezoning to CB-5 had challenged the wisdom of expanding the downtown to the east rather than to the south as had long been planned, and they had argued the eastern edge should continue to be a transitional zone between downtown and the residential areas farther to the east. They had also argued the City should have rezoned the land prior to issuing the RFP. Fourth, the 2030 Comprehensive Plan Update, which we had literally just adopted, also indicated that this site should ensure quality design and make an appropriate transition to the lower-density residential neighborhoods that border it. In the end, however, the council defeated the proposed rezoning with only Michelle P. and me voting in favor.[31] It seemed very likely that the Chauncey would proceed, but many additional steps would have to be taken in the coming year.

* * *

Selecting a developer for the College and Gilbert Street site was part of an overall effort to make downtown more attractive to visitors and residents other than University of Iowa students. A key part of this effort involved transforming the streetscape.

In April 2013, we hired a consulting firm to help us develop a new master plan for the downtown streetscape. I subsequently participated in many discussions about the proposed plan, as well as in many meetings of an advisory committee which had been created to assist the consultant. It could become a very expensive, multiyear project, and some residents claimed—especially after the council had approved the Chauncey and the new 14-story building on the Pedestrian Mall—that the city council was focusing too much attention and money on the downtown. In November, the City staff and the consultant held a public open house about possible design improvements to the downtown's streetscape.

The streetscape planning effort was largely inspired by a desire to transform the downtown away from one dominated by student bars and transient/homeless people. In late June 2013, the owner and manager of two of the bars downtown successfully submitted to the City a petition to reverse a 21-only ordinance which had barred people over 19 but under the legal drinking age, 21, from being in places with liquor licenses after 10 p.m., with limited exceptions. The council decided to ask voters if they wanted to repeal the 21-only ordinance. In November 2013, voters upheld the ordinance 66 to 34 percent.

Shortly before the vote on the 21-only ordinance, the council became deeply immersed in a debate over whether to further regulate the behavior of homeless/transient people on the Pedestrian Mall. In mid-August, City staff reported there had been a growing number of complaints about behaviors downtown and especially on the Pedestrian Mall. The complaints highlighted aggressive behaviors, loud and vulgar language, storage of personal property in public spaces, smoking, littering, aggressive panhandling, and obstruction of public walkways and public amenities (e.g., benches and planters) in a manner than prohibited use and enjoyment by others. City staff indicated that both the City and the Downtown District felt that non-regulatory approaches had been exhausted, and that we needed to consider ordinance modifications aimed at mitigating the behaviors. The proposed ordinance would limit the storage of personal property, prohibit lying on benches (except late at night) and on planters, and prohibit soliciting near parking meters and at entrances to the Ped Mall. It would also limit the use of electrical outlets only to those who had obtained written permission.

The staff's memo consistently stated that "the City" thought this and that, but our council had not even discussed it in a work session. Some people, myself included, often felt uncomfortable when walking past certain people downtown, and some thought downtown was dirty and dangerous, partly because of the presence of clusters of people who appeared to be homeless. However, the fact that some of us felt uncomfortable did not mean that specific individuals in this specific location were dangerous. How could we appropriately distinguish between what makes us *feel* uncomfortable and what *is* dangerous? I believed that the people of concern were fellow human beings and part of the Iowa City community.[32] They had as much right to the city as any other resident. Moreover, some of the chaos and congestion people complained about in that part of the Pedestrian Mall was caused by the construction staging area that had been created for the new 14-story building's construction. Might the problem become less serious once the construction was completed? Also, two council members (Terry D. and Connie C.) and Mayor Matt H. owned businesses located just a few doorways away from that main entrance to the Ped Mall. Furthermore, prohibiting certain behaviors on the Ped Mall would simply shift them to other parts of the city. What should be done in those locations? To the extent that the "offending" people were homeless, I thought we should look back at the information and advice we had received from the director of the city's primary homeless shelter and others several months before.[33] I doubted that this proposed ordinance was consistent with the advice they gave.

These points did not carry any weight with other council members. In a very long mid-August meeting, we voted in favor of the ordinance 6:1, with me against. We did not get to the ordinance pertaining to homeless people until 10:30 p.m. and did not vote on it until shortly before midnight (Hennigan, 2013c). A couple of weeks later, I spoke at a public event to a group of roughly 50 people who opposed the Ped Mall ordinance.[34] The council adopted the ordinance 4 weeks later. The tenor and tone of the discussion had a significant effect on me, especially with regard to perceiving a clear class bias in favor of business interests on our council and consequently in City government's policies and practices.

• • •

The council's actions pertaining to the 14-story building on the Pedestrian Mall, the Chauncey project, and cleaning up the downtown were consistent with the council's 2012 Strategic Plan and were strongly supported by the major economic development organizations, but the council's actions had also elicited diverse kinds of opposition from people who had different ideas and

visions about how the city should change over time.[35] How the tension between conflicting visions should be resolved was the subject of the 2030 Comprehensive Plan Update (City of Iowa City, 2013a), which the council had
adopted immediately before voting on the CB-5 rezoning for the Chauncey.

City planning staff drafted the 2030 update after conducting two public
workshops early in 2012, engaging in extensive public outreach, and using an
online participation tool. The staff found "a tension between the small-town
character that people value and identify as being quintessentially Iowa City
and the uncertainty that comes with change in a growing community" (p. 5).
The tension existed largely because the city is the home of the University of
Iowa. "The question," the staff planners stated, "seems to be how and where to
strike a balance between preservation [of the city's small-town character] and
change [growth and investment that brings big-city vitality]" (p. 6). According
to the plan, application of "sustainability" would enable "the community" to
strike the balance.[36] How would this balance be struck? Readers had to infer
the answer.

No members of the public spoke during our public hearing on the 2030
update. However, we did receive a small amount of correspondence pertaining
to it. Some urged us to reduce greenhouse gas emissions and promote buildings which had "net zero" energy use. Another person drew attention to the
update's quiescence about homelessness, crime, social service needs, and how
to improve life chances for lower-income people in general. Other than Mayor
Matt H. and I, no members of the council expressed their views about the plan.
The motion to approve the updated plan passed unanimously.

When the mayor spoke, he highlighted all the City had been doing in the
name of sustainability over the past few years. I thought the 2030 update improved on the 1997 Comprehensive Plan and therefore expressed my support
for it. But I also noted ambiguity in the update about how the council would
strike the balance each time the council interpreted the plan and made key
decisions on behalf of the City government.[37] I had observed that, with occasional exceptions, council members were strongly inclined to defer to the professional staff. The update implicitly treated the council's process for "striking
the balance" as a "black box" which converted values and information presented by diverse publics into an authoritative decision without clarifying what
would guide "the City's" decision. In council discussion about the proposed
update, I argued that we needed to actively solicit the views of diverse publics
prior to striking the balance with regard to any major action. This would mean
soliciting the views of not just those who routinely participated, but especially
those who did not—that is, working people, diverse ethnic groups, students,
older people, environmental groups, newcomers, and others. We needed to
give them ample opportunity to express their own views and, especially, to
give them good reasons to know they might be able to influence the final
decision. I did not realize it at the time, but I was essentially saying conflict is

an important part of democratic governance, and we needed to find a way to enable conflicting visions of the city's future to be contested politically, not simply through City government's formal decision processes.

• • •

The Riverfront Crossings (RFC) District would present a key site for testing the council's willingness and ability to strike a good balance between preserving Iowa City's small-town character and promoting growth and investment that brings big-city vitality.

Newly named, the district was a 76-acre area located immediately south of downtown. City planning staff had briefed us, late in September 2012, about a proposed Downtown and Riverfront Crossings District Master Plan (City of Iowa City, 2013b), and the council considered adoption of the plan 4 months later. Informed by a consultant's market yield analysis and influenced by a visioning process plus a significant amount of public input, the RFC District Master Plan identified key framework elements that would guide redevelopment within the district and eight subdistricts, highlighted 13 primary development opportunities, and included design guidelines to use until a form-based code (FBC) could be adopted. As expressed materially in Figure 2.2, the 13 development opportunities were: (1) infill development that is contextual in nature; (2) housing options throughout the study area, including condominiums, town homes, apartments, live–work units, cottage homes, senior housing, and student housing;[38] (3) a new regional park on the former site of the North Wastewater Treatment Plant; (4) restoration of Ralston Creek; (5) enhancements to the pedestrian environment along heavily travelled Burlington Street; (6) transformation of Clinton Street into a multimodal promenade; (7) a new "Clinton Plaza" at the northern end of the Clinton Promenade; (8) a "Station Plaza" connecting a proposed regional passenger rail station with a proposed light-rail stop;[39] (9) transit-oriented development adjacent to transit stops; (10) an arts district on the southeastern edge of the district; (11) transformation of a north–south street (Gilbert Street) into a "Main Street" with active street fronts; (12) redevelopment of commercial uses along a north–south road on the west side of the river; and (13) improvement of the aesthetics and pedestrian environment along that road. The staff had conducted numerous public meetings about this new plan, and the public had responded quite positively to it. I thought it was an excellent plan and supported it quite enthusiastically. The council unanimously approved it.

In April 2013, we learned about a development proposal that would jump-start the new RFC District Plan. It was oriented around a complicated private agreement between the university and a major local bank in which the university would obtain a key downtown property owned by the bank. This would permit the university to use that site for a new music building, replacing one

FIGURE 2.2 The 2013 Downtown and Riverfront Crossings District Plan (north on left).

Source: City of Iowa City, 2013b, p. 25.

that had been flooded in 2008, and, in return, the university would transfer to the bank ownership of a 1917 school site located in the middle of the RFC District. Prior to transferring ownership of the site, the university was required to demolish the aged building to make room for a new 580-space parking structure lined with townhouses on the exterior. The bank would build a new five-story office building next to that parking structure in the center of the RFC District. Owners of the bank would not be seeking TIF support for the new building, but they would need access to City-owned parking. In mid-May 2013, the council unanimously supported this proposal. I disliked the idea of demolishing the old school building, but I voted for it because I saw the redevelopment as an important part of our Riverfront Crossings initiative, which I supported. Getting the first developments right on the main north–south (Clinton Street) corridor were crucial for the plan's success.

Seven months later, one of the City's senior planners (Karen H.) briefed us about the new form of zoning, form-based codes, which the staff would be proposing for the RFC District. Her briefing was needed, for many council members were completely unfamiliar with the concept. In essence, ordinary zoning separates land uses (residential, commercial, industrial, etc.) from one another and then regulates the density of the uses. An FBC, on the other hand, uses physical form rather than separation of uses as the organizing principle. FBCs also include standards intended to enhance the walkability and appeal of the streetscape while providing potential property owners and developers with clear guidance about what they must do to develop their properties.

On the same night that Karen H. briefed us about FBCs, the council authorized the staff to apply for a $9 million grant from the Iowa Flood Mitigation Board to transform the southernmost part of the RFC District. The grant would enable the City to demolish the City's North Wastewater Treatment Plant and administration building (both of which had been flooded in 2008), create a 5-acre wetland on part of the treatment plant's site, stabilize the banks of a creek which ran through the district, and, hopefully, produce a new regional park.

Racial Equity and a Proposed Justice Center

None of the economic development efforts just described focused on improving the lives of Iowa City's lower-income residents, especially those who were black. So, let me turn now to the fourth major topic the city council encountered in 2012–2013: the City's responses to demands for racial equity in relation to Johnson County's planning for a new justice center.

On February 26, 2012, a neighborhood watch member shot and killed a young black man named Trayvon Martin in Sanford, Florida. Martin, a 17-year-old African-American high school student, had been visiting a friend with his father and was unarmed. The watch member claimed he shot Martin in self-defense and, in mid-July, he was acquitted of second-degree murder based on Florida's "stand your ground" law. The fatal encounter and the subsequent trial sparked outrage and protests throughout the country.

Trayvon Martin's murder also provoked a strong reaction in Iowa City. On March 26, several hundred people gathered on the Pedestrian Mall to demonstrate in a "Million Hoodie March." In a work session roughly 1 week later, I asked the council to support a resolution expressing our dismay and outrage about the senseless killing of this young man. The mayor, mayor pro tem, and other council members hesitated to have the council express its views on national rather than local issues, but the council did agree to discuss during our next work session the possibility of adopting some kind of resolution. I emphasized that my proposed resolution did have a local focus. In part, it read: "Martin's killing has caused grief and outrage among many Iowa Citians," and "Iowa Citians have a long and admirable history of resisting racism and racial profiling." The proposed resolution also criticized "stand your ground" laws (Hennigan, 2012b). Two weeks later, the council suggested that councilman Rick D. and I work with City staff on crafting a revised resolution.[40] On May 1, the council formally appointed Rick D. and me to prepare a resolution rejecting racial profiling and relating to diversity issues in the Iowa City community.

I asked the organizers of the multiracial CRJ to invite a group of black Iowa Citians to meet with Rick D. and me. When we met with 18 black residents at First Baptist Church early in May, we listened to them narrate their personal stories about being black in Iowa City. Many of those stories focused on interactions with police officers. Building on that conversation and my earlier draft resolution, Rick D. and I negotiated a revised resolution pertaining to "diversity issues." The council discussed it during a work session later in May. Rick D. stunned me right off the bat by saying that none of the "whereas" (justification) clauses in the proposed resolution mattered much to him. And then Connie C., the long-serving member, said she wanted to drop almost all the "whereas" clauses. The mayor and council member Michelle P. seemed to agree. I said—calmly, but feeling quite upset—that all of the "whereas" clauses came from the conversation we had with minority members of the community; we didn't dream them up. The mayor pro tem suggested that we retain a couple whereas clauses, and so we agreed to a watered-down resolution expressing our intent to establish an ad hoc committee to study City law enforcement and transportation operations as they related to minority populations, with a view toward promoting just and harmonious interaction between local government and minority segments of the community.

I was really upset at Rick D. I thought he and I had co-drafted a resolution, but, instead of arguing for it, he had tossed half of the resolution out the window right at the start. I was so upset I almost flew out of my chair, saying "F—k it! This is a waste of time!" There were about ten observers in the crowd from the CRJ, and it seemed very clear to me they were extremely disappointed in the council's unwillingness or inability to face the situation forthrightly. I had to walk around for a half-hour between the work session and the formal meeting just to calm myself down, reminding myself all the time that politics is the art of the possible. During the formal meeting, I thanked the people Rick D. and I had spoken with. He basically said, "This stuff is very hard to talk about." No, it isn't, I thought. One simply has to be honest, speak from one's own experience, and deal with the emotional intensity of the topic. I biked home around 9:30 p.m., had a scotch, and ranted to my wife about the evening's experience.[41]

Not long before the Million Hoodie March and our council's first discussion about it, Johnson County government had proposed to build a new $47 million justice center. The proposal would include renovating the existing county courthouse and attaching an entirely new five-story jail and office structure to it. It soon became clear there were important connections between the County's proposal and local response to Trayvon Martin's death.

The existing jail, which was built in 1981 and was located in the middle of the City's proposed RFC District, had a capacity of about 90 beds, whereas its occupancy rate was running between 160 and 190 inmates per day, and the county sheriff's office projected a large increase in inmates over the coming years. County officials and representatives from the legal community argued the existing jail and courthouse were unsafe and did not have enough space.

Moreover, the county was paying to transport and house overflow inmates elsewhere, and the existing jail's design did not allow for easy monitoring. The courthouse also lacked a secure entrance, and court officials said there was a great need for more courtrooms and storage and office space. The proposed five-level justice center building would include a 240-bed jail, the county sheriff's office, six more courtrooms, a new clerk of court office, and other court-related space. The existing courthouse, which was on the National Register of Historic Places, would be renovated and continue to be used. A diverse mix of opponents claimed the plan was too costly, the proposed jail was too large, and the county needed to address unnecessarily high arrest rates in general and disproportionately high arrest and incarceration rates of racial minorities in particular before building a new jail. In order for the county to pay for its new justice center, county voters would have to approve a bond issue of up to $47 million. A super-majority 60 percent would be required (Hennigan, 2012c).

Was the proclaimed need for a new jail linked to the Iowa City Police Department's arrest practices pertaining to black people? Would our proposed resolution concerning "diversity issues" have any significant effect on those arrest practices and, ultimately, on the need for a new jail? Our council did not explicitly address these questions, but they were lurking under the surface.

We discussed the purpose, size, composition, and other details of the possible "Ad Hoc Committee on Diversity Issues" during a work session early in June. Two weeks later, we officially created the committee. We charged it with reviewing the policies, practices, and procedures within the Police and Transportation Services Departments with the intent of providing a set of recommendations to the council on diversity-related matters. Two weeks later, the council considered 14 applicants for seven positions on the new committee. The chair would be a young African-American lawyer (Kingsley B.) who worked for the county auditor's office and had recently been appointed to the City's Police Community Relations Board.

Four months later, our council considered a resolution supporting the referendum authorizing the county to sell bonds to pay for the justice center. When thinking about whether or not to support the resolution, I asked myself four questions. First, would the proposed center improve the health and safety of the inmates; ensure the safety of jurors, courthouse employees, and the general public; and improve the efficiency of the court's and jail system's operations? Second, were the 150 additional jail beds needed? Third, were the estimated costs reasonable for accomplishing these purposes? And last, would the physical design of the new justice center enhance the appeal and long-term prosperity of the RFC District south of downtown? I was persuaded that the first criterion had been met, but not the other three. My concerns mainly had to do with arrest rates. Having been working with the CRJ on these matters, I understood that Johnson County had the highest rate for arresting African-American and Latino youth in Iowa. We had recently been told that, in 2009,

African-American youth in particular were nearly nine times more likely to be arrested than their white counterparts, and Latino youth were almost three times more likely to be arrested (Coalition for Racial Justice, 2013). I also had not yet seen any data comparing the costs of transporting inmates to other jails with the costs of operating the new jail. Last, I was not persuaded that the proposed physical design of the justice center would be compatible with our plans for revitalizing the RFC District. Consequently, I had not yet decided whether I should support the proposed justice center, and so I abstained on the resolution.[42] In Iowa City, abstaining counted as a vote for the motion.

Roughly 2 weeks later, I travelled to Cincinnati to participate in the Association of Collegiate Schools of Planning's academic conference. One afternoon, my wife and I walked through the Over-the-Rhine neighborhood north of downtown. We stopped in a lovely little café embedded in a cluster of renovated older brick buildings and new shops. Young, mostly white, hip people were sitting inside, while black people, most of them younger men, were walking on the sidewalks outside. I could only guess, of course, but to my eye they looked unemployed, alienated, and possibly outraged. The experience reminded me of segregated and impoverished neighborhoods I had visited in Detroit, St. Louis, and Chicago, and of my discipline's past role in creating such neighborhoods. In my view, white people in positions like mine should feel a moral imperative to do what we could, as allies, to improve the lives and neighborhoods of low-income and minority populations.

A few days later, the county's bond referendum for the new justice center failed: 56 percent of voters supported the referendum, just 4 points shy of the required 60. Shortly thereafter, the county proposed a revised $44 million plan, which included a new 195-bed county jail and four new courtrooms, plus space for other court functions and the ability to add more beds and courtrooms later. Once again, opponents argued the plan was too costly, the jail was too large, and the county needed to address excessively high arrest rates in general and the disproportionately high arrest and incarceration rates of racial minorities in particular. The referendum on the revised plan would take place early in May 2013.

Over the many months the county's plan and referendum was being discussed, I had become persuaded that building a new jail and renovating the courthouse were warranted, but I could not support investing in a new jail until I was convinced that everyone in the local criminal justice system (the cities' police departments, the county sheriff, the county attorney, and others) had done everything reasonably possible to reduce disproportionate minority contact throughout the system and to create ways to divert troubled individuals away from the jail and the emergency wards of hospitals. By "everyone in the system," I meant myself as well. Consequently, in the first few months of 2013, I worked with several friends in the CRJ to craft and hopefully complete a CRJ report about race and poverty in Iowa City.

The Ad Hoc Committee on Diversity met for 8 months and submitted its recommendations at our work session on April 9, 2013. With regard to law enforcement, the committee reported that minority community members were either unaware of or lacked faith in the City's Police Community Relations Board. The committee also indicated that the City's police department needed to build better relationships with minority communities and to adopt a "customer service" attitude—that is, to shift from a "control and monitor" to a "protect and serve" culture. The committee also found a lack of consistency in how police officers performed their duties (when stopping drivers, for example) and a lack of understanding within the minority community about individuals' rights and responsibilities. The committee provided detailed recommendations for each of these topics and attached a report from the U.S. Department of Justice about community-oriented policing. With regard to transit services, the Ad Hoc Committee made recommendations pertaining to weekend services, the difficulty of getting to and from work, how public transit passengers were treated, and related topics. One of the related topics involved improving conditions at the City's transit interchange downtown so that boisterous black teenagers would not be singled out as troublemakers. Last, the committee recommended that the city manager's office prepare an annual equity report.

Having heard the Ad Hoc Committee's recommendations, the council directed the City staff to review the recommendations and return to us with the staff's responses and recommendations. I was pleased with the report and its recommendations, especially the ones concerning law enforcement. Likewise, I thought the transit recommendations were reasonable, although I doubted some of them were practicable. I also thought we should consider appointing a new temporary Ad Hoc Committee to consider the housing challenges faced by African-American and Latino residents, along with ways of diversifying the employee mix in City government. At the time, in 2011, only 11, 10, and 2 of 459 full-time City employees were black, Hispanic, and Asian, respectively.

On May 7, county voters again chose not to approve the referendum, with only 54 percent of voters backing the bond issue (Hennigan, 2013d). County officials expressed dismay but also recognized they would have to rethink their plans.

During our work session 1 month after the bond issue's defeat, the city manager and police chief presented the staff's recommendations about how to implement the Ad Hoc Committee's recommendations. The city manager had created a diversity task force consisting of City staff and had appointed an equity director to ensure the recommendations would be implemented and comply with the city council's goals. She would also be responsible for preparing an annual equity report. The council unanimously approved the staff's recommendations later that evening (Hennigan, 2013e).

I supported many of the staff's recommendations. However, as a general matter, I thought we should ask the Ad Hoc Committee members what they thought about the recommendations before we adopted them. As I read it, the written text of the Police Department's response basically said, "we'll continue doing what we've been doing." If I understood the Ad Hoc Committee correctly, that was not what the committee wanted. It was definitely not what I expected. I strongly believed we should be seeing a more active indication of what the Police Department would change, not what it would continue doing. Making this point during the work session led to a fairly tense interaction between the city manager and me.

On July 23, the CRJ held a press conference releasing its Racial Equity report (Coalition for Racial Justice, 2013). The report received a substantial amount of public attention. Broken down by race/ethnicity, it presented data pertaining to education, juvenile justice, adult criminal justice, economic well-being, housing, and representation in community leadership. Based on these data, the CRJ report found troubling racial disparities in each of those areas and it called for action to reduce them. The CRJ would continue to advocate for the needed actions, but several leaders in the black community decided they needed to create their own advocacy group as well. This new group called itself the Black Voices Project (BVP).

The November 2013 Council Elections and Beyond

After several months on the council, I had established cordial relationships with other council members, but I felt little sense of political camaraderie. Partly for this reason, after 15 months or so on the council, I also thought that I was not being as effective a council member as I would like. I felt a modest sense of accomplishment with regard to changing the City government's approach to racial equity. But I also thought the progress had been quite slow and barely adequate and I was struck by the complete disconnect between the City's economic development efforts and the day-to-day lives of black Iowa Citians. Moreover, I gradually realized that there were very few opportunities for members of the council to initiate action. With the important exception of racial equity, I constantly felt that I was reacting to proposals the staff brought to us rather than working with other council members to initiate new policies and actions. I would read the information the staff provided, think about it, talk with people who were likely to be affected by proposed actions, pose questions for the council and staff, and often end up feeling like I was whistling in the wind. What could I do differently?

By mid-2013, the situation had led me to begin having exploratory conversations with possible candidates for city council. One was Kingsley B., the young black chairman of the Ad Hoc Committee on Diversity. Another was Rockne C., the young lawyer who had been helping people challenge the Chauncey development. And a third was a black woman, Royceann P., who played a significant leadership role within the black community and helped create the BVP. I hoped to identify at least one new person who might be a political ally on the council. Somewhere around the end of 2012, I had also started attending meetings of a new Center for Worker Justice (CWJ) and recognized that I shared their desire to assist immigrants and recent refugees. I sensed lots of great new energy among the 30 or so people who attended those meetings.

As the November 5 election approached, four people were vying for the two at-large positions: an incumbent (Susan M.), Rockne C., Kingsley B., and a downtown business owner (Catherine C.) who was the daughter of the long-serving council member who would be departing the council. For the District B position, the incumbent downtown businessman (Terry D.) was running against Royceann P. The referendum about eliminating the under-21 bar ordinance was also on the ballot, which was likely to increase voter turnout significantly. I provided considerable help and encouragement to Kingsley B. and Rockne C. and I told people (who asked) how I intended to vote, but I did not publicly endorse anybody. I also offered some help and encouragement to Royceann P. in her bid to defeat the incumbent downtown businessman, but I was concerned that she had not yet learned enough about the range of topics council members typically had to deal with.

In the end, slightly under 11,000 people voted in the election, which constituted a 22 percent turnout. The race for the two at-large positions turned out to be quite close. Susan M., the incumbent financial analyst, was chosen on 42 percent of the ballots, just 1 point ahead of Kingsley B. The downtown business woman and the young lawyer finished third and fourth, with 38 and 33 percent. The downtown businessman, Terry D., was reelected after being named on 58 percent of the ballots, to 40 percent for Royceann P. Voters soundly defeated the effort to overturn the under-21 ordinance by 66 to 34 percent.

Reflecting Back, Looking Ahead

As the first 2 years of my council term neared their end, I was far too busy to think systematically about what I had learned. Even so, a few basic facts stood out. First, being a good council member was hard work both intellectually and emotionally; it is far more difficult than the general public imagines.

Second, I remembered something that I first learned in the mid-1990s: to function effectively as a member of the council, one must pay close attention to the flow of action pertaining to each of the topics that come one's way. By "flow of action" I mean that each topic has its own starting point, sequence of events, decision points, and outcomes. Some of these topics can be devilishly complicated both technically and politically, as the Gateway project exemplifies quite nicely. Consequently, council members need help. The City's professional staff provide much of the needed support, but council members cannot and should not rely exclusively on what the City staff tells them. Instead, council members must call upon interested members of the attentive public to provide information and highlight values the staff has missed or marginalized, to test alternative ideas, and to assess the feasibility of proposals.

Third, council members cannot focus their attention on everything; rather, they must learn how, as much as possible, to focus attention on what really matters. This requires knowing or discovering what one values. Of all the topics that came our way in 2012 and 2013, the four discussed earlier in this chapter struck me as being most important. Although I had begun my council term intending to be a team player, I learned by engaging these issues that my values and priorities differed in key respects from those of my fellow council members. The extent of the difference varied by topic.

With regard to the two flood mitigation projects, my sense was that we council members had arrived at reasonable decisions through a process in which each individual member made a valuable contribution. I also learned how complex and difficult some decisions can be, and about how many diverse actors can have a hand in shaping the ultimate decisions. Ever so gradually, I was searching for, but had not yet found, a word that might express this multiplicity.

I also was reminded how important the School Board's decisions were for the health and sustainability of Iowa City and its neighborhoods and, conversely, how important our investments in Iowa City's neighborhoods and our decisions about making all of our neighborhoods healthy, diverse, and inclusive were to the quality and equity of education in the School District's schools. Consequently, I enthusiastically joined the mayor and other council members in supporting the School District's efforts to pass the referendum on its revenue purpose statement and to develop (and mobilize public support for) its FMP. However, based on many conversations with affordable housing advocates, I also grew increasingly concerned that a growing number of Iowa Citians— many of whom were recent immigrants or refugees who spoke little or no English—were unable to find decent housing they could afford. Much more needed to be done, and I was beginning to wonder how firmly committed the council and city manager were to taking on the challenge.

I felt a modest sense of accomplishment with regard to changing the City government's approach to racial equity. My efforts had helped the CRJ complete its influential report, and I had helped our council take a cautious but non-trivial step toward improving racial equity by creating the Ad Hoc Committee on Diversity and then responding positively to some of its recommendations. But much more needed to be done.

As we approached the end of 2013, I had also developed a more precise understanding of what the rest of the council had in mind with regard to developing the downtown and near downtown areas. Gradually, I was realizing that I did not share the council's and staff's vision of the kind of city we should be creating. The process by which the council made its decision about the Chauncey, the ways in which some council members marginalized opposing views coming from the general public, the stark class bias I witnessed when we were deciding about homeless people downtown, and the council majority's determination to dramatically transform the downtown area in the name of sustainability, while disregarding the social and environmental components of that concept, all led me to this conclusion.

And last, I gradually learned that many issues were interconnected at a very complex and detailed level. There was, for example, the connection between the City's policies concerning the spatial distribution of affordable housing and the School District's difficulty in reducing the disparities in FRL rates among schools. This, in turn, was connected to the outrage and fear that black residents displayed after the killing of Trayvon Martin early in 2012, and to Johnson County's unsuccessful effort to develop a new justice center and a greatly enlarged jail. The proposed construction of this new justice center was, in turn, connected to the City's efforts to redevelop the area south of downtown; to council-led efforts to remove homeless people from the Pedestrian Mall downtown and, thence, to the council's approval of TIF for the new 14-story building on the Ped Mall; and to the council's initiation of an expensive project to rebuild the downtown streetscape. For me, these interconnections made Iowa City look more and more like Jane Jacobs's "problems in organized complexity." Although my background in urban planning helped me deal with narrowly defined issues within this complexity, it was less helpful with regard to dealing with the complex interconnections among issues. There was much I needed to learn.

I could not claim I had been right in every instance, but I trusted my own knowledge and instincts and concluded that changes were needed. I remained hopeful that the Riverfront Crossings District Master Plan we had adopted early in 2013 would turn out quite well. And I was looking forward to having Kingsley B. join the council. Perhaps, with his help, we could make considerably more progress toward making Iowa City a safer and more welcoming place for all its residents. If we could also make it a more sustainable place, so much the better. I was looking forward to it.[43]

Notes

1 Local governments frequently use TIF as an economic development tool. Although specific features vary from state to state, the TIF process typically begins with the city establishing an "urban renewal area" (URA) and then diverting taxes on increased property value in the URA (the tax increment) from the city's general fund, school districts, and counties to the city's TIF fund. The city must spend those diverted taxes on development projects within the URA. In practice, cities often use the diverted tax increment to enable construction of desired projects, either by providing predetermined up-front "gap financing" to developers or rebates of taxes paid by the developers. Once a predetermined amount of TIF support has been paid or rebated, all property taxes revert to the city, the county, and the school district. A key question to ask is, would the project be built if TIF assistance was not provided?
2 Implicitly at least, their views were strongly influenced by urbanist Richard Florida's (2002) ideas about "the creative class."

3 In lay language, I understood a sustainable place would be one in which its residents thrive over the long term and do so without dumping their wastes and problems onto future generations or onto other people and species in other places. This kind of sustainability involves a combination of economic vitality, social justice, and ecological health. Planning scholar Scott Campbell (1996) provides a more rigorous explication.

4 My thinking about conflict resolution was heavily influenced by Fisher, Ury, and Patton (1991), Susskind, McKearnan, and Thomas-Larmer (1999), and LeBaron (2002), and by teaching for several years a graduate course in negotiation, mediation, and consensus-building.

5 In the U.S., the collapse and recession contributed to the rise of the Tea Party and, at the other end of the political spectrum, the Occupy Wall Street movement, which sought to draw attention to the massive disparities among households in terms of income and wealth. It had a fleeting presence in Iowa City from late 2011 until spring 2012.

6 At that moment, my thinking about justice was influenced by political philosopher Michael Sandel's *Justice* (2008).

7 See Jacobs (1969/1970, 1984/1985, 1992/1994, 2000, 2005). Although Iowa City is hardly the kind of city Jacobs had in mind when she wrote *Death and Life*, many residents seemed to be aware of her work.

8 See Bryson (2007) for details about strategic planning by public and non-profit organizations. Iowa City officials used strategic planning to provide short-term policy guidance to City staff. The strategic plan did not have the force of law behind it.

9 Joint Cities meetings involved elected officials from all local governments in Johnson County, including the Iowa City Community School District's Board of Directors. The Joint Cities group had no formal authority; it met only to share information of mutual interest.

10 For details, see Connerly, Laurian, and Throgmorton (2016).

11 This memo and all other relevant Gateway Project documents can be found at: www.icgov.org/gateway-project-planning-information

12 Early in 2013, City staff reported that 150 of the Peninsula Development's planned 410 units had been built, construction of buildings in the southern half would begin in the spring, and a commercial building seemed likely. Consequently, ensuring access to the development during floods seemed important. For background about the Peninsula project, see Franklin (2003).

13 See "A Tough Decision about a New Levee" at: https://persuasivestorytelling. wordpress.com/2012/11/28/tough-decision-about-building-a-new-levee/

14 In making this claim, I drew upon the National Research Council's (2012) report, *Disaster Resilience*.

15 The term "500-year flood" means there is a 0.2 percent probability (based on the historical record) that such a flood would occur in any year.

16 The City engineer's references to increased precipitation and severe weather events raised big red flags for me. Having been greatly influenced by Hansen (2009), I thought the 1993 and 2008 floods and another serious flood earlier in 2013 were consistent with the scientific literature about climate change. And yet, I also thought that Hansen and most other climate scientists missed something important about the relationship between scientists and the public in democracies. To think purely in terms of educating the public was to ignore a large body of scholarly literature about the nature, complexity, and importance of communication; e.g., Lakoff (2010).

17 In lay language, a deck girder bridge is basically flat with no ornamentation, whereas a through arch bridge traverses through arches on both sides of the bridge.

18 In the 2012–2013 school year, about 34 percent of the district's students had been approved for free or reduced lunch. At the elementary level, the percentages ranged from 6 to 79 percent. The difference in FRL percentages at the district's three

junior high schools and two comprehensive high schools was considerably smaller (Iowa City Community School District, 2013).

19 Sometime in 2013, I began meeting with Sally S., a researcher who worked at the university's Public Policy Center and who had organized a group that eventually coalesced into the Johnson County Affordable Housing Coalition. I normally participated in its monthly meetings.

20 The Facilities Master Plan and related details can be found at: www.iowacity-schools.org/Page/15773

21 One of the suburban schools would replace an older eastside elementary school which the district's FMP had scheduled for demolition. This decision greatly upset parents who lived near the older school.

22 See "Crafting Deft Transitions" at: https://persuasivestorytelling.wordpress.com/2013/04/27/crafting-deft-transitions/

23 When making this argument, I was unaware that the City staff planned to recommend that the site be upzoned to CB-10. City Code limits the height of buildings in the CB-5 zone to 75 feet and a maximum floor area ratio (FAR) of three. There is no height limit in the CB-10 zone, but the maximum permissible FAR is 10.

24 See "A Major Redevelopment Project near Downtown Iowa City" at: https://persuasivestorytelling.wordpress.com/2012/12/19/a-major-redevelopment-project-near-downtown-iowa-city/

25 I had recently read the last volume of Christopher Alexander's, *The Nature of Order*. On the whole, I found his work to be inspirational and right in almost every respect. But I also thought his recommendations were radically at odds with conventional planning and zoning and, hence, would be very difficult to act upon.

26 The U.S. Green Building Council's Leadership in Energy and Environmental Design (LEED) program is a widely used rating system. It provides independent verification of a building's or neighborhood's green features—e.g., its resource efficiency.

27 Quotations from city council meetings here and elsewhere in this book come from the City's official transcripts. The transcript for this work session can be found at: www.iowa-city.org/WebLink/DocView.aspx?id=1280665&dbid=0&repo=CityofIowaCity

28 Council member Michelle P. recused herself from the vote because she worked for the company that owned part of the property that would be purchased and rezoned.

29 For details, see: "A Major Development Mistake on the Eastern Edge of Downtown Iowa City" at: https://persuasivestorytelling.wordpress.com/2013/01/09/a-development-mistake-on-the-eastern-edge-of-downtown-iowa-city/

30 I met with the city attorney prior to this meeting (and one more time later in the year) about whether I should recuse myself from votes pertaining to the Chauncey because of my attendance at Trinity. Having no financial stake in, and occupying no leadership role at, Trinity, I decided not to recuse myself and explained my rationale publicly during the meeting.

31 Later in 2013, Rockne C. and the Iowa Coalition against The Shadow (ICATS) filed a petition with the Iowa District Court for Johnson County for a writ of *certiorari* asserting the denial of the rezoning application was arbitrary and discriminatory because the council had already prejudged the issue and intended to grant CB-10 zoning to accommodate the Chauncey development. The petition included additional claims.

32 Early in August 2013, I attended a memorial service for a young homeless woman who had died on July 31.

33 In November 2012, I had urged the council to invite some knowledgeable people to enlighten us about the problem of homelessness in Iowa City. Not long thereafter, three such individuals spoke to us during a work session. They told us that

"panhandlers" constituted a very small fraction of the total homeless population, and that many of them tended to be service-resistant and often were not homeless. They also told us that incarceration was not the answer for that population; instead, there was a need to address the chronically homeless, perhaps by providing for a "housing first" facility, which would provide them with temporary housing, followed by implementing a frequent users service enhancement initiative, which would enable such people to access needed services.

34 For details, see "Regulating Behavior in Downtown Iowa City" at: https://persuasivestorytelling.wordpress.com/2013/09/19/regulating-behavior-in-downtown-iowa-city/

35 The debate over the Chauncey, its design, and its compatibility with the neighborhood to its east alerted me to the lack of well-informed architectural and urban design criticism in the Iowa City area. In the fall of 2013, I joined with a local architect in creating DesignIC, an informal group of professionals who were knowledgeable about urban design.

36 The 2030 update defined sustainability as "meeting the needs of the present without compromising the ability of future generations to meet their own needs." It identified three interrelated factors that together create healthy and thriving communities: environment, economy, and society. And it noted that the City had begun using sustainability indicators to assess the city's sustainability status.

37 What constitutes a good plan? To the best of my knowledge, there are very few exemplars of what might be called "urban criticism" to draw upon for insight. Architectural criticism provides one model. But urban criticism requires more. First, one must learn how to read plans (Mandelbaum, 1990). Beyond that, one possible way of assessing an *adopted* plan's merits would be to use explicitly defined, "objective" criteria to evaluate how well it achieves its stated purposes (Laurian et al., 2004). But assessing the merits of a *proposed* plan calls for a different process, which would assess its normative purposes as well as its feasibility, cost, and other criteria. Experimenting with the idea of urban criticism, I found it fruitful to interpret the 2030 update through a lens provided by literary criticism, especially Terry Eagleton's (2013) *How to Read Literature.*

38 The plan encouraged the university to build new residence halls within certain parts of the district or to sponsor privately developed dorms.

39 By this time, we had learned that opposition from Republican legislators and the Republican governor had caused the state government to reject $53 million in federal funds which, when combined with $23 million in matching funds from Iowa, would have enabled construction of an Amtrak rail line connecting Iowa City with Chicago to the east and Des Moines and Omaha to the west. This eliminated the centerpiece of the Riverfront Crossings Plan.

40 Just a few days after this meeting, I watched a new play at a local theater which explicitly focused on race relations in Iowa City. Titled *Mayberry* (Lewis, 2012), it enabled a diverse array of characters to narrate their stories about race, racism, and fear in Iowa City.

41 Not long after that night's meeting, I read Michelle Alexander's (2012) *The New Jim Crow* and Fergus M. Bordewich's (2012) *America's Great Debate* about the Compromise of 1850. Reading these two books and Daniel Walker Howe's (2009) *What Hath God Wrought?* deepened my understanding of systemic racism in the U.S.

42 For details, see "Justice Center Proposal Needs Three Changes" at: https://persuasivestorytelling.wordpress.com/2012/10/24/justice-center-proposal-needs-3-changes/

43 I was also aware that my health had deteriorated somewhat over the preceding 2 years. I was 69 years old at the end of 2013 and I had begun to experience worrisome deterioration in my vision due to macular degeneration.

References

Alexander, M. (2012), *The New Jim Crow: Mass Incarceration in the Age of Color Blindness*, The New Press, New York (NY).

Bordewich, F. M. (2012), *America's Great Debate: Henry Clay, Stephen A. Douglas, and the Compromise That Preserved the Union*, Simon and Schuster, New York.

Bryson, J. (2007), *Strategic Planning for Public and Nonprofit Organizations* (3rd ed.), Jossey-Bass, San Francisco (CA).

Campbell, S. D. (1996), "Green cities, growing cities, just cities: Urban planning and the contradictions of sustainable development", *Journal of the American Planning Association*, v. 62, n. 3, pp. 296–312.

City of Iowa City (2012), Power Point presentation by The Chauncey LLC during a City Council work session on November 26, rendering by Rohrbach Associates; available at: www.iowa-city.org/WebLink/0/doc/1272866/Page1.aspx (last accessed May 6, 2021).

City of Iowa City (2013a), IC2030 Comprehensive Plan Update, Iowa City (IA); available at: www8.iowa-city.org/weblink/0/edoc/1965450/Comprehensive%20Plan%20Updated%2010.2020.pdf (last accessed January 3, 2021).

City of Iowa City (2013b), *Downtown & Riverfront Crossings Master Plan*, Iowa City (IA); available at: www.iowa-city.org/weblink/0/doc/1482448/Electronic.aspx (last accessed January 5, 2021).

Coalition for Racial Justice (2013), "Racial Equity in Iowa City and Johnson County", Iowa City (IA); available at: https://www.racialequitytools.org/resourcefiles/Iowa-racial-equity-report.pdf (last accessed December 21, 2020).

Connerly, C., Laurian, L. and Throgmorton, J. A. (2016), "Planning for floods at the University of Iowa: A challenge for resilience and sustainability", *Journal of Planning History*, v. 16, n. 1, pp. 50–73.

Eagleton, T. (2013), *How to Read Literature*, Yale University Press, New Haven (CT).

Fisher, R., Ury, W. and Patton, B. (1991), *Getting to Yes: Negotiating Agreement without Giving in* (2nd ed.), Penguin Books, New York (NY).

Florida, R. (2002), *The Rise of the Creative Class*, Basic Books, New York (NY).

Franklin, K. (2003), "The Peninsula", in B. Eckstein and J. A. Throgmorton (eds.), *Story and Sustainability: Planning, Practice and Possibility for American Cities*, MIT Press, Cambridge (MA), pp. 193–204.

Hansen, J. (2009), *Storms of My Grandchildren: The Truth about the Coming Climate Catastrophe and Our Last Chance to Save Humanity*, Bloomsbury, New York (NY).

Hawkinson, E., and Garza, K. (Circa 2016), "Housing and equity in Iowa City", University of Iowa Graduate Program in Urban and Regional Planning, Iowa City (IA).

Hennigan, G. (2012a), "Iowa City bypasses petition, Oks altered TIF deal", *The Gazette* (July 10); available at: https://www.thegazette.com/2012/07/10/iowa-city-bypasses-petition-oks-altered-tif-deal (last accessed on December 18, 2020).

Hennigan, G. (2012b), "City council member proposes I. C. response to Trayvon Martin." *The Gazette* (April 3); available at: www.thegazette.com/2012/04/03/city-council-member-proposes-iowa-city-response-to-trayvon-martin-shooting (last accessed on December 18, 2020).

Hennigan, G. (2012c), "Officials tout need for Johnson County justice center at forum", *The Gazette* (October 1); available at: www.thegazette.com/2012/10/01/

officials-tout-need-for-johnson-county-justice-center-at-forum (last accessed on December 18, 2020).

Hennigan, G. (2013a), "Iowa city schools revenue vote passes despite controversy over diversity policy", *The Gazette* (February 5); available at: www.thegazette. com/2013/02/05/iowa-city-schools-revenue-vote-passes-despite-controversy-over-diversity-policy (last accessed on December 18, 2020).

Hennigan, G. (2013b), "Iowa City council likes 20-story building for downtown site", *The Gazette* (January 8); available at: www.thegazette.com/2013/01/08/iowa-city-to-pick-20-story-building-for-downtown-site (last accessed on December 18, 2020).

Hennigan, G. (2013c), "Iowa City moves on ordinance aimed at downtown behavior concerns", *The Gazette* (August 21); available at: www.thegazette.com/2013/08/21/ iowa-city-moves-on-ordinance-aimed-at-downtown-behavior-concerns (last accessed on December 18, 2020).

Hennigan, G. (2013d), "Johnson County justice center comes up short", *The Gazette* (May 7); available at: www.thegazette.com/2013/05/07/results-johnson-county-justice-center-comes-up-short (last accessed on December 18, 2020).

Hennigan, G. (2013e), "Iowa City gets recommendations from diversity committee", *The Gazette* (June 18); available at: www.thegazette.com/2013/06/18/ iowa-city-gets-recommendations-from-diversity-committee (last accessed on December 18, 2020).

Howe, D. W. (2009), *What Hath God Wrought: The Transformation of America, 1815–1848*, Oxford University Press, Oxford (UK).

Iowa City Community School District (2013), "Enrollment, Demographics, and Class Size Report", Iowa City (IA); available at: www.iowacityschools.org/site/handlers/ filedownload.ashx?moduleinstanceid=763&dataid=3951&FileName=2013-14-Enrollment-Demographics-and-Class-Size-Report.pdf

Jacobs, J. (1969/1970). *The Economy of Cities*, Vintage, New York (NY).

Jacobs, J. (1984/1985), *Cities and the Wealth of Nations: Principles of Economic Life*, Vintage, New York (NY).

Jacobs, J. (1992/1994), *Systems of Survival: A Dialogue on the Moral Foundations of Commerce and Politics*, Vintage, New York (NY).

Jacobs, J. (2000), *The Nature of Economies*, Vintage, New York (NY).

Jacobs, J. (2005), *Dark Age Ahead*, Vintage, New York (NY).

Lakoff, G. (2010), "Why it matters how we frame the environment", *Environmental Communication*, v. 4, n. 1, pp. 70–81.

Laurian, L., Day, M., Backhurst, M., et al. (2004), "What drives planning implementation? Plans, planning agencies and developers", *Journal of Environmental Planning and Management*, v. 47, n. 4, pp. 555–577.

LeBaron, M. (2002), *Bridging Troubled Waters: Conflict Resolution from the Heart*, Jossey-Bass, San Francisco (CA).

Lewis, S. C. (2012), *Mayberry*, Working Group Theater, presented under commission by Hancher Auditorium, Iowa City (IA).

Mandelbaum, S. (1990), "Reading Plans", *Journal of the American Planning Association*, v. 56, n. 3, pp. 350–356.

National Research Council (2012), *Disaster Resilience: A National Imperative*, The National Academies Press, Washington (DC).

Sandel, M. J. (2009), *Justice: What's the Right Thing to Do?* Farrar, Straus, and Giroux, New York (NY).

Susskind L., McKearnan, S. and Thomas-Larmer, J. (eds) (1999), *The Consensus Building Handbook: A Comprehensive Guide to Reaching Agreement*, Sage, Thousand Oaks (CA).

Throgmorton, J.A. (2012), "For TIFs, Iowa City needs to allow more time for debate." *Iowa City Press-Citizen* (June 27), 7A.

3
TURNING TOWARD THE JUST CITY, 2014–2015

As 2013 ended, I thought I had learned much of value over the previous 2 years. On the whole, I felt good about the contributions I had made and was looking forward to the next 2 years. But I also had learned that my values and priorities differed in key respects from those of my fellow council members. Moreover, I was beginning to see my city as a complex whole. That sense came from being immersed in the flow of action involving the multiple diverse, and yet highly interconnected, topics we had to process every other week, as well as from getting to know the city better by spending more time out in the field.

As actions unfolded over the next 2 years—especially during the winter of 2014–2015—the conflict between what I (and many other Iowa Citians) valued and what the council majority was doing became increasingly apparent. If I believed the people of Iowa City would be better served by taking the city in a different direction, then I needed to step up, make my case, and let the public decide which direction they wanted to go in. Put simply, I would have to forsake the managerial mode of governance that traditionally marked the behavior of council members and which obfuscated the political stakes of our actions. At this moment, I would instead have to think and act in a more explicitly political way. Consequently, and to my surprise, the next 2 years became a story about shifting from managerial governance to explicit political engagement—that is, about turning toward "the Just City."

Picking Up Where We Left Off

The city council opened 2014 by holding an organizational meeting in which the council reelected Matt H. and Susan M. to 2-year terms as mayor and mayor pro tem, respectively. We also considered changes to the council's strategic plan

DOI: 10.4324/9781003160991-3

and reviewed the staff's proposed budget and capital improvements plan. In preparation for our strategic planning session late in November 2013, the staff invited each of us to respond to a lengthy questionnaire. I submitted a lengthy response highlighting several key issues and opportunities, including: greatly improving our local response to the threat of global climate change, fulfilling the Riverfront Crossings District Plan's enormous potential, and inventing better ways of responding to the growing percentage of residents who were black, Hispanic, and/or recent immigrants. I also listed several actions the City should consider taking in the next 2 years. For example, I thought we should embed goals concerning social/economic justice and long-term prosperity/sustainability into the City's budget, CIP, zoning code, and economic development policy. In the end, however, the council stuck closely to the strategic plan we had adopted in 2012.

Over the next 2 years, we continued to be inundated, week by week, by a diverse array of topics, including the steady stream of requests to rezone properties, mostly for developments on the outer edge of the city. We also took on several important new tasks which, regrettably, I do not have space to discuss here. For example, the City Charter required us to appoint a commission which would review the current charter and recommend possible changes. Likewise, we created the Ad Hoc Committee on Senior Services to review the City's senior center and consider better ways of providing services to senior residents.

Four of the topics we focused on were continuations of ones we had addressed in 2012–2013. We had to complete our preparations for the Gateway project and take further action on the Chauncey project and the Downtown and Riverfront Crossings District Master Plan. We also continued working with the School District on its facilities master plan and considering ways to help make its new diversity policy succeed. And we needed to follow through on commitments made about improving racial equity. One new topic demanded our attention as well: we had to decide how to respond to state-mandated property tax reforms and consequent reductions in the City's anticipated property tax revenues.

Finalizing Design Parameters for the Gateway Project

By the end of 2013, we had completed most of our work pertaining to the Gateway Project. But we had not yet decided whether to accept or modify the staff's recommendations about how high to raise Dubuque Street and the new Park Road Bridge—that is, how much flood protection to provide. And there were further aesthetic considerations we would need to resolve.

We turned to the roadway and bridge elevations during our mid-January work session and formal meeting just days after Kingsley B. (the young black lawyer) had replaced Connie C. on the council. Staff reported that the Federal Highway Administration had signed the Finding of No Significant Impact, which permitted us to move forward with the project. Now free to proceed, staff recommended that we approve the 2008 + 1 foot roadway elevation, a 200 + 1 foot bridge elevation, and either a through arch or deck girder bridge, with the estimated cost being $38 million or $35 million, plus the cost of the bridge.

To cut to the quick, we council members asked many questions during this meeting and, I think it is fair to say, we felt as though the staff and consultant had answered our questions well. But, in the end, we voted unanimously for the 100 + 1 roadway elevation and the through arch bridge (Hennigan, 2014).[1] We chose this level of protection (less than the 200 + 1 alternative) because we had concluded that elevating the roadway higher would cause additional damage to the wooded hillside without producing commensurate benefits in terms of the avoided number of days of flooding. I was very pleased with this decision, but understood (and said publicly) that we should expect the elevated roadway to flood in the future. If the past 20 years provided a good guide, it would flood slightly less than 0.1 percent of the time. If the 100 + 1 alternative would have entailed extensive or lengthy flood damage, I would have said the roadway must be higher. But we had received no evidence to indicate that would be the case. To the contrary, the higher we elevated the roadway, the more construction damage would occur. We still were not done, though. At some point later in the year, we would need to decide on a few key aesthetic components of the project.

In the middle of the year, we discussed those aesthetic components. We started doing so just days after we had experienced a flood that narrowly exceeded one that had occurred in 2013 and thereby became the third highest flood in the history of Iowa City's river gauge. These two consecutive major flood events caused me and many other Iowa Citians to (at least temporarily) lose trust in the Corps of Engineers' management of the Coralville Dam and Reservoir, which is located just a few miles upstream from Iowa City.

In our mid-July work session, we focused on a variety of aesthetic measures, including the appearance of a retaining wall to be built along the Dubuque Street side of the river and other topics. We also had to decide on speed limits, lane widths, roadway crossings, safety measures, and other topics. Two months later, we (minus the mayor, who could not attend) unanimously approved a resolution establishing the design elements for the Gateway Project. Lots of staff work remained to be done, though, including identifying the construction firm or firms that would do the work. That work proceeded.

Considering Adoption of a Local Option Sales Tax

One of the most important tasks we chose to undertake was to explore how to respond to the property tax reforms the state legislature had passed in 2013. These reforms changed residential assessments and how they were assessed; reduced commercial and industrial property taxes by incorporating a "rollback" feature; and reduced property taxes for multi-residential properties by reclassifying them from commercial to residential. The state promised to "backfill" a portion of the revenues local governments would lose owing to the first two reforms, but overall we could expect to see a loss of $52 million in property tax revenues over the next 10 years minus an estimated $15 million if the state lived up to its backfill promise. Some of the reforms would be phased in, but, by Year 10, we could expect to lose 8–10 percent of the property tax revenue we would otherwise expect to receive. As roughly 75 percent of the City's general fund (which funded police, fire, library, and other basic services) came from property taxes, we would need to cut services or else find replacement sources of revenue. And we could not count on the state's promised backfill.

From early March through mid-August 2014, the council deliberated about possible ways of replacing that lost revenue. We focused primarily on whether to ask voters to approve a 10-year, 1 percent local option sales tax (LOST) and on determining the particular features of the proposed tax. We did so partly because existing state law about the adoption of a LOST established conditions favorable to Iowa City. Iowa City and four contiguous cities would vote as a block, and a simple majority vote of all votes cast in those five cities combined would determine whether a LOST would be established in all five of them. LOST revenues collected in jurisdictions that approved the tax would go into one pool of funds, and the funds would be distributed only to those jurisdictions that had voted in favor of the tax. The funds would be distributed among those cities in accord with a formula that benefitted Iowa City. A 1 percent LOST would generate approximately $9 million–$12 million per year for Iowa City, depending on how many other cities participated, and the resulting $90 million–$120 million over 10 years would far exceed the property tax revenue we expected to lose as a result of the state's reforms. Moreover, our city manager advised that using LOST revenues to reduce property taxes would improve Iowa City's ability to retain businesses and attract new investment and, therefore, improve our ability to compete economically with Coralville and other nearby cities. The city manager and an exploratory committee consisting of a few City staff members and Mayor Pro Tem Susan M. recommended allocating 60 percent of the City's share of LOST revenues to property tax reduction, 30 percent to street maintenance, and 10 percent to affordable housing.

When we first began our internal negotiations, I indicated my unwillingness to support the LOST because I knew that many people in Iowa City saw it as taxation of the poor in order to reduce taxes for wealthy property owners at the same time as the City was planning to give a wealthy developer a large amount of money to build the Chauncey. After considerable internal negotiations within our council, we decided to allocate 40 percent to property tax reductions, 50 percent to street maintenance, and 10 percent to affordable housing. I agreed to vote for this proposed allocation primarily because other council members had been willing to compromise by reducing the percentage that would go toward reducing property taxes. But I stated more than once that putting the LOST referendum on the ballot without first soliciting public input and advice was a political mistake, and that acting without first consulting and negotiating with the other contiguous cities would only exacerbate preexisting conflicts with Coralville over its aggressive use of tax increment financing. In the end, 54 percent of voters in the five contiguous cities voted no in the November 2014 election. Voters in Coralville and North Liberty overwhelmingly opposed the LOST, and only 52 percent of Iowa City voters supported it (Schmidt, 2014). Iowa City government's relationship with Coralville's officials probably reached its lowest point during the months the LOST was being considered.

The fact that voters rejected the LOST mainly meant we would have to increase our property tax levy, reduce expenditures in one way or another, or increase the tax base by stimulating more land development.

Densifying the Downtown Area

Recall that the city council had adopted a new master plan for the Riverfront Crossings District at the start of 2013 and, later in the year, had received a briefing from one of the City's senior planners (Karen H.) about a key tool, a form-based code (FBC), which the staff wanted to use in implementing the plan. In conventional planning language, the proposed FBC would "implement" the RFC District Master Plan. As action unfolded, though, I gradually concluded that the council's adoption of the proposed FBC had transformed the master plan into an "aspirational" document which justified very large increases in allowable density and, thereby, enabled property owners and developers to maximize their profits.

Early in 2014, Karen H. met with the Planning and Zoning (P&Z) Commission and described the specific version of the FBC the staff was proposing for the RFC District. One member of the commission, John T., was the landscape architect who had done such good work on North Market Square Park a few years earlier. Karen H. reported that the proposed FBC included a regulating plan; subdistrict standards; standards pertaining to frontage type, building type, and parking type; and more. The regulating plan specified boundaries for seven subdistricts, primary street frontages, building heights, parks and open space, and specific conditions and requirements for the subdistricts. She noted that the proposed code would permit the transfer of development rights (TDR) and would authorize developers to apply for height bonuses totaling one to seven stories in return for incorporating one or more public benefits into their proposed buildings.[2]

The commissioners posed many questions and expressed some concerns. They wanted, for example, to ensure the FBC was consistent with the RFC District Master Plan. Some asked what was likely to happen to older buildings in the district and worried that redevelopment of the area might produce a new "student ghetto." And some commissioners wanted some affordable housing built in the area, whereas others thought increased land costs would make that quite difficult. The commissioners discussed the proposed code again at subsequent meetings until mid-February, when they recommended approval (with numerous amendments) 6:1, with landscape architect John T. against. He thought the FBC should produce mid-rise structures throughout most of the district, partly because they are more energy-efficient than high-rise structures and would be more consistent with the scale of buildings in the RFC District Master Plan and Iowa City as a whole. To the best of my knowledge, the staff had not held any public workshops about the FBC, and virtually no members of the public had spoken about the proposed code during the commission's public hearing.

The proposed RFC District FBC came to the council for a public hearing and first consideration in mid-April, at which time the director of the new Neighborhood and Development Services (NDS) Department, Doug B., recommended we defer our first vote to the following meeting.[3] Much like she did for the P&Z Commission, Karen H. guided us through the proposed FBC.[4] (By this time, Kingsley B. had replaced the long-serving downtown business owner on the council. He, too, was completely unfamiliar with the purpose, structure, and processes associated with FBCs.) She showed us many architectural renderings and appealing photos of the diverse kinds of buildings that would be authorized by the FBC—for example, rowhouses, apartment buildings, mixed-use buildings, and liner buildings (residences wrapped around parking structures). She closed by highlighting the proposed FBC's numerous benefits: higher residential densities, greater diversity of uses, reduced vehicle miles travelled, lower parking requirements, reduced risks for developers and long-term residents, a larger customer base for local businesses, increased property values, and increases in the tax base.

In general, I thought the draft FBC was likely to provide a far better way of guiding redevelopment in the district than existing zoning. However, the proposed code was extremely complicated and left many uncertainties about how it would be administered and what effects it would produce once adopted. Moreover, the proposed FBC authorized a massive "up-zoning" throughout the district, primarily through its treatment of maximum building heights. It specified maximum building heights for each of the subdistricts, varying from three stories for the Gilbert Street subdistrict to eight stories for the South Downtown and West Riverfront (river frontage) subdistricts. But it also delineated a two-stage process by which height bonuses could be permitted, with the staff having the authority to grant up to two stories in bonuses and council approval being required for bonuses up to

BASE   BONUS

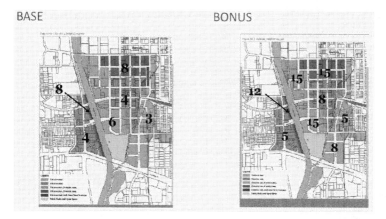

FIGURE 3.1 2014 Riverfront Crossings District form-based code's maximum
building heights: base versus bonus.
Source: City of Iowa City, 2018.

five additional stories. Once these height bonuses were included, the maximum building heights rose to 15 stories in the South Downtown, University,
and Park subdistricts, and to 12 for West Riverfront (see Figure 3.1). With
these height bonuses, the maximum permissible heights would end up being
roughly double what the RFC District Master Plan had anticipated. Consequently, I thought the council needed more time to digest the proposed code
and to discuss our responses to it.

We considered the proposed FBC during three meetings in May and June.
As I worried might happen when we considered adoption of the 2030 Comprehensive Plan Update, my fellow council members seemed inclined to defer
to the staff's judgment and asked very few questions. One notable exception
had to do with affordable housing. Members of the Affordable Housing Coalition had urged us to provide incentives for affordable housing in the district.
Discussion during our first meeting in May led us to direct the staff to initiate
a process that might result in mandatory "inclusionary housing" within the
RFC District.

Unlike the other council members, and surely because of my background
in urban planning, I had a long list of questions about the proposed code—for
example, how would the transition from existing zoning to the FBC subdistrict
zones occur? Why does the draft code not explicitly require achievement of
Gold or Platinum levels in order to obtain Leadership in Energy and Environmental Design (LEED)-related bonuses? Why does the staff recommend such
large height and density bonuses? Other council members seemed not inclined
to consider these concerns, though someone did ask whether speculators might

drive up the cost of land in the district. During the first meeting in May, the council asked me to share my questions in a memo so that the City staff would have an opportunity to respond. I did so. The director of NDS responded to my questions constructively in most cases, but some of his responses called for a deeper discussion than other council members wanted to have.

Recognizing the council had little appetite for probing these questions, I ultimately reduced them to three possible amendments to the proposed code. One of the amendments had to do with the FBC's proposed height bonus for affordable and workforce housing. I thought we should require the affordability of the units to be maintained for a minimum of 15 years rather than, as the staff had recommended, letting the City staff and developers negotiate the duration of the requirement.

Another of my amendments pertained to the building height limitations and bonuses. During one of the meetings in May, I said my personal preference was for the heights not to exceed five to seven stories, mainly because very livable development density could be achieved within those height limitations. But I was not a purist on this point. I was willing to accept the proposed maximum post-bonus heights for the South Downtown subdistrict. However, I thought 12- and 15-story heights were not warranted anywhere else in the district. Specifically, I thought the maximum post-bonus height for the Park District and the west side of the river should not exceed 10 stories. I did not want to provide incentives for tall buildings in which only wealthy people could live. Moreover, 15-story buildings in those subdistricts would be completely out of scale with what one typically found in Iowa City; I understood the average height of buildings downtown was only two to two-and-a-half stories.

Other council members rejected my proposed amendments. During our early June formal meeting, Rick D., Michelle P., and Susan M. all indicated they did not want to constrain the staff in its future negotiations with developers. The mayor indicated he did not want to adopt any of the amendments and have to start the whole process over again. Rick D. brought things to a close by saying it was important for us not to micromanage what the staff did. My motion to amend failed 1:5, with Kingsley B. being absent.

The negative vote on my proposed amendments notwithstanding, I decided to join all other council members (minus Kingsley B.) in voting to adopt the new FBC. I did so primarily because I thought an FBC would be a great improvement over existing zoning and because our discussion might lead to the production of affordable housing in the district. But I was also aware that, other than the Affordable Housing Coalition and its allies, we had received virtually no comment from the general public either for or against the proposed code or the height bonuses. In effect, I learned there was no well-informed political constituency for good urban design in Iowa City.[5] Such a constituency would have to be created.

In the end, we adopted a new regulatory code which was extremely complicated, full of uncertainties, and likely to have a dramatic effect on a large part
of the city immediately south of downtown. I doubted that any of us council
members could imagine how the district would actually change in response to
the FBC. What seemed clear was that the new code would stimulate a lot of
development activity in the RFC District over the coming years. Would the
people of Iowa City like it? Would I?

• • •

Shortly after adopting the FBC, we began receiving proposals from land developers. In mid-September, we were asked to rezone a small parcel of land in
the Central Crossings subdistrict. This rezoning would permit the developer
to construct a new four-story residential building, preserve (through historic
landmark designation) a building located next door to it, and, as authorized
by the new FBC, transfer the development rights for that historic building to
some other location in the RFC District.[6] On that same night, we considered a
staff-initiated proposal to rezone roughly 26 acres in the Riverfront Crossings
District to RFC–SD (South Downtown) and RFC–CX (Central Crossings).
After two more readings, the council unanimously approved the rezonings.

One of the South Downtown subdistrict rezonings pertained to a site the
City owned at the corner of Court and Linn Streets in the northeast corner
of the RFC District. Just a few weeks after we approved that rezoning, and
just 2 days after the LOST referendum failed to pass, we began considering a
staff-initiated process for redeveloping the site. Early in November, the City's
economic development administrator, Jeff D., initiated a special work session
by providing us with an overview of the site and the process which had led to
the night's meeting. The parcel had been the parking lot for a church until the
building was destroyed by a tornado in 2006. The City had acquired the parcel
and been planning to use it as the site for the City's s next multilevel parking
structure, but those plans changed after an Iowa-based bank (MidWestOne)
proposed to construct its new office building in the middle of the RFC District.

As Jeff D. continued, we learned that, in May, the City staff had issued a
request for proposals from potential developers about how to use the land. (I do
not recall seeing the RFP before it was issued.) Six developers had submitted
proposals, and the staff wanted us to winnow the number down to three. A
committee consisting of ten staff members, two council members (Susan M.
and Kingsley B.), and a consultant from the National Development Council
had reviewed the six proposals. The committee evaluated them in light of
four criteria: the developer's experience and capabilities, the market and economic viability of the project, the long-term fiscal benefit to the City, and how
the project would help achieve the City's economic development and Riverfront Crossings goals.[7] The economic development coordinator reported the

committee had unanimously recommended that three teams should be invited for interviews: CA Ventures, HUB at Iowa City (Core Campus), and Sherman Associates. None of the firms were locally based. The committee highlighted four points. First, a project of this scale requires an experienced developer with a proven track record who can bring the required financial capacity to the project. Second, the site might be an appropriate location for high-density student housing in order to take pressure off established older neighborhoods near downtown. Third, even though a proposal which emphasized senior housing had not been included as a finalist, there still was interest in senior housing in this vicinity. And fourth, there was a tradeoff between the amount of financial assistance the City would be asked to provide for higher-risk uses—such as affordable housing, speculative office space, and hotels—and lower-risk uses, such as student housing, which might not require public subsidy. Ultimately, the economic development coordinator told us, this tradeoff presented a political question for the council to answer.

Several issues arose as we discussed the six proposals, including: the mixed blessing of having a large amount of student housing located there, the potential for including affordable housing, the sufficiency of the projects' sustainability features, and the effects of the FBC's height bonuses and their relationship with developers' expectations about receiving TIF subsidies. I noted that, to the best of my knowledge, we had not seen the RFP before it was sent out. Nor had we had a chance to determine how to weight the criteria. After discussion, we decided to include the proposal which emphasized senior housing and had been submitted by a local development team (CG/Hanson) in our final review.

We discussed the four proposals during a special work session in mid-November. Core Campus (Hub at Iowa City) was a $92 million project containing 325 student-oriented residential units with about 630 beds, a 170-suite hotel, and two floors of Class A office space plus many amenities. CA Ventures's project (the Rise) was very similar to Core Campus's project. Also oriented primarily toward university students, it would be a $97 million project containing about 300 residential units and 525 beds, a 130-room hotel, 20,000 sq. ft. of office or convention space, and a substantial amount of space for amenities. Sherman Associates' proposed project would contain a 124-unit hotel, about 90 units of upper-scale housing, 23,000 sq. ft. of retail/office space, and shared courtyard space in two five-story buildings. They would need City financial assistance to fill a $10 million–$12 million gap.[8] The project's spokesperson said, if you want a quality hotel and market-rate housing on this site, you have to provide some financial support; a large student-oriented project and the tax benefits associated with it would get built somewhere else in the city. You need to decide, he said, what kind of neighborhood you want to be creating. And, last, CG/Hanson's Court–Linn Lofts project would contain two 12–15-story towers. One of the towers would include a mixture of market-rate and aging-in-place housing, and potential workforce housing, along with commercial, retail, and possible wellness, medical, and office space. The other building would be dedicated to professionally managed high-quality student housing. A spokesman for the $90 million project said it would be built and backed by an all-local team, the same one that would be building a new structure at 316 Madison Street (see below). Several council members expressed concern about ambiguities associated with this particular proposal.

My sense was that we faced a very difficult choice. Two of the possible projects would consist of 15-story buildings designed to appeal primarily to students. Upon completion, they would immediately begin generating a large amount of property tax revenue without requiring public subsidies. A third project had a much more appealing scale and mixture of uses, but also would require a large financial subsidy from the City; when compared with the first two proposals, the foregone tax revenues associated with this one would be enormous. And the fourth would include student housing in one building and high-amenity housing for retirees from the university in another. Although I thought we should support construction of this kind of project near downtown, in this particular case, the developers' ideas seemed too incomplete and in flux.

We decided about the Court and Linn Street project during our work session on December 2. The city manager recommended that we narrow the competitors down to two so that the staff could negotiate the best possible offer for the City. He also noted that building high-quality, high-rise student housing in this part of the RFC District would take pressure off residential neighborhoods located close to the downtown. This proved decisive. In the end, I preferred to narrow our choice to CA Ventures or CG/Hanson's Court–Linn Lofts, as did Terry D., but the other five council members preferred to go with CA Ventures and Core Campus. Kingsley B. suggested it would be good to have some affordable housing be a part of the winning project. "It's all a negotiation," the city manager replied. We agreed the winning proposal should not include a TIF subsidy, and the winning developer should pay the City for the land.

• • •

That was not the only difficult topic we had to deal with on December 2. We also had to decide whether to approve a seven-story height bonus for a professionally managed mixed-use building at the 316 Madison Street site we had recently re-zoned in the northwestern corner of the RFC District.[9] With the bonus included, this project would be a 15-story building of 160,000 sq. ft., with ground-level retail and about 250 bedrooms for students. The staff recommended approval of a five-story bonus for professionally managed student housing and two stories for designing the project to be equivalent to LEED Gold.

The staff had placed this seven-story height bonus in our consent calendar, which implied they thought the project would not need careful scrutiny by the council or the public. This really upset me because this was the first time we would be considering a Level II density bonus in accord with our new FBC, and because I could see several important questions that needed to be asked and answered in public, including: was the council legally required to approve what the staff FBC committee recommended, or did we have some flexibility and discretion in deciding, for example, how many bonus stories to authorize? The City attorney told us it is a discretionary decision on the part of the council, but we could not be arbitrary. And, I asked, would the developer be requesting TIF or other direct financial support from the City? My sense was that it would be completely unnecessary and inappropriate to provide TIF assistance for a project on property which had significantly increased in value as a result of the up-zoning we had recently approved and which would be receiving a very large height bonus. I also thought that the developer's plan differed significantly from the RFC District Master Plan, most importantly by concentrating so much housing into one 15-story structure instead of dispersing it into four separate 4–7-story buildings organized around a quad. In the end, I joined the other council members in voting for the height bonus while saying I was not willing to approve a subsequent TIF subsidy.

• • •

Sometimes, major turns result from seemingly small events. On that same December 2 night, the council entered into an intense conflict over a proposal to demolish three small 160-year-old working-class cottages located in the middle of the RFC District. In the days immediately preceding that meeting, we had received a large number of emails opposing destruction of the buildings. To judge by the flood of emails, many of them angry or sad, various people were acting quickly, both within and outside City government. We also had received a petition signed by well over 500 people asking us to withdraw a notice of violation the City's building inspection staff had sent to the owner of the cottages. I was struggling to understand what was going on and what, if anything, I or we could do. I had to do some quick research.

Three months after we adopted the FBC, a private developer had applied to have the site of the three cottages rezoned to a Riverfront Crossings–Central Crossings (RFC–CX) zone in order to build an apartment complex. Demolition of the cottages would be required. If the rezoning was approved, the cottages were demolished, and the planned project was completed, the assessed value of the property would increase from about $4 million to about $14 million. On November 24, the City's building inspection staff had ordered the tenant in (at least) one of the cottages to vacate his building not later than December 8 because, according to an assessment prepared by a structural engineer hired by the owner, the building presented a health and safety hazard. Friends of Historic Preservation (FHP) had another structural engineer look at the building. This assessment concluded the building was structurally sound. FHP asked the City to withdraw its notice of violation.

During our brief work session on December 2, development services coordinator John Y. told us that—based on the first structural engineer's report—the notice of violation required the property owner to vacate the properties and abate the violation, and abatement could involve either repair or demolition. "And whose discretion is that?" the city manager asked. John Y. responded, it is "the property owner's decision."[10] If, on that night, we scheduled a public hearing on the landmark designation, there would be a 60-day moratorium on the issuance of a demolition permit. Noting that the owner had already applied for a permit, it dawned on us that we would have to meet very soon to decide whether or not to schedule a public hearing. Puzzled, Kingsley B. questioned why public concern over these three cottages had arisen so quickly. Susan M. responded by saying, all across the country you see people trying to block actions they do not like. The council directed the city clerk to schedule a special meeting prior to December 10 at a time which would work for all of us.

FHP quickly applied to have the cottages designated as local historic landmarks. They also applied for historic preservation overlay zoning for the site. However, the owner formally protested the FHP's proposed rezoning. Because his property constituted more than 20 percent of the property within 200 feet of the site to be rezoned, Iowa law required a super-majority vote (6:1 or greater) from the council to approve the rezoning.

All that information (and more) was swirling around in my sleepy head as the mayor opened our special formal meeting at 7 a.m. on Monday, December 9. Roughly 25 interested members of the public were present. The question before us was, did we want to schedule a public hearing on possible historic landmark designation for the three small cottages? Eleven people spoke during the 1-hour-long public hearing, including the director of FHP, the owner's structural engineer, Rockne C. (who was representing two of the tenants), a commercial real estate appraiser, a tenant who had been living and working in one of the cottages for almost 30 years, two other residents of the city, the owner of the cottages (Ted P.), the attorney for the owner, and a resident who wondered why the owner had let the property deteriorate so much over such a long period. The real estate appraiser told us the assessed value of the property would increase by at least $10 million. "In short," he said, "it is about the money."[11]

The mayor terminated public discussion at this point and called for council discussion. Susan M. expressed her concern about "kind of the 11th hour approach on this" and about how additional efforts to tell property owners what to do might happen in the future. In her view,

> it is imperative that people … who support … historic preservation in this community … get out in front of these issues … and do your due diligence and start that process before the 11th hour of a property owner trying to move forward with plans for their properties.

Michelle P. said, "I … agree that the property owner has rights that are kind of being tramped on with this process." Pressured by the council's self-imposed 8 a.m. deadline for ending the meeting, the voting went quickly. The mayor, mayor pro tem, Michelle P., and Terry D. voted no, and so the motion to schedule a public hearing failed 3:4. On the next day, the owner received a permit to demolish the three cottages. The permit would be valid for 180 days. Shortly thereafter, an orange plastic fence was placed around the southernmost cottages.

I emailed the city manager the next day to express my puzzlement over part of the staff's review process concerning the three cottages. Knowing that the City's building inspection staff had routinely inspected the cottages over a period of years, I asked, how could it be that those inspections did not reveal that one or more of those buildings were in such a state of disrepair that they constituted an immediate danger to occupants' health and safety, and, hence, that the structures would need to be vacated and the nuisance be abated, either through repair or demolition? And, how could it be that such a state of disrepair was identified only when the owner of the property wanted to demolish the buildings, sell the property, and greatly profit from enabling construction of a much larger structure?

After a contentious public hearing on December 11, the Historic Preservation Commission unanimously voted in favor of the historic landmark designation. Eleven members of the public spoke at the hearing, including Alicia T. of FHP, the owner's son, two owners of businesses located in the cottages, and others.[12] The owner's son roundly condemned those who wanted to preserve the buildings, saying,

> this whole fight is a repository for all the anger and resentment about other rezoning and development around Iowa City. … [I]t is just one example among many of intentional manipulation by the organizing groups to foment public outcry against allowing the owner to do what he wishes with the property.

The commission's chair, Ginalie S., said what slows processes down are things like lack of historic preservation staff, lack of money or funding, needing consultants to do the work, lack of volunteers, and so on. Moreover, preservation efforts are often "eleventh hour," because that is when the public first learns about the planned demolition.

Five days later, a December 3 memo from City Attorney Eleanor D. appeared in a late handout for our meeting on December 16. This new memo stated in part:

> City staff cannot and need not make a determination as to which [of the structural assessments] is the better or more valid report. … City

enforcement staff will not dictate which option is chosen. That determination can be made by the property owner and is likely governed, in part, by whatever leasehold interest the tenants may have in the properties.[13]

I did not question the City attorney's *legal* interpretation. As a practical matter, however, I found her claim to be completely unpersuasive. My sense was that the City staff *did* choose which is the more valid report by issuing a notice of violation and a vacate and abate order.

On December 18, the P&Z Commission held a public hearing on adoption of the historic landmark overlay zone. Staff planner John Y. told the commission that the Riverfront Crossings Plan states: "preservation of these structures [the cottages] should be a goal. In order to encourage their preservation, it is recommended that a density bonus be granted for their preservation and renovation." He also indicated, as he did several times in this whole process, *"The plan is simply a vision, highlighting certain areas. The decision to redevelop is ultimately up to the property owner* [emphasis added]."[14] Hold on, I thought. The plan is "simply a vision," or, as I later heard, "merely aspirational"? Does the plan not express what the people of Iowa City aspire to? Does that aspiration have no bearing on what the property owner can do?

Eleven members of the public spoke during the public hearing. Alicia T. and Ginalie S. both emphasized that protecting these cottages has been in line with the City's Comprehensive Plan and strategy for at least the past 20 years. Alicia T. responded to the claim that preservationists were intervening at "the 11th hour" by recalling all the commission's efforts over the previous 15 years to get this part of the district surveyed, and by saying, "Historic preservation does take time, what does not take much time in Iowa City is demolishing a building that only has a seven day waiting period." The owner referred to "this last minute process," "scare tactics," and "a circus" and said he and his family had been vilified in the media, and the scare tactics had upset his tenants. In his view, it appeared everyone had more rights in this situation than the property owner. During the commissioners' discussion, one of the commissioners noted there was a specific illustration in the 2013 Riverfront Crossings Plan which showed these three cottages had potential historic significance, and he emphasized that the plan had been approved after a 2-year-long public engagement process. The P&Z commissioners unanimously recommended adoption of the overlay zone for the site.

Four days later, Rockne C. began filing a series of motion of court petitions in the Johnson County District Court on behalf of the tenants (the owners of two small businesses) in the two northernmost cottages. Sometime before 8 a.m. on December 26, however, the owner had the southernmost cottage demolished. As the year ended, it was not entirely clear what would happen next.

On January 2, I had another frank and enlightening conversation with the city manager about the City staff's actions pertaining to the cottages. The conversation led me to wonder about the various parties' best alternatives to a negotiated agreement (BATNAs) and to suggest it might be possible to resolve the multi-party conflict over the three cottages—now two—in a mutually acceptable way. He replied skeptically.

During the council's formal meeting 4 days later, we set a January 20 public hearing on the historic landmark designations. By this time, the issue had become far more contentious and emotional than it had been just 1 month before. The escalation in emotional intensity became even more evident when we held the public hearing on January 20. Emails, letters, guest opinions in the newspaper, and word of mouth had signaled that many people would be coming to the hearing. Many developers, builders, and property owners were interpreting the proposal as an attack on property rights, whereas many other members of the public were defending the historic character and importance of the cottages and their immediate neighborhood. Hyperbole abounded. By the time the formal meeting began, at least 60 people had gathered in the council chambers, with many others watching the meeting on a television screen located in the entryway to City Hall. Many supporters of the cottages' preservation were wearing stickers that read, "Save the Cottages."

Staff planner John Y. spoke first and summarized the application. Contrary to what the staff normally did, he did not recommend either approval or denial of the rezoning. After him, 29 members of the public spoke. As best I could count, 19 of them favored the landmark designation. It was a long public hearing, and I found it very hard to maintain my concentration and pay close attention to everything everyone said so late in the evening. I was ready to vote. But the City attorney reminded us that, if it looked like we would be disagreeing with the P&Z Commission's recommendation, we had to offer to consult with them before voting. Susan M. and Rick D. indicated they expected to disagree; consequently, we continued the public hearing and deferred the first vote to our next meeting. One might think our meeting ended at that point. It did not. In fact, it continued for another 2 hours and ended around 11 p.m. I drove home, poured myself an Irish whiskey, ate three small slices of reheated pizza, went to bed, and slept very poorly.[15]

On February 9, we consulted with the P&Z Commission about the two remaining cottages (see Figure 3.2). Commissioners articulated why they had voted for the historic landmark overlay zone designation. Council member Michelle P. stressed the rights of the property owner, but the chair of the commission retorted that the council was not legally required to approve requests for rezoning. Immediately after that consultation, we continued the public hearing during our formal meeting. Around 55 people filled the council chambers. Staff planner John Y. began the hearing by briefly speaking on behalf of the staff. After him, 21 members of the public spoke. Roughly two-thirds spoke in favor.

FIGURE 3.2 Two working-class cottages still standing.
Source: Photo by author, January 26, 2015.

Once the public hearing was closed, we council members began discussing our responses.[16] I drew upon my prepared comments, but modified them considerably on the spot in light of what speakers had said. As I saw it, three major questions had to be answered: (1) would the rezoning violate the owner's property rights, (2) had preservation advocates disrupted the process by intervening at "the 11th hour," and (3) were the cottages significant enough historically to warrant preservation? I answered by saying the owner had the right to demolish his buildings at any time until they were designated historic landmarks, but the owner did not have a right to have his property rezoned to RFC–CX; whether it should be rezoned was a judgment for the council to make. Preservation advocates did intervene at a late hour, but they had no other choice. And the record amply documented the case for preserving the cottages. Regardless of how we voted that night, however, the underlying conflict would remain. And it was likely to become increasingly polarized and virulent unless we found a satisfactory way to resolve it. In my view, the way out of the conflict would begin with everyone understanding that, first, the owner did not have a right to have his property rezoned to RFC–CX without conditions; second, the cottages faced a perilous future unless the owner chose not to demolish them; and, third, our shared lives together would be worse if we did not collectively invent a mutually satisfactory solution.

Other council members then expressed their views, with Susan M., Terry D., and Michelle P. indicating they would oppose the rezoning. Susan M. put a great deal of weight on the part of the RFC District Master Plan which stated, "The plan is simply a vision, highlighting certain areas. The decision to redevelop is ultimately up to the property owner." In the end, she basically claimed the council needed to strike a balance between development and preservation, and for her that balance meant voting no. Kingsley B. said he would vote in favor, Mayor Matt H. said he had agonized over this but eventually decided to vote no. Rick D. said he would vote in favor. Needing a 6:1 vote to pass, the motion failed on a 3:4 vote. At the very end of our discussion, Kingsley B. reported he felt very confused about many of the terms being used—for example, about goals being "aspirational," and about the ultimate decision being in the hands of the developer. At that point, I said something like, "Ultimately the meaning of a plan lies in the actions taken. We're taking an action right now."

· · ·

This passionate debate over three small working-class cottages had a huge effect on me. My sense was that an "old-boy" network combined with a desire to maximize profit to produce a decision that would take the city in an undesirable direction. I began thinking that the transformation we (myself included) had initiated in the RFC District might prove to be equivalent to "Urban Renewal 2.0." In my view, it was not the RFC District Plan that would be taking us in the wrong direction; however, the way the council "struck the balance" after adopting that plan would be. Throughout the debate over the three cottages, the City staff and council majority interpreted the plan and used their discretionary powers to favor the private landowner and developer. The RFC Plan clearly stated that preservation of the cottages "should be a goal." If the staff wanted to fulfill the plan's stated goal, it should have guided the owner toward producing a development concept that would achieve both profitable redevelopment and preservation of the cottages. Instead, the City staff's and council majority's choices encouraged the owner to act precipitously in the direction he preferred. Those choices transformed what could have been a both/and decision into an either/or one instead. After the decision was made, an Iowa City resident asked me, why should anybody care about three small, old cottages? In my view, this heated debate over the fate of three small cottages was actually a debate over the future of Iowa City. Who are we? And what kind of city do we want to be living in?[17]

· · ·

My thoughts about this conflict became clearer when, later in February, we considered a development agreement involving a $5 million TIF for the 316

Madison Street project. The council approved the proposed agreement 6:1, with me voting no. The development would be a 15-story, 150-unit, $40 million multi-family/student housing project. We had recently indicated our intention to adopt an "inclusionary housing" ordinance, which would apply to any residential or mixed-use project seeking rezoning to an RFC District zone. In light of that likely ordinance, the developer had voluntarily agreed to provide a mix of affordable units and "fee-in-lieu-of" payments equivalent to 10 percent of the project's unit count. As partial compensation for this voluntary action, the developer had increased his TIF request. We also learned that the developer would proceed with a conventional five-story building if we did not approve the TIF. After the City's director of development services talked us through financial machinations and told us the TIF would be paid off in 21 years, he concluded, "Realistically this is a 100-year building, steel construction ... that will then have this much larger tax increment associated with it, as opposed to the five-story building tax increment."[18] I felt quite confused by this project and development agreement. When commenting, I said,

> we've done so much good work tonight ... it really disappoints me that I have a fairly negative view toward this particular project. ... In many ways I feel like Alice in Wonderland who's just fallen down a rabbit hole and things look curiouser and curiouser. I cannot make sense out of this project as something that should be supported financially by the City.

Why should we provide TIF support for a student-housing project? Why should we provide TIF support for a project that had recently been rezoned to a much higher allowable density? And why should we provide TIF support for a project we had recently given a seven-story height bonus? Beyond that, it puzzled me why the staff supported this project when it, at least to my Alice-in-Wonderland eyes, appeared not to be very consistent with the RFC Master Plan. The RFC Plan displayed four photos of the kinds of student housing it encouraged for the South Downtown subdistrict. It also presented a bird's-eye view showing four buildings of four to seven stories in height surrounding a courtyard, with an estimated market yield of approximately 110 units (see Figure 3.3).[19] "So, something strikes me in my Alice in Wonderland, tumbling down the rabbit hole view, as being oddly out of sync between this project and the Riverfront Crossings Plan we adopted in 2013." Mayor Matt H. disagreed. He thought the project was consistent with the plan. Mayor Pro Tem Susan M. emphasized that we would start receiving full property taxes from the 316 Madison Street development in 21 years. I countered by saying this presumed we knew what the situation will be like 21 years from now. The city manager emphasized that land assembly costs need to be considered: to achieve the scale of development envisioned in the plan, the developer would have to purchase two lucrative adjacent properties. The director of development services told us

SD-2: Clinton Street Promenade

SD-4: Capitol Street Student Housing

FIGURE 3.3 Bird's-eye view of Clinton Street promenade and Capitol Street student housing.
Source: City of Iowa City, 2013, p. 61.

the height bonuses made the project much more expensive, which justified the TIF. Responding to a question from Kingsley B., the city manager said,

> when you're creating a public purpose [such as requiring the inclusion of affordable housing], the public has a responsibility to participate in the cost of that public purpose. To not do that, you're going to drive development to neighboring jurisdictions that have no commitment to affordable housing.

I said, the site was not blighted, the project would not help develop the local economy, and I could not support the proposal.

So, I opposed the development, largely because it was not, in my view, consistent with the RFC District Master Plan. However, it was consistent with the FBC, which I too had voted for just a few months earlier. Back then, I had tried to amend the maximum post-bonus heights in some subdistricts, but I had lost. And I had not fully understood how the FBC would encourage redevelopment at a much taller and denser scale than the RFC Plan envisioned. My bad, for sure. But what I now saw emerging from the FBC being combined with TIF subsidies was not what I had enthusiastically supported when we adopted the RFC District Master Plan. It looked to me like the ultimate purpose actually was to maximize the properties' market value and property tax revenue.

• • •

Conflict over development projects intensified even more in the spring of 2015, especially with regard to the Chauncey. Recall that, in January 2013, the council had selected it as the preferred development for the College and Gilbert Street site. Selection only started the process; many more steps had to be taken in order for that project to be completed. Many of the necessary steps involved detailed staff work and negotiations with the developer. But the council also had work to do.

From a council member's point of view, the first step was to respond to an application from the staff early in the spring of 2015. It proposed to add a three-block stretch immediately east of downtown to the Downtown and Riverfront Crossings Master Plan. The Chauncey site was located in that stretch. The proposed action would also identify the land use in this three-block stretch as "civic/mixed-use." The staff's application included a map, which showed 7–12-story buildings on corner properties along Gilbert Street, with mid-rise heights along much of the remainder of the block. Staff planner John Y. noted that the P&Z Commission had failed to approve the proposed action by a 1:5 vote after a motion to defer failed 3:3. This meant that a super-majority vote from the council was required to approve the recommended change.

Early in March, we held a public hearing on the proposal. It proved to be very contentious. Roughly 70 people were in the room, and approximately 30 of them spoke during the hearing. As had been the case back in 2013, they and others who had written to us were sharply divided. Spokespersons for major economic development organizations (the Convention and Visitors Bureau, the Chamber of Commerce, the Downtown District, the Home Builders Association, and the Iowa City Area Development Group), realtors, downtown business owners, FilmScene supporters, and residents of buildings owned by the developer of the Chauncey vigorously supported the proposal, whereas many residents of neighborhoods north and east of the area, as well as members of Trinity Church, opposed it. The supporters thought we should enable construction of very tall mixed-use buildings which would attract high-tech businesses, "creative class" workers, and wealthier residents and would expand the tax base, whereas the opponents preferred a mixture of uses in two-to-six-story buildings and wanted a more sensitive transition between the new and the old and between the downtown and eastside residential neighborhood. Everyone wanted a lively and thriving downtown.

Given the P&Z Commission's 1:5 vote, I thought we should defer voting and invite the commissioners to consult with us. But a majority of the council preferred to move ahead with the vote. Just prior to voting, I said: "[A]lmost everybody in this room has expressed their love for the city … and talk about the city as it is now! But we're not deliberating about what the city is like now. We're talking about the future."[20] Many supporters had argued that developing at high density in the downtown area would reduce sprawl, as if we faced an either/or choice between much higher-density new development downtown or a sprawling periphery. I rejected that reasoning, saying:

> I can tell you there's no bigger advocate of higher density than me. … But there's a big difference between … mixed use density … in two to six story buildings and a few highrise towers. … Moreover, if the purpose of the proposed amendments is to help avoid further sprawl, then we would not have already been supporting new suburban developments on the periphery. … We would instead be investing in and strengthening our older core neighborhoods.

In the end, I voted against the proposal and, much to my surprise, so did Kingsley B. Lacking the required super-majority support, the proposal was defeated.

Two weeks later, the council majority chose not to reappoint the landscape architect (John T.) to the P&Z Commission. They did so for what seemed to me to be obvious but unstated reasons having to do with John T.'s deliberative style and votes on the Chauncey and the three cottages. Susan M. recommended appointing new people, stating that, "some of the things are getting bogged down at P&Z," and there is a "need for, I think, a variety of opinions there to really represent the community."[21] Terry D. agreed, saying he had attended the commission's most recent meeting and "was almost shocked about how little got done … the meetings just went on for two and a half hours, for three subjects! … [W]e have to do something," he said, "when we're wondering why things don't get through to the Council, there's such a time lag." I disagreed, saying I had not seen any evidence that the current commissioners were delaying anything. If we're not going to reappoint John T. (the landscape architect), I said, "we should be very clear about why he is not being reappointed." Kingsley B. agreed with me, saying, "I'd hope that we would say something to them before penalizing or changing our past practice [with regard to reappointing a member who has reapplied]." Michelle P. agreed with the mayor pro tem. So did the mayor. He said,

> I think there's a level of dysfunction right now … on that commission … both internally and in terms of its interaction with City Hall, including … the Council … I mean, you can see it in the minutes! … [I]t's distressing … and it's not something that I think advances the City's interests, and the only thing I can come up with to do is to try some new blood.

Our heated discussion went back and forth this way, with members restating the views in different ways, until Rick D. agreed with the other four council members. The council decided not to reappoint the commissioner.

To my ears, it sounded as though the council majority wanted to have a more compliant, business-friendly commission that would speedily ratify the City staff's recommendations. When connected with the council's earlier actions concerning the Chauncey, the three working-class cottages, and several other matters, this decision persuaded me to seek reelection and try to move the city in a different direction. (I discuss this further near the end of this chapter.)

Two weeks after the council chose not to reappoint John T. to the P&Z Commission, we approved a development agreement with Iowa City Hotel Associates LLC for a proposed 12-story, 140-room Hilton Garden Inn Hotel on Clinton Street just south of downtown. The proposed agreement included a $9 million TIF rebate from the City, a tax increment grant from the new art museum the university was planning for an adjacent site, and a partial rebate of hotel-motel taxes. The hotel would be located at a major intersection on the southwest corner of downtown, directly across Clinton Street from the university's new School of Music building and immediately south of the proposed museum. It was a perfect location for a new hotel. Precisely because of that, I could not understand why financial support from the City was required. I voted "no."[22] On a related topic, that evening, the staff recommended that we select CA Ventures as the preferred developer for the Court and Linn Street site. We directed staff to begin negotiating a development agreement with the firm.[23]

. . .

As the council's actions on the three cottages, 316 Madison, the Rise, the Hilton Garden Inn, and other projects demonstrate, developers were responding enthusiastically to the market opportunities created by the City's RFC District Plan, FBC, and willingness to provide TIF subsidies.[24] As a result, the city would be changing quite rapidly and in ways I thought deserved far greater democratic debate in the public arena. My views about this became even stronger late in May when our council turned its attention back to the Chauncey.

On May 24, just 3 days before I planned to announce my candidacy for reelection, we held a public hearing and first vote on the staff's proposal to rezone the College and Gilbert Street site to CB-10. (Earlier in May, a District Court judge had supported the City's denial of Iowa Coalition against the Shadow's application to rezone the property to CB-5.) This would allow for the construction of the Chauncey, now proposed to be 15 stories tall after negotiations between the City staff and the developer. However, a complication had arisen: in April, Trinity Church had, with the assistance of Rockne C., filed a formal objection to the proposed rezoning, which potentially would require a super-majority vote to approve the rezoning. (The super-majority requirement would be invoked if the owners of 20 percent or more of the property located within 200 feet of the outer perimeter of the project objected.) However, another twist emerged when, on April 30, I learned by reading the *Iowa City Press-Citizen* that the staff was preliminarily estimating that Trinity owned only about 7 percent of the property located within 200 feet of the site. A subsequent memo from the director of development services to us affirmed that Trinity alone did not own enough property adjacent to the site to invoke the requirement.

Because I attended Trinity with my wife (who was a member of the church's vestry) and had friends there, I decided to make a public statement at the start of the public hearing about a possible conflict of interest or appearance thereof. I reported that I had met with the City attorney and concluded that I had no troubling conflict, legal or otherwise. Trying to be as transparent about my situation, I reported that I attended Sunday services at Trinity, contributed modest amounts of money to it, had many friends there, and had heard many Trinity parishioners express their views (both pro and con) about the proposed rezoning and the Chauncey in particular. But I also indicated I was not a formal member of Trinity, had no personal financial stake in its well-being, and did not hold nor had ever held any official positions on Trinity's governing committees. I had met with Trinity's rector in mid-April to explain the rezoning process and what Trinity's rights were within it, but I did not provide her with any advice about what Trinity should do.

The director of development services, John Y., reviewed details about the proposed project and highlighted the project's consistency with the Comprehensive Plan. He also spent a substantial amount of time presenting an analysis of the project's shadowing effects on Trinity Church, which had been prepared by the project's architect. Forty-two other people spoke during the hearing, 21 in favor and 21 opposed. Several Trinity people were among the opponents. The council decided to continue the public hearing and defer the first vote on the rezoning.

The staff's decision to include City-owned right-of-way as part of the property located within 200 feet of the project's outer boundary was part of a string of actions pertaining to the Chauncey that troubled me. Nothing about the string of actions was illegal, but it just did not feel right to me. The council had chosen the Chauncey as the preferred developer after there had been virtually no council discussion about the relative merits of the final three competitors, without the project first being consistent with the Comprehensive Plan, and without the site first being rezoned to CB-10. And now, the City, which was the applicant, had prepared a staff report recommending approval of the proposed rezoning, had decided that City-owned streets and right-of-way should be included as part of the property located within 200 feet of the site, and would be deciding whether or not to approve the rezoning. And it had taken these actions while largely discounting the concerns of northside and eastside neighbors and Trinity parishioners. Moreover, the developer's description of the project stated, among many other things, that the mixture of arts and entertainment in the building would create a destination location for people of all ages. Yes, I thought, but it will not be a destination location for low-to-moderate-income people. The class bias embedded in this project really disturbed me.

One week later, we continued the public hearing and took our first vote on rezoning the site. Responding to prior questions from the council, the director of development services noted that most of the existing buildings downtown were between two and four stories tall, while three were over 10 stories. He also said that it was standard City practice to include City-owned property in 200-foot calculations pertaining to proposed rezonings. Roughly 25 people spoke after him. A spokesperson for the Chamber of Commerce emphasized the project would constitute the highest and best use of the land. Rockne C. objected that he and the public had not yet had a chance to see the proposed development agreement for the project, which apparently would require a $14 million TIF. However, City Attorney Eleanor D. said the proposed agreement had been on file in the city clerk's office since May 28, and, therefore, the public had had a chance to read it. Some speakers claimed the project contained an insufficient amount of affordable housing and responded inadequately to the climate crisis. Trinity's rector thought proponents for the project were speaking from a position of privilege, whereas opponents wanted a project in which all citizens would feel they had a rightful place.

During the council's discussion, I posed two questions pertaining to the TIF component of the development agreement because there had been no opportunity to do so when the council first selected the Chauncey as the preferred project early in 2013. I displayed a chart I had drawn which compared property tax revenues that would be generated by a generic five-story building over the first 20 years as compared with the Chauncey (once TIF support was included). It showed very clearly that a generic five-story building would, over the first 20 years, generate about $3 million more in property tax revenue than the Chauncey. More important, a well-designed, modest-scale, mixed-use, no-TIF alternative would do even better. Shortly after Year 20, if there were no negative surprises, the Chauncey would begin generating far more than the generic building. I also stated we had not publicly discussed in January 2013 why we thought the various development proposals were worth, or not worth, the TIF subsidies that would be needed. "It was," I said, "as if we had walked into a car dealership, swooned over the many extras associated with one car, and never talked about whether those extras were worth the price."[25] For me, the core question before us was:

> are the attributes of the Chauncey worth forgoing at least $2.8 million in City tax revenue over the next 20 years, in terms of discounted present value, and should we rezone this property to CB-10 in order to make that happen?

My answer was no. I thought the site should be treated as part of a transitional zone between downtown and the residential neighborhood to its east, and that any building on this site should be at a scale, height, and mass that enabled the project to be a good neighbor. I also thought that we should not be subsidizing the construction of luxury penthouses and other condos in which most of our residents and workers could not afford to live. Last, I thought that any subsidized development on the site should achieve a higher level of energy efficiency and sustainability than proposed.

> [A]ssuming … we do vote to approve the rezoning, I would hope the City staff and the developer take a few key steps to help us move ahead together as a community. Most important, I hope that both will take the initiative to reach out to the objecting neighbor, acknowledge the important contributions that Trinity and other faith-based institutions make to the downtown and our city, and constructively respond to many of the concerns they have expressed.

Despite these and other objections expressed by the public, the motion passed 4:2, with Michelle P. recusing herself, and Kingsley B. and me against.

During a very brief special meeting on June 4, the council voted second consideration on rezoning the site to CB-10. The motion passed 4:1, with me against and Michelle P. and Kingsley B. being absent. Four days later, the council would be voting third and final consideration of the proposed rezoning. But first we had to vote on the proposed development agreement.[26] The City's economic development coordinator made a long presentation, followed by the director of NDS, a financial expert from the National Development Council, the City's finance director, and the City attorney.

The City's economic development coordinator described the details of the $49 million, 15-story, mixed-use proposal. Along with other features already described, it would contain five affordable housing units, which would be sold to the City for public housing. The developer was requesting a $12 million up-front TIF to fill the "gap" between the project's cost and available financing. She then explained how TIFs work. The owner would pay a little over $1 million in property taxes (cumulatively to the City, the county, the school district, and other taxing entities) on a minimum assessment of $31 million every year. The state-mandated "protected debt levy" would constitute approximately $250,000 of that total annually, whereas "the TIF levy" would account for the remaining $900,000. (This was the first time I recall hearing of a "protected debt levy.") The TIF levy would be used to pay back the City's up-front financing. Once all the TIF debt had been paid off, which would be not later than 2046, then all $1 million per year would flow to the taxing entities.

Doug B., the director of NDS, spoke after the economic development coordinator and pointed to the various investments the City had made in affordable and workforce housing over the past couple of years. He then reported the Chauncey's five affordable units, costing a total of $1 million, would be owned by the Iowa City Housing Authority, would probably be occupied by elderly and/or disabled residents, and would be paid for with federal public housing funds coming from the 1995 sale of several public housing units located in the southeastern part of the city.

The representative from the National Development Council then described in detail the assumptions he made when assessing the financial justifications for the requested TIF. One of the assumptions was that the developer would expect a 7.5 percent internal rate of return. (By this point, it had become clear that the data I had used did not match the more current data contained in the development agreement. Inclusion of "the protected levy" accounted for part of the difference, as did the way the City staff counted the project's TIF levy payments.)

The City's finance director followed the NDC representative. Among many other things, he reminded us that the economic development grant to the developer would include funds from a $12 million revenue bond, sale of the land on which the Chauncey would be built (roughly $2 million), and sale of easements to build geothermal wells in an adjacent City-owned park. He then described in detail how the bonding process would work. The City attorney concluded these presentations, mainly by identifying key steps that would have to be taken before the City would be obligated to sell the property and before the developer would be obligated to purchase it.

We council members began asking questions. Kingsley B. asked several pertaining to affordable housing. I followed with several others, one of which was, "what happens in the event something unexpected goes wrong … for example, a global financial crisis or some other thing that we can't fully anticipate at the moment?" The City attorney essentially said, they will have to be dealt with when they come up using the remedies available to the City.

Let me now inject a point from the future. The proposed development agreement was an extremely complicated document, one which would be very difficult for any non-professional person to read and understand. And yet, the City attorney had told us the proposed agreement had been available for public review since May 28. That meant people, myself included, had only about 4 days to learn of, read, comprehend, and form coherent thoughts about it while doing all the other things people normally have to do. What kind of democratic practice is this?

The mayor opened the floor to public comment. Roughly 25 people spoke and, once again, they were equally divided between supporters and opponents. One speaker, who was a retired law professor, condemned the hypocrisy of free-market advocates using taxpayers' money to subsidize private enterprises, as well as city councils giving money to their friends for private projects on a whim. TIFs are unnecessary, he said.[27] The second speaker noted that the developer's Plaza Towers structure on the Ped Mall had a 15-year TIF, but the developer had been able to pay it off in 5 or 6 years. The third speaker basically said that this project would not benefit working people. The fourth praised the developer for being a local resident who was trying to improve the city and emphasized that people who lived in other cities would love to have a project like this one. A couple of other speakers supported a TIF for the project, whereas another person said the payoff is too far down the road to be grasped, and the rewards go to too few while the rest of us pay the price. A member of Trinity said the project should express a vision for the children of the future and the future of the planet, not just for profit in the present; consequently, this project should do far better than LEED Silver and include more affordable and workforce housing. Rockne C. described Iowa City was increasingly becoming a tale of two cities and said the council should stand with the entire community rather than the privileged few. The rector of Trinity said this would not be an appropriate use of public funds. Several business owners and representatives of economic development organizations supported the use of TIF for the project. Some of the speakers understood how TIFs work; most did not. The developer, Marc M., was the last person to speak. Among many other things, he reported that private property in the entire downtown was assessed at roughly $200 million. Three of his buildings accounted for $45 million of that total, and, with the Chauncey included, his buildings would account for $84 million. He did not explicitly say so, but this meant he would own at least 35 percent of the property value downtown.

At that point, council members weighed in. Kingsley B. wanted to increase the amount of affordable housing in the project. He also said he had spoken with a lot of people who told him: do what you want, I don't have any skin in this game. Is this building, he asked, going to be for the entire community? Affordable housing is number one, Terry D. said, but he thought the $1 million targeted for it could be spent more effectively than the City staff proposed. Otherwise, he was fully supportive of the TIF. Looking to the future, he said, kids and grandkids throughout the town are going to benefit from it. Mayor Matt H. stressed how infrequently Iowa City used TIF; Iowa City accounted for only about 2 percent of the total value of TIF-fed property in the county, and other cities (by which he meant Coralville) had been using TIF and other incentives in a predatory way. Beyond that, he reiterated what the staff and Marc M.'s supporters had said concerning the merits of the project while also suggesting that opponents were "insufficiently pragmatic" and "ignorant." I delayed speaking because I was feeling tired, had an aching lower back, had just listened to the staff spend an hour advocating the development agreement, and was feeling undermined by the finance director's written critique of my chart comparing the Chauncey's property tax revenues versus those of a generic five-story building. But I said the following, which I had written pretty much on the fly while I was listening to the other speakers:

> [I]t' s not the way I would invest the City's limited public funds. Instead of investing them on this project … in a way that will not fully pay off its TIF debt for … maybe up to 27 years, and will largely be focused on providing space for wealthy people and an elite class of highly trained workers, I'd spend those funds on improving the lives of people … in the bottom half of the income bracket. That is on job opportunities, living conditions, affordable housing … improving the neighborhoods they live in, and … improving transportation related access to and from jobs and

school and so on. … But the question is, should we spend $14 million … on this particular TIF for this particular project, given the agreement that's been worked out, and I think the answer's no.

Susan M. spoke right after me and said,

> The problem is that people forget key points here and … they keep getting this confused over and over. Number one, we don' t even have these dollars unless the project is built. And number two, the project won't be built unless we have a TIF.

Rick D. said the discussion had revealed three realities: Iowa City is a progressive community, we live in a capitalist democracy, and tax increment financing is underutilized in Iowa City. "This democracy has scrutinized this capitalist, and this project is worth our investment." The council approved the resolution 4:2, with Kingsley B. and me against, and Michelle P. recused.

We then took our third and final vote on the proposed rezoning. Once again, the vote was 4:2, with Kingsley B. and me against, and Michelle P. having recused herself. My "no" vote subsequently generated a lot of praise from a substantial number of people but also the ire of (or disappointment from) many others. For me, the rezoning felt like the tail wagging the dog. Riding home on my bike after the meeting, I felt pretty crummy. It was not that I expected to see a different outcome, for the decision had pretty much been made back in November, 2012, if not earlier. But I felt that I had failed to rise to the occasion, and a bit like a boxer who had just been beaten up in the ring. As far as the Chauncey was concerned, I thought, it's time to let it go and move on.

Many months later, during our last formal meeting in 2015, the council considered minor amendments to the development agreement about the project. This forced me to consider once again whether I should recuse myself from the issue. Shortly after the election, I learned that, on October 22, the District Court had ruled in the City's favor and had concluded the City's rezoning of the College and Gilbert Street site had been lawful. But I also learned that Trinity was likely to appeal the Court's decision. Shortly thereafter, I received a text message and a phone call which led me to conclude that a story was going around town that I and/or my wife (who once, but no longer, held a formal position on Trinity's vestry) were manipulating Trinity's decision-making. Recognizing that the results of the November council elections had altered the context, and in light of the text message, I spoke with our City attorney and decided to recuse myself from any future City decisions pertaining to the Chauncey owing to the *perception* that I had a conflict of interest. Consequently, I recused myself from participating in the discussion and vote on the minor amendments. I later learned the developer had requested a change in certain deadlines owing to the lawsuit Trinity Church had filed and to the church's appeal of the District Court's opinion. Several council members expressed disappointment at Trinity Church's decision to file suit and then appeal the court's decision, and the developer stated the delay had already cost more than $1 million. The council voted 5:0 in favor, with Michelle P. and me recusing ourselves.

Taking Steps to Improve Racial Equity

Who are *we*? And what kind of city do we want to be living in? Surely our ability to imagine future possibilities depends to a great extent on who *we* are and on the conditions of our day-to-day lives. Much of what I have described, especially the council's efforts to redevelop the area south of downtown and to bring the Chauncey to life, would have very little direct effect on the daily lives of Iowa City's minority communities. For the city's black residents in particular, the sense of being treated unfairly or unjustly was a profoundly troubling feature of their lives, and, in their view, we in City government had not been paying sufficient attention to how those conditions could be improved.

To fully understand what this meant for Iowa City, it is important to know that the city's black population lives primarily in the southeastern part of the city, and that some (mostly white) people have been speaking fearfully about that part of the city ("the southeast side") for at least 25 years, primarily because some of the people living there are lower-income African-Americans. Those fearful race-related claims about "those people from Chicago" increased significantly after a few large fights involving black youth occurred in 2009 ("the Mother's Day riots") and especially after the owner of an apartment building was murdered, allegedly by a 17-year-old black youth. In response, the city council imposed a citywide curfew on youth 17 years old and younger. The curfew took effect late in December 2009 (Throgmorton, 2010; Gutsche, 2014).

With this as context, recall that, in May of 2012, councilman Rick D. and I had heard 18 black residents narrate their personal stories about being black in Iowa City. Many of them focused on their interactions with police officers, including being stopped by officers for "driving while black." Recall too that, in April 2013, the Ad Hoc Committee on Diversity Issues had made several recommendations concerning law enforcement and public transit services, and that the council had adopted the staff's advice about how to implement the committee's recommendations.

Almost exactly 1 year after the council adopted the City staff's advice, we focused a special mid-June work session on what came to be known as the St. Ambrose Traffic Study (Barnum et al., 2014).[28] The study had been prepared by Dr. Christopher Barnum, an associate professor of sociology and criminal justice at St. Ambrose University, and two graduate students. Dr. Barnum, who knew policing well from having been a police officer for 25 years, focused the study on traffic stops by Iowa City Police Department (ICPD) officers and subsequent outcomes (such as citations, arrests, consent searches, and "hit-rates").[29] Much to our surprise, or mine at least, we learned that he had previously collected data for the years 2005–2007 and 2010–2012, with 2008–2009 being excluded owing to data management conversion problems. In order not to let the study influence behavior, neither he nor the police chief had informed the officers that the study was being conducted. The key question was, is there disproportionality in how the ICPD officers treat minority drivers as compared with white ones? In brief, Dr. Barnum's answer was, yes, there is.

With regard to *stops*, the report indicated that, from 2005 through 2007, the disproportionality was comparatively low: roughly 14 percent of the traffic stops involved "minority" drivers, as compared with the 10 percent of all drivers who were minorities. However, the disproportionality increased in 2010 and remained stable through 2012: roughly 19 percent of the stops involved minority drivers in those years. Dr. Barnum attributed the increase, in part, to the establishment of a new patrol beat (Beat 2-A) in southeast Iowa City and an escalation of patrols in that area. With regard to stop *outcomes*, the report found,

> On average across all years of the study the odds were about three times greater that minority drivers would be arrested on a traffic stop in comparison to others. Likewise, the average odds for consent searches were about three and a half times greater that ICPD officers would request a search from minority drivers compared to others, this despite hit rates that were actually lower on average for minority drivers.
>
> *(Barnum et al., 2014, p. 8)*

The St. Ambrose study also analyzed stops and subsequent outcomes on an officer-by-officer basis (without identifying the officers). It reported considerable variation in "disparity index values" and noted that the index values were higher for officers assigned to Beat-2A and many "Beat-5 SCAT [Special Crime Apprehension Team] officers," and it suggested a couple of possible explanations. I suggested a third possible explanation: individual officers simply varied in how they exercised their discretion about whether or not to stop a driver who was black.[30] Last, when conveying the St. Ambrose study to us, the police chief had stated that any inappropriate officer behavior had resulted in personnel action. But he provided no details, which made me wonder how many inappropriate behaviors (pertaining to the subject of the report) had resulted in personnel actions over the past few years, and what actions had been taken.

Along with other council members, I was very pleased to learn that the police chief had commissioned the study. It meant that Iowa City was one of only two cities in Iowa that systematically studied disproportionality in traffic tops and arrests. I wanted to believe that our officers would respond effectively to serious crimes while not engaging in racial or ethnic profiling. For me, the ICPD's guiding philosophy should be to "serve and protect" so that Iowa City would be a safe and welcoming place for all. During the work session, I drew attention to the way the study interpreted trends over time. According to the study, the estimated violent crime rate in Iowa City during this period had trended sharply downward from roughly 650 such crimes per 100,000 residents in 1999 to roughly 250 per 100,000 in 2012. However, it also reported that the rate had sharply increased in 2008 and 2009 and then had resumed its downward trend through the rest of the decade. In his oral presentation, Dr. Barnum noted that the 2008–2009 spike had been accompanied by a disproportionate amount of media coverage, which had framed the "crime problem" in Iowa City as predominantly a product of illegal activity occurring in the southeastern part of the city. In his opinion, political pressure had caused the ICPD to create the new Beat 2-A and do more intensive patrolling ("hot spot policing") to reduce crime in that area. Kingsley B. asked, what was the connection between stopping drivers and reducing violent crime? "[G]iven the structure of that neighborhood," Dr. Barnum responded, "traffic stops is the main modality that would be used to do zero tolerance policing." Following up, Kingsley B. asked, do traffic stops reduce crime? "I don't know," said Dr. Barnum.

We understood that the St. Ambrose study would continue, and that reports would be submitted to the council annually. I was very pleased to hear this, for my sense was that it provided information *we* needed to respond effectively to community concerns about how our police officers were treating black drivers. (What I routinely heard from black friends was, this study reports what we already know: being stopped for "driving while black" can be dangerous.) I also realized this was the first time our council had looked carefully at any aspect of police work. Up to then, for me at least, it felt as though the ICPD was almost a separate institution being run by its own rules. I needed to learn more about what being a uniformed police officer entailed, and where, specifically, ICPD policies and practices permitted, for good or for bad, officers to exercise discretion about when and how to the enforce the law.

It would take another jolt to focus our attention on race-related inequities in the City's policies and practices more broadly.

On August 9, 2 months after we received the St. Ambrose study, another white police officer killed another black man. This man was Michael Brown, and the killing took place in Ferguson, Missouri. Brown's death at the hands of a white officer immediately led to mass protests, demonstrations, and destruction of property in Ferguson. The national news media repeatedly showed video images of angry people torching parts of the city.

These events provided much of the context for a work session we held at the start of September. We had received two reports from the City's equity director (Stefanie B.): a 2013 Equity Report and a memo from her summarizing the National League of Cities (NLC) Institute for Youth, Education & Families' 2012 action guide, "City Leadership to Promote Black Male Achievement."

As the Coalition for Racial Justice's earlier report had done, the 2013 Equity Report revealed many important race-related disparities. Iowa City's median household income in 2008–2012 was about $42,000, but, for black people, it was about $19,000. Black people (just under 6 percent of the city's total population) constituted 29 percent of all people our police officers arrested in 2013. Of the City's permanent employees in 2013, only 15 out of roughly 580 (less than 3 percent) were black, 17 were Hispanic, and 6 were Asian. Only 1 of 56 Fire Department employees and 6 of 82 police officers were black, Hispanic, or Asian. Just two of the police officers were black. There were approximately 130 seats on the City's boards, commissions, and the city council. According to voluntary responses to a survey of people occupying those seats, 6 of 80 respondents were black, and 67 were Caucasian.

The equity director's summary of the NLC report highlighted several key facts and made numerous recommendations. Across the nation, black (especially male) youth had been experiencing large disparities in comparison with youth who were not black. The disparities could be seen in poverty rates, educational success, political exclusion, and high death rates. Moreover, black children were more likely to be placed in foster care, be suspended from school, be incarcerated, and not complete postsecondary education after enrollment. The situation called for city leadership, the NLC's report said. City leaders could draw needed attention to the disparities, allocate funding, pool resources, garner support, and collaborate with other municipalities and organizations to advocate changes in local, state, and federal policies. Municipal leaders should also carefully assess the effect local policies have on outcomes for black male youth. The NLC report also identified specific actions a city might take with regard to families, education, and work. In the end, our equity director's memo stated,

> The importance and influence of city leadership is crucial for any success in combating disparities. ... [T]he City (both staff and Council) needs to work towards identifying disparities, understanding the roots of the disparities and working collectively as a community to resolve racial disparities.[31]

We did not discuss the equity director's two documents that night. Mayor Pro Tem Susan M., who was chairing the meeting, suggested that we place discussion of the reports on our long list of pending work session topics. Kingsley B. and I argued we needed to discuss the reports soon, and we needed to allocate enough time to discuss them thoroughly. Kingsley B. also wanted us to acknowledge that disparities exist, and that we were committed to reducing them. I noted that we had taken several good first steps, but everyone I had talked with in the African-American community thought they were "just baby steps," and there was a real sense that we were not taking this issue seriously enough. This led to a rather heated discussion among council members about whether the steps we had taken thus far were mere "baby steps." In the end, the council decided to hold a special work session 2.5 months later. I drew attention to the big gap between the Equity Report's focus on City government operations and the NLC report's focus on reducing disparities more generally throughout the community.

During our mid-November work session, just a day after we had held the long and complicated discussion about the finalists for the Court and Linn Street project, we discussed the two reports our equity director had given us. She made a very long statement summarizing both reports and identifying several possible topics for council/staff action. Owing to the length of her presentation, we council members were left with only a few minutes to respond. Displaying his frustration (which I shared) about the length of her presentation, Kingsley B. urged us to schedule a follow-up work session in which we could explore possible actions more thoroughly. Mayor Matt H. suggested we email our recommended actions to the council as a whole.

I responded to the mayor's request 3 days later by suggesting we needed to take three actions pertaining to equity and diversity: (1) build stronger bonds based on mutual trust (between City government and the city's black community); (2) address the deeper inequities in education, employment, income, housing, incarceration, and so on presented in the equity director's two reports; and (3) devise programs that could potentially be funded with revenues generated by a revised LOST. With regard to building trust, I argued that having good data—such as one could find in the Equity Report—was important for management and policy-making purposes, but it was not sufficient as a response to public concerns. Building trust throughout the community was at least as important. We council members and key staff needed to get out of City Hall, meet with black residents who distrusted local government, and do so in places where they felt most comfortable. To develop mutual trust, we needed to identify intermediaries or liaisons—that is, black adults who came from lower-income backgrounds and who black youth trusted. With regard to addressing the deeper race-related disparities, I claimed the data concerning those disparities did not explain themselves. Diverse people might agree the data showed large disparities and yet disagree about what produced them and, hence, what should be done in response. I thought, therefore, that future versions of the City's Equity Report should focus greater attention on those deeper inequities, especially as they pertained to lower-income black residents. And we needed to devise actions that would reduce those deeper disparities. Drawing upon the good ideas contained in the NLC report, the City would have to work with community members to collaboratively devise some community-based programs that increased employment opportunities and practical, hands-on educational opportunities for lower-income residents, especially those of color. We would also need to allocate funds sufficient to fund the programs.

Kingsley B., who had recently been appointed equity director in the School District, shared his recommendations with the council a week or so later. He urged us to take six actions: first, to publicly acknowledge there were racial inequities and disparities in our city and to identify actions the council could take to eliminate or minimize them; second, to add public oversight or inclusion in the City's Diversity Task Force; third, to use Seattle's Racial Equity Toolkit or something like it when making budget and policy decisions; fourth, to develop different ways to engage and include the minority community; fifth, to work with other governmental entities on racial equity; and, sixth, to follow through with an overall action plan to reduce racial/ethnic disparities in the ICPD's actions.[32]

While we were talking, actions were taking place in the streets. A little over 2 months after Michael Brown was killed in Ferguson, and just 4 days after we held our work session late in November, more than 200 people gathered on a cold night in front of the university's Old Capitol building downtown to protest against racist police and the grand jury's decision not to indict the officer who had shot and killed Michael Brown. They marched through the downtown to City Hall chanting, "Hands up! Don't shoot!" (Jordan, 2014).

The November protests provided further justification for holding a special council work session focusing on the equity director's two reports. On December 2, just as we were choosing two preferred developers for the Court and Linn Street project and just as we had begun hearing angry complaints about the possible demolition of three working-class cottages, we had a frustrating work session discussion about when to hold that work session and how to conduct it. Moreover, instead of discussing the two reports in the abstract, we would inevitably have to consider them in relation to the events that had recently occurred in Ferguson, Missouri, and New York City.[33] Councilman Kingsley B. and I wanted to hold a focused work session in the very near future. After considerable discussion concerning competing demands on our time, the council decided to schedule one for mid-January.

Just a few days before our January 13 work session, we held a special work session concerning the proposed budget for FY 2015–2016. With regard to racial equity, I recommended that we direct more funds to people in the lower half of the income bracket and the neighborhoods in which they live. To that end, I suggested we should reduce by 10 percent (or almost $2 million over the next 5 years) the amount of capital being directed toward the downtown streetscape project, and we should redirect that money toward the southeastern part of the city. As I saw it, the particulars of this initiative could be developed over the coming year and begin in FY 2016–2017. A majority of the council declined to redirect the funds.

Three days later, we held the special work session on equity and diversity issues. To help us prepare for the session, the assistant city manager, the chief of police, and the equity director had sent us a memo recommending actions, with a focus on building relationships and communication channels. It specifically recommended that the council hold listening posts in various locations during the year, with two council members attending on a rotating schedule. It also recommended that the city manager convene small, regularly scheduled roundtable discussions with the directors of relevant community organizations—for example, the Black Voices Project (BVP) and the Center for Worker Justice (CWJ). It also recommended continuing the St. Ambrose study and requiring police officers to use body cameras. And it asked the council to review the metrics contained in the 2013 Equity Report and to specify any new measures that should be included. We also had in hand the memos Kingsley B. and I had shared with the council several weeks earlier. By this time, I had learned that the BVP and the CRJ strongly supported Kingsley B.'s recommendations and wanted white allies to avoid speaking during the work session until black residents had spoken. I also knew they had identified policing, housing, schooling, and jobs as priority issues, and they wanted the council to identify key indicators for each of the priorities, to examine progress on them at least quarterly, and to invest the necessary funds to fully implement the six actions. With all this in mind, I saw the staff's and Kingsley B.'s recommendations as good steps in the right direction.

When we assembled for the January 13 work session, around 40–50 people were in the council chambers. Some 10–15 of them were black, and many of the attendees were affiliated with the CRJ. More people trickled in as the meeting proceeded. I could feel considerable tension in the room, partly because a group of black students (led by Vinson C.) had conducted a Black Lives Matter protest demonstration outside City Hall shortly before our meeting.

The City's equity director opened the meeting by reporting that the City had been trying to increase the diversity of representation on the City staff and the City's boards and commissions. In addition, the City had started training City staff on cultural competency and hoped to begin "implicit bias" training later in the year. The ICPD had started participating in jail diversion programs and had begun more community policing. It had also been participating in the St. Ambrose study for several years, and it had been trying to build relationships with youth of color. City Manager Tom M. followed the equity director and essentially repeated the points made in the memo we had received a few days earlier. He also suggested that community members could be invited to participate in "ride-alongs" with police officers, and he reported that City staff expected to purchase a body camera system for the City's police officers. He urged us to invite council members in nearby cities to consider establishing community police review boards like ours. He also indicated that City staff supported the county's proposed "Community ID" program, and he urged the council's representative on the county's Criminal Justice Coordinating Council (Kingsley B.) to report to the council on a regular basis.[34] We cannot resolve the situation all at once, he said, for "The issues are systemic and individual. They're national and local. They're long-term and they're immediate."[35]

According to my notes, 17 members of the public addressed us after the staff had finished. Roughly two-thirds of the speakers were black, roughly half were directly affiliated with the CRJ, and roughly half were well known within the community. LaTasha D., a black resident who was active in the CRJ and had served on the Ad Hoc Committee, spoke for many when she applauded the work that had already been done, thanked the council for listening actively to what people had to say, and told us the CRJ supported the six actions Kingsley B. recommended. Other speakers typically reinforced what she had said but drew attention to specific details. An older Sudanese-American resident thought the staff's recommendations lacked specificity and were just a public relations gesture. He urged us to reach out to immigrant and refugee communities, which faced formidable language and cultural barriers. A woman who coordinated a healthy reentry program for people who are coming out of prison urged us to reduce disproportionality in police contacts. "When the cards are stacked against you," she said, "it's difficult to be optimistic about your future." Royceann P., who was a member of the City's Community Police Relations Board and had been a council candidate in 2013, commended us for convening the work session and told us that people of color have lots of ideas about how to make Iowa City a great place to live. A young white woman who directed the CWJ urged us to strengthen the Community Police Relations Board, work with the county to implement the new Community ID program, and extend our efforts to include the quality of jobs and livable wages. A young white man told us that black drivers were eight times more likely to be arrested for possession of marijuana, and the resulting felony record made it harder for arrested persons to get a job. He thought we should tell the police chief to make arresting people for nonviolent offenses the police's lowest priority. An older white woman who was a member of the CRJ and also served on the county's Criminal Justice Coordinating Committee hoped we would partner with other governmental entities to bring greater racial equity into the criminal justice system. She also drew our attention to a new organization called the Government Alliance on Race and Equity (GARE) and urged us to connect with it. She thought the Equity Report was excellent: "[I]t feels to me like we've come a long way," she said, "and the tone of the discussion has changed." Speaking on behalf of a local black leader, Henri H., another black man told us that people of color who were trusted in the community needed to be on City staff in order to bring people of color's concerns into City government. Two young black women from Black Hawkeyes urged us to "keep intersectionality" in mind and to recognize that black people can be queer, disabled, or transgendered, and are not necessarily Christian in their faith. A long-time black resident who had often been critical of black people disagreed with almost everything the other speakers told us. In his view, the biggest problem facing black people in Iowa City was poor leadership within the local black community.

At this point, we council members began discussing how we should respond. Kingsley B. stressed the importance of using a racial equity review toolkit. Recognizing the strong support Kingsley B.'s recommendations received,

I sought to reinforce him. But I also emphasized a couple of the actions mentioned in my earlier memo to the council—for example, future versions of the Equity Report should focus more on deeper inequities, especially as they affected lower-income black residents. Michelle P. agreed up to a point, but also said there were some things City government had no control over. Kingsley B. said we have always had data and recommendations; what we needed now was effective action. In response, the city manager told us that collecting valid data was the first step toward accomplishing goals (such as reducing disproportionality in traffic stops and arrests). Mayor Matt H. argued we needed to be acting in partnership with other jurisdictions and major organizations throughout the region. I reiterated my memo's claim that knowing facts is not sufficient. What was required was trust between the people who presented facts and the people who received them. "[I]f we don't have that bond of trust from the git-go," I said, "they're just numbers."

After a few other council members commented, the mayor noted that some additional people in the audience wanted to speak. One young woman told us she felt afraid to be alone in a police car with an officer. Immediately following her, Venson C., the young black man who had helped lead the protest demonstrations and was accompanied by other several other black students, told us we were not getting to the root of the issues. "[W]hat just happened [the entire discussion] for me was a failure. Period, point blank!" Susan M. tried to interject, but Venson C. cut her off. "I'm very clear when I'm done," he said as he continued speaking. At this point, I could feel tension escalating in the room. You don't need another equity report, he said, you need an equity plan so that we can be clear about what steps you are going to take to reduce inequities.

After Vinson C. finished speaking, we council members brought our discussion to a close. As the meeting was winding down, it had become clear there was unanimous council support for accepting the City staff's recommendations. The city manager elaborated on the challenges associated with diversifying the 600-member City staff and the ICPD's 82 uniformed officers. Civil Service Commission processes and union contracts posed the major challenge. Management did not have as much discretion on hiring decisions as people thought, he said, but we could diversify the staff more as positions became vacant. The work session ended after 2.5 hours of discussion. However, several black residents (led by Vinson C.) apparently felt the council had not taken them seriously and walked out of the meeting.

Consistent with our discussion that night, we unanimously approved a resolution adopting a 2015 Equity Report Action Plan 6 weeks later.[36] The action plan identified top priorities and related initiatives designed to promote racial and ethnic equity and to improve communications and relationships within Iowa City. I thought it was a good and necessary but insufficient step. If we wanted to avoid another jolt, we would need to do more.

Another jolt came when, in the last half of June, we began hearing from community members about an incident that had occurred in mid-June at the City's Robert A. Lee Recreation Center, which is located just across a street from the Chauncey's site. The complaints included a petition signed by 100 people emphasizing "Black kids play too." The petition told us we should "End discrimination against black youth in Iowa City and its public spaces." It demanded that the council, the city manager, the police chief, the Community Police Review Board, the Human Rights Commission, and the Parks and Recreation Department staff take a series of specific actions. Most important, all ICPD officers must be retrained so they could build authentic, positive, reciprocal relationships with community members, especially children, and such training must include "de-escalation" techniques and many other interventions appropriate for children.

The petition came as a surprise, and, much as had been the case with the three working-class cottages, I had to learn what motivated the petition. The city manager explained what had happened in a memo to us shortly prior to our next formal meeting late in July. An ICPD officer had forced a black juvenile to the floor, taken the juvenile to the ICPD's offices, and charged the juvenile with interference and criminal trespass. The city manager noted that most of the event had been recorded on a cell phone and later posted on the internet, but it was also recorded on Recreation Center cameras. Two days after the incident, the police chief met with interested community members and showed them videos of the event. The community members found the videos to be quite upsetting and they shared numerous thoughts and opinions about how the police officer could have handled the situation better. Given the recent death of young black males in other parts of the country, and especially in light of the June 17 murders of nine people at Mother Emmanuel African Methodist Episcopal Church in Charleston, South Carolina, the police chief committed to reviewing the incident and reporting back to community members. According to the city manager, the ICPD recognized the officer had moved very quickly to a control technique that was likely not the most effective way to deal with the situation. Consequently, the ICPD had modified its arrest procedures to deploy "de-escalation" techniques prior to, and hopefully instead of, using force. The city manager concluded his memo by indicating that appropriate corrective action and additional training would be provided to modify any unacceptable police conduct. Further, the Parks and Recreation staff would also undergo further training.

A large crowd of people gathered in front of City Hall prior to our July 27 meeting, and around 100 people came into the council chambers just prior to its start. It was the same night on which we approved the development agreement for CA Ventures' large project at Linn and Court Streets. By this time, the petition had been signed by more than 850 people. Some were carrying signs which read, "#BlackKidsPlayToo" (Schmidt, 2015). I counted

21 people who addressed us during the community comment period at the start of the meeting. LaTasha D. presented the petitioners' demands. Most of the subsequent speakers were black residents who narrated stories about how they or their children had been treated inappropriately. One of the speakers, an older white man affiliated with the CRJ, said he watched the videos carefully and concluded the youth had not been aggressive and did not deserve the treatment he received. Even so, the young man had been arrested and charged with two offenses, and he would become part of the disproportionality statistics. There should be a way, he said, of removing record of the young man's arrest in circumstances such as this. Royceann P. said she had not heard anybody in City government apologize to the young man. So, she turned toward the youth (who was sitting at the front of the audience) and apologized to him.

Mayor Matt H. made a long statement in response, the essence of which was that the City staff's response subsequent to the incident had been immediate, professional, and genuine. In his view, City government had done a lot over the past couple of years to restore trust with the community, but we needed to keep improving. I said I wanted to speak from a gut level as a white man. As a white man, I had been horrified by the cascade of incidents involving the deaths of black men and women around the country.

> [W]hen I try to take a very big leap and imagine myself to be a young black man ... I would be fearful! ... And I would not react very well. ... So I think we need to look carefully ... at the petition we've received and ask ourselves ... What steps remain? What else should ... must we be doing.[37]

Kingsley B. essentially said we should not just kick the can down the road and keep having these kinds of conversations whenever something traumatic happens. Susan M. said it is important to recognize that all of us carry implicit biases within ourselves, biases which remain at a subconscious level. She also noted that her husband was a black man and together they had four biracial children. Rick D., Michelle P., and Terry D. did not comment.

• • •

Attending meetings and reading reports and memos is one thing. Seeing action on the ground is quite another. On the night of the first weekend of the university's fall semester, I spent several hours doing a ride-along with an on-duty uniformed police officer, Officer Doug R. As the evening unfolded, we had several encounters which reflected the diversity of experiences that our officers have: for example, responding to a complaint about loud music coming from an apartment and observing another police officer stop a vehicle and ultimately cite two of the occupants for PAULA (Possession of Alcohol under the Legal Age). But two incidents really got my attention.

Officer Doug heard a report on his radio about a loud kerfuffle in front of a house on the eastern end of Hollywood Boulevard in the southeastern part of the city, so we drove there. When we arrived, two other officers were talking primarily with a black woman who was barbequing ribs in front of her house. One of the officers wanted to go inside to look for a younger person who had apparently tried to hide when they arrived. Two other black women were re-inforcing the first woman's words and tone. Several children were running around the area. Two SCAT members were present too. The situation appeared to be escalating and looked to me like it might quickly spin out of control, but Officer Doug tried to calm things down, to de-escalate the situation. He went inside the garage to talk with the woman. The garage door closed behind them. This made the other officers very nervous. But eventually he came out. Things calmed down. We and the other officers decided to leave.

The second incident involved a call for help from officers on South Keokuk Street, which also is in the southeastern part of the city. It struck Officer Doug as important, so we drove very rapidly to an apartment complex near the 2100 block. Other officers from the Hollywood Boulevard encounter were there, along with at least one other officer. We walked through the dark looking for a male who had tried to kick a door in and reportedly wore a long brown coat. Talking, flashlights darting around, looking for movement. We didn't see anybody and left. While driving back on Keokuk, we encountered the same officers talking with a black woman and man who had been walking along the sidewalk. The officers had stopped them because the man was wearing a long brown coat. As Officer Doug and I started walking toward the couple and the officers, I saw the woman crumple down and fearfully say, "Don't shoot me." The officers had a dog in the car. It was barking pretty loudly. Eventually the officers decided the two people had not been involved in the alleged break-in and let them walk away.

The whole night emphasized for me how challenging it is to be a good po-lice officer. It also emphasized how important it is for officers to be well trained about how to use good judgment and discretion when enforcing laws in par-ticular circumstances. And the two encounters revealed how important it is to de-escalate tensions rather than let them build and explode. Images from the evening are riveted in my memory, especially seeing the black woman cringing as she fearfully said, "Don't shoot me."

• • •

A couple weeks later (mid-September), we received the 2014 Equity Report from the equity director.[38] At roughly the same time, we received a September 22 email, from a white resident of the southeastern side of the city, complaining about the lack of police response to unruly young people in his neighborhood. He wanted a City grant to pay for additional (overtime) police patrol on weekends during the summer. In part, he wrote:

> We have experienced many incidents of young people having no respect for property, authority or residents. This has also been experienced all over town at Robert A. Lee, Mercer, the public library, the Ped Mall, our City Parks, City busses, school busses, schools and our neighborhoods in general. The general response has been to protest the way Police are handling the individuals who are committing the crimes or being unruly and unresponsive to Police requests. … I keep hearing from people who should know that the police are being told to back off arresting or confronting these kids. … Since our request for additional patrols has gone unanswered I am going to assume that things are not good between our officers and the City and that they are being told to back off. Congratulations, you have now even managed to alienate our Police force and make my neighborhood a less safe place to live this summer.

The writer included an email from an Iowa City police captain, which indicated that some officers were reluctant to confront unruly youth because of the perceived backlash following the recent incident at the Recreation Center.[39]

I found these to be a very disturbing but not surprising pair of communications. They supplemented other communications we had received over the preceding couple of months in which white property owners had complained about "disorderly conduct" at Wetherby Park and the lack of effective response from the ICPD. One of those writers wanted us to install a 6-foot-high chain link fence and lighting at the east entrance to the park, and to adopt a City ordinance against loitering. The first writer wanted City police to force black youth to respect authority, residents, and property, without ever identifying any actions that constituted criminal offenses. Moreover, he claimed to be speaking on behalf of Grantwood/Wetherby neighbors without showing he had made any effort to involve black neighbors in crafting his proposal. In addition, by including an email from one of our higher-ranking police officers, the writer had used that officer's response and hearsay about the views of lower-ranking officers to promote his own preferred actions. If enacted, I thought, his proposals would mark a step toward transforming Iowa City into a police state.

As 2015 neared its end, I thought we had made some good changes, but there was much more we needed to do. We were simply reacting to events, both near and far. As the events in Ferguson, the mid-summer incident at the Recreation Center, and my encounter with the black woman who feared being shot revealed, a Ferguson-type event could occur in Iowa City at almost any time. If we wanted to avoid that, and if we wanted to avoid a backlash from fearful white people, we needed to improve fundamental conditions for black residents, especially with regard to education, employment, income, health, home ownership, and wealth. I also realized that we in City government routinely told a continually unfolding story about the good steps we were taking to improve racial equity, but there was a massive gap between the stories we were telling ourselves and the stories that black Iowa Citians were telling about their experiences on the ground. How could we bridge that gap?

The School Board, Diversity, and Affordable Housing

How could we improve fundamental conditions for Iowa City's black residents? In part, the answer had to do with the intersection of housing and education. Recall that the School Board had adopted a diversity policy early in 2013. From the School Board's point of view, that policy was intended to ensure all students would receive a high-quality education. In part, this meant ensuring there was a sufficiently diverse mix of students in each public school. As discussed in the preceding chapter, the board's diversity policy raised a key question for Iowa City: what could we do to ensure that housing low-to-moderate-income households could afford was distributed fairly across the city and, ideally, across the district?

This question demanded our attention when, in mid-October 2014, the president and the administrator of the School Board sent a letter to all mayors in the district, as well as the County Board of Supervisors, which asked each municipality and the county to "codify policies regarding inclusionary zoning, re-invest in areas of our community where there is socio-economic isolation, and place restrictions on rental units and rental density" (Lynch and Murley, 2014); that is, they urged us to ensure that new developments contained a socio-economically diverse mix of residents and to avoid concentrating rental apartments for lower-income residents in any particular parts of our cities.

This was a regional issue which, ideally, required a regional solution. Consequently, the multi-jurisdictional Joint Cities group discussed the School Board's plea later in October. Designed to enable entities to share information of mutual interest, and lacking authority to compel action, the group decided to let individual entities determine their own ways of responding.[40] In a late-December memo, our city manager provided some information for us to consider when responding. He argued that, while the goal of greater socio-economic balance across the district was laudable, the zoning-related solutions the School Board proposed were decades-long processes, whereas the detrimental effects of the current imbalance among schools were immediate. He thought that requiring additional affordable housing in some of Iowa City's growth areas, such as the area near the new elementary school in our South District, might make the imbalance even worse. And he thought any effective "inclusionary zoning" effort would need strong buy-in from all local governments in the school district; having just one city adopt it would have little effect on the district's ability to achieve its diversity goals. Even so, just a few days after we received the city manager's memo, the director of the City's Neighborhood and Development Services department told us that the substantial up-zoning authorized by the RFC District FBC had created a favorable environment for requiring afford-able housing to be included in new developments. He recommended that we authorize the staff to assemble an ad hoc committee to study and develop a proposed "inclusionary housing" requirement for any future up-zonings in the district. We agreed to do so.[41]

How we should respond to the School Board request for help became a moot question after the U.S. Department of Agriculture informed the board that using Free and Reduced Lunch data as the board intended violated the department's FRL rules and might cause the district to lose millions of dol-lars in FRL subsidies. Given that news, the School Board decided to rescind its diversity policy and try instead to achieve better socio-economic balance among the schools by modifying school attendance area boundaries. If past efforts were a good guide, changing those boundaries was likely to prove very controversial.

As discussions about how to respond to the School District's plea drew to a close, council members Michelle P., Kingsley B., and I began discussing pos-sible ways of enabling the private market to increase the supply of market-rate housing lower-income households could afford. These March and April dis-cussions led us to propose a set of eight actions to the city manager and council in mid-April. The proposals included (1) reducing initial costs of development (e.g., by changing the minimum lot area and lot width requirements in RS-5 zones), (2) identifying privately owned land in Iowa City that would be suitable for redevelopment as lower-cost neighborhoods with small houses, and (3) in-structing City staff to identify which of those privately owned parcels the City could possibly purchase for redevelopment. During our work session a few days later, we asked the council to schedule a work session focusing on our recom-mendations. The director of NDS told us the City already permitted some of the actions we recommended, but "the trick is how do you make that [smaller houses on smaller lots] attractive to the private sector to take that risk to build that unit?" I replied, "we need to try to think outside the box a little bit here." The council asked the staff to prepare a memo responding to the suggestions so that we could discuss them further at a later date.

Two months later, the lead organizer of the Affordable Housing Coalition (Sally S.) supported our affordable housing initiative while expanding upon it in ways I thought were potentially quite fruitful. For example, the coali-tion strongly supported our proposal to have the City identify publicly owned land—or to purchase privately owned land—and work with both private and non-profit developers to develop affordable and market-rate housing on it. Par-cels could include medium houses on medium lots, small houses on small lots, market-rate rentals, affordable rental units (duplexes, fourplexes), and shared green space. These ideas connected nicely with what I had been learning about "missing middle" housing.[42]

During our September 2015 work session, City planner Karen H. responded to the recommendations Kingsley B., Michelle P., and I had made. She reported that, as part of an overhaul of the Zoning Code in 2005, the City had made a series of changes to create more opportunities for lower-cost housing. She told us that much progress had already been made over the past 10 years, but the staff also saw three opportunities for improvement. However, she did not address our suggestion about using City funds to buy land, issuing an RFP to potential private developers indicating how we wanted that property developed, choosing the best developer, and thereby increasing the supply of affordable units and providing a model for how things can be done. Karen H. said the staff had not addressed this possibility because it was a policy decision best left to the council. In the end, a majority of the council expressed an interest in having the staff investigate the first and second of Karen H.'s recommendations, but not the one Kingsley B., Michelle P., and I had made.

By the end of 2015, I had gained a deeper understanding of how wicked the affordable housing problem was. So long as the market economy produces vast differences among households in income and wealth, and so long as black/white racial disparities remain large, and so long as city leaders let their actions be dominated by the neoliberal idea that their cities must compete against one another to attract higher-income residents, and so long as single-family zoning (e.g., RS-5) makes it virtually impossible to insert affordable housing into existing neighborhoods, the affordable housing problem would remain insoluble. Additional steps should be taken in Iowa City, but they would inevitably be quite small in relation to the scope of the problem.

Four Years of Climate [In]action

The 2008 flood had been Iowa City's second "100-year flood" in 15 years, and we had two other severe floods in 2013 and 2014. Those floods were symptomatic of (or at least consistent with) global climate change. The City had focused considerable attention on flood recovery projects, each of which was consistent with adapting to a changing climate and mitigating against future damage. But the City had been doing very little to reduce the total amount of carbon and other greenhouse gas (GHG) emissions caused by actions taking place within Iowa City's city limits.

This did not mean that City government had literally done nothing relating to climate change. In 2007, as part of the U.S. Conference of Mayors, Iowa City's mayor had signed the Mayors' Climate Protection Agreement, signaling Iowa City's first commitment to reduce GHG emissions. A year later, Iowa City joined the Cities for Climate Protection Campaign, which committed the City to inventory emissions, adopt a reduction target, develop a plan, implement the plan, and monitor progress. In 2009, Iowa City became the first city in Iowa to complete a community-wide GHG inventory. One staff member had been up-dating that inventory annually and, beginning in the spring of 2013, preparing an annual "Sustainability Assessment" report. And more.

By themselves, these were good actions; however, the City's efforts to re-duce GHG emissions had focused exclusively on emissions generated by City government—for example, by the City's landfill, wastewater treatment plant, and City-owned buildings, which constituted less than 5 percent of the total emissions generated by all public and private activity taking place within the city. It had done nothing to reduce those emissions, and citywide emissions had actually increased slightly from 2008 through 2014.

From 2012 through 2015, I consistently argued whenever possible that we needed to do more, especially with regard to reducing emissions generated by actions taking place within Iowa City. But, whenever the council discussed this possibility, the City staff and other council members essentially said, we should not do anything unless other local government entities do so as well. From a climate change mitigation point of view, these were essentially 4 lost years.[43]

Turning toward the Just City

From my point of view, the third year of my council term had ended on a somewhat troubled note. Voters had rejected the LOST, primarily, I thought, because key people had not been adequately consulted. Moreover, I was be-ginning to sense that the RFC District FBC was likely to yield development projects significantly taller and denser than visualized in the 2013 Riverfront Crossings District Master Plan. Our responses to concerns about racial inequity had been good but nowhere near sufficient, and the three cottages situation seemed to be turning into a heated conflict. What would 2015 bring? I did not know, but I soon found out.

The period from early December 2014 through July of the following year proved decisive and, ultimately, led me to shift from participating in mana-gerial-style governance as a member of an ostensibly apolitical city council to acting in an explicitly political way. The public debate and council's actions concerning the three historic working-class cottages, the Chauncey, and public response to the events in Ferguson and elsewhere played key roles in persuading me that we needed to alter course.

By the time we were considering TIF support for the 15-story student-hous-ing project at 316 Madison Street late in February, I had shifted from thinking of myself as "a team player" to someone who was feeling like Alice in Wonder-land. This sense of being in a very confusing "Wonderland" largely stemmed from finding myself in a world consisting of a swirling array of complex City codes and policy instruments. I struggled to make sense of how the instruments were being used and gradually concluded that the FBC we had adopted for the RFC District was producing a scale and intensity of redevelopment that significantly exceeded what the RFC District Master Plan had envisioned and, I think, the people of Iowa City had expected. The complexity of these codes and instruments was also systematically undermining the ability of the public to engage knowledgeably in democratic debate about economic and land development issues. As Susan M. put it during the 2012 debate over the Chauncey, "I don't believe economic development can be done by the public-vote process."

My sense of feeling immersed in a confusing Wonderland also derived from seeing key decisions (especially with regard to the Chauncey and the three cottages) being made in staff deliberations behind the scenes and during the staff's negotiations with property owners/developers. For example, it was normal practice for the staff to work with developers to refine their proposals before formally applying for rezoning, but I saw no indication they had sought to negotiate with the owner/developer a settlement which would have resulted in preservation of the cottages. Instead, preservationists learned about the proposed development late in the process and then were lambasted for intervening "at the 11th hour." And, last, I was struck by how much attention we paid to land development versus grappling with the core causes of racial inequities.

I had been pondering these still inchoate concerns in mid-March when my wife, daughter, and I took a spring break trip to Zion National Park in southern Utah. While there, I basically decided not to seek reelection. Why continue slogging through emotionally and intellectually painful council processes when I could be immersing myself in beautiful places like Zion? However, shortly after we returned, the council majority chose not to reappoint the landscape architect (John T.) to the P&Z Commission.

When coupled with several actions the council had taken over the preceding 3 or 4 months, especially ones concerning the three cottages and rezoning the College and Gilbert Street site, this decision not to reappoint the commissioner led me to feel increasingly distrustful of the staff and at odds with the council majority.[44] It also played a major role in my decision to seek reelection in the fall of the year and to campaign around the theme of helping to build a more "Just City." I firmly decided to seek reelection and do everything I could to increase the number of allies on the council. Shortly thereafter, I wrote an op-ed for the *Press-Citizen* titled "2 Contending Visions for Iowa City's Future" (Throgmorton, 2015a).

Three days after we held a public hearing and first vote on the staff's proposal to rezone the site for the Chauncey to CB-10, I rode my bike to a popular hang-out spot for people with disabilities located near the middle of the Riverfront Crossings District. There, I formally announced to a small audience of roughly 25 people that I would be seeking reelection in the fall of the year. The timidity of 2011 was gone. "With your help," I said to them, "we can build on what's already great about Iowa City and lead it toward becoming a Just City, a place that's good on the ground for all, both now and in the future." While highlighting good things we in City government had done over the past 3.5 years, especially taking steps to improve racial equity, I claimed that, to a great extent, we Iowa Citians had also lost our way. Consequently, we now stood at a crossroads, conflicted over which direction we wanted to go in the coming years. "Two contending visions might guide the way," I said:

> One vision might be called "Boomtown." Guided by a desire to expand the economy and increase the tax base, this Boomtown vision has been invigorating parts of our city in ways that many people like. And those who benefit most directly from this vision claim that all we need to do is stay the course. If it ain't broke, they say, don't fix it. But for far too many Iowa Citians, our city is broken! For them, the Boomtown vision accommodates the interests of a few while ignoring those of the many. It's rapidly changing the city they love into a place that will soon be unrecognizable. And by dramatically discounting the risks of climate change and the long-term value of biodiversity, it's undermining our children's prospects for a healthy future. The second vision might be called the "Just City." Those who share this Just City vision believe that Iowa City should be good on the ground for all, both now and in the future, and that the long-term health of our community depends upon it.[45]

Largely as a result of what I had been observing and learning over the previous 3.5 years, I had by this time developed a preliminary set of ideas about the role local elected officials play in guiding the transformation of their cities. Wanting to share my experience with other planning scholars, I expressed these ideas in a paper I presented at the Association of European Schools of Planning's July meeting in Prague, Czech Republic (Throgmorton, 2015b). I suggested that cities "unfold," with elected officials and other human and non-human actants being part of a never-ending and very complicated process of co-crafting the direction of a city's step-by-step unfolding. Feedback at the conference helped me refine my ideas.

By mid-October, the city council election was fully underway. As an incumbent council member seeking reelection, I constructed my campaign narrative around the Just City vision I had articulated when announcing my candidacy in May.[46] In part, this Just City vision was inspired by urban scholar Susan Fainstein's (2010) *The Just City*. But mostly it was rooted in my own observations and experiences as a politically active resident of Iowa City and almost 6 years as a city councilman.[47]

At first, I just wanted to increase the relevance of this Just City vision by facilitating the election of at least one additional sympathetic council member, as had occurred in 2013. To enable this, I made a strategic decision to move out of my District C seat and instead seek election to one of the two available at-large positions. One other incumbent (Michelle P.) and two new candidates (a young realtor, Tim C., and the young lawyer, Rockne C., who had played a major role during the debates over the Chauncey and the three cottages and had been a strong social justice advocate for issues pertaining to immigrant rights and racial equity) also competed for those two positions. This move made space for John T., the retired landscape architect who had served on the P&Z Commission, to run for the seat I was vacating. He faced one opponent, a building contractor (Scott M.), who also was a new candidate. The District A seat was also in play, and I helped recruit a new candidate (Pauline T., who was a retired nurse with strong ties to local labor unions) to challenge that district's incumbent, Rick D.

Early in the campaign season, I loosely aligned myself with the retired nurse, retired landscape architect, and young lawyer. But, for the most part, each of us focused on constructing our own campaigns and emphasizing our own themes. In the last few weeks before the election, though, those three candidates and I began coordinating some of our efforts and jointly participating in campaign events. The fact that we were linking our efforts became quite visible when we and our supporters marched together during the university's homecoming parade early in October. (See Figure 3.4.) Someone labeled this loose coalition "the Core Four," and the label stuck throughout the remainder of the

FIGURE 3.4 "The Core Four" campaigning after the University of Iowa's Homecoming Parade.

Source: Photo by Barbara Eckstein, October 9, 2015.

campaign. Opponents began criticizing us for having formed a "slate," which ran counter to Iowa City's unofficial norm of candidates constructing their campaigns on an individual, nonpartisan basis.

Late in the afternoon on an unusually balmy and beautiful November 6, my wife and I walked from home to a popular local restaurant/bar (the Sanctuary) for our election night party. While walking, I sensed that we had had the wind at our back over the past several days, and so I had a good feeling about how the election would turn out. I was very confident that I would do well, and I thought that Rockne C. would be elected too. I doubted that John T. or Pauline T. would win, though I expected the first's election would be close. The Sanctuary was filled with friends and supporters. When precinct results started flowing in after around 8:30 p.m., one could feel surprise and happiness starting to build.

Holy sh_t! All four of us were elected, and two incumbents were defeated, an outcome no one expected. When the final results appeared, euphoria reigned. It was tremendously pleasing to see so much joy on friends' faces. Slightly under 7,000 people had voted. In the race for the two at-large seats, 62 percent of them voted for me, 50 percent for Rockne C., 42 percent for Tim C., and 35 percent for Michelle P. In the District A race, Pauline T. soundly defeated incumbent Rick D. by 55 to 45 percent, and John T. narrowly outpolled Scott M. by 51 to 48 percent. Observers immediately began suggesting that the winners would have a 5:2 majority on the new council.

To an extent, this victory resulted from my effort to forge a political coalition based on face-to-face relationships I had built over the past two decades. But the victory of all four candidates also reflected a confluence of at least four forces and unexpected events, including: (1) Pauline T.'s deep connections with a re-energized local labor movement; (2) the Center for Worker Justice's very successful advocacy on behalf of Hispanic and refugee communities through its Community ID and minimum wage campaigns; (3) widespread animosity toward the council's use of TIF for a few favored projects downtown; and (4) the council's temerity in responding to race-related tensions pertaining to the 2012 killing of Trayvon Martin, Michael Brown, and other young black men. Ironically, a guest opinion in the *Press-Citizen* by the outgoing mayor shortly before the election seemed to undermine his own preferences. Implicitly criticizing me for wanting "to issue public debt to fund his [my] pet causes," he wrote, "If this slate wins, the next mayor will likely be Jim Throgmorton. We will return to the anti-growth, micromanaging city hall of eras past" (Hayek, 2015).[48]

Other than preparing for the last two council meetings, I spent most of November and December thinking about the probability I would be elected mayor and considering what that would entail. I also focused a lot of my attention on enabling a good transition from the outgoing council to the incoming one. This would be challenging and involve many face-to-face conversations. In the 60 or so days after the election, I met with four present council members and all incoming ones, sometimes more than once; with the city manager and City attorney (separately) several times; and with the city clerk. I also met with two of the defeated candidates and with the directors of the major economic development organizations. Stepping beyond these predictable conversations, I also met with leaders in the black community, a Coralville council member, a local architect/developer, the owner of the *Corridor Business Journal*, a leader of senior citizens, two labor union leaders, a former council member, interviewers on KXIC Radio, and many others.

While doing all these things, I pondered what kind of mayor I wanted to be. I had not sought reelection in order to become mayor, had never been a mayor before, and had not carefully studied exemplary mayors in other cities. But I had served under three mayors in Iowa City, and I met with the outgoing mayor to seek his advice. Given all that, I had to draw upon my experience as a council member, what I had learned as a scholar of urban planning, my own values, and my emerging set of ideas about what cities are and how they change over time. The City's Charter created a "weak mayor" form of government, but I wanted to be the strongest weak mayor I could be. Moreover, as implied by the presentation I had made in Prague during the summer, I wanted to use my position as much as possible to lead Iowa City step-by-step toward becoming a more Just City.

As I thought about the kind of mayor I wanted to be, I also drew upon key things I had learned over the previous 2 years. First, council members do not simply make decisions on specific topics, with the City's planners and other professional staff assisting them as "skilled-voices-in-the-flow." Rather, they also must consider the ways in which specific topics are part of a continually evolving and interwoven array of complicated and emotionally challenging topics—that is, are part of Jane Jacobs's "problem in organized complexity."

Second, most members of the general public know very little about the flow of action pertaining to specific topics. Nor do they have the background information that City staff and council members draw upon when making decisions in that flow. Standard ways of informing the public through the news media about the complexities of this flow provide little help. Consequently, the general public remains largely in the dark until some particular issue grabs their attention. The sparse media coverage of the RFC District FBC and, therefore, the public's general lack of knowledge and comments about the FBC's origins, purposes, key features, and likely consequences exemplify the point. Consequently, when members of the general public become involved, they typically frame their advocacy either in terms of testimonial storytelling based on their own lives and those of their close relatives and friends, or else in terms of generalized opinion remotely connected to the specific decisions at hand. Examples abound, but the two that were most prominent in 2014 and 2015 involved black residents narrating personal stories about being stopped, or frisked, or worse by white police officers; and Mexican and Central American immigrants narrating their tales about employers stealing their wages or about close friends or relatives being arrested and deported by U.S. Immigration and Customs Enforcement officials. Unless council members get out of City Hall and go beyond the normal conventions, therefore, the council's decision processes can be highly exclusionary.

Third, my immersion in this flow of interconnected topics enabled me to clarify further my own values, priorities, and ideas about what needed to be done in Iowa City. Actions the council majority took from December 2014 through July 2015—especially ones concerning the three cottages and rezoning the College and Gilbert Street site—led me to conclude that the council majority was enacting the policy priorities of the local growth machine while the City staff was enacting a neoliberal, entrepreneurial form of planning that, in my judgment, seemed highly unlikely to lead Iowa City toward becoming a more equitable and sustainable place.[49] Debates over these controversial projects and actions went to the heart of two critical questions: who are we? And what kind of city do we want Iowa City to become? Awareness of how much the growth machine's answers to these questions differed from mine and allied groups' persuaded me to seek reelection and to campaign around the theme of helping to build a more Just City.

Fourth, I learned by observing Kingsley B.'s presence on the council in 2014 and 2015 how important adding just *one* new member to a seven-member body like our council can be. Suddenly, two of us were advocating for improved racial equity and for more significant action on affordable housing. Moreover, Kingsley B. often joined me on key votes pertaining to major development projects, including the one concerning a three-block stretch just east of downtown, and the rezoning of the Chauncey's site to CB-10. The lesson? Adding *at least one more* political ally to the council could produce an even greater difference.

And fifth, I began formalizing a set of ideas about how cities change and how that change could be guided. If a city is a problem in organized complexity, consisting of an interwoven array of topics and issues, then the future of the city cannot be formally planned. Rather, a city unfolds step-by-step, with each actor (elected officials, professional staff, business people, nongovernmental organizations, and others) trying to guide the unfolding in the actor's preferred way. But, acting in the context of organized complexity, each actor's steps affect other actors who respond in terms of their own interests, values, and stories. All of these actions produce effects that bleed across territorial and functional boundaries, escape the control of the initiating actors, and ultimately cause the city to unfold. In our case, two floods, a major fire at the City's landfill, at least one severe storm, police officers killing black men in Ferguson and other cities, and the state's decisions to adopt property tax reforms and not to support the Amtrak line through Iowa City also affected how Iowa City unfolded from 2012 through 2015. In brief, I concluded that Iowa City was unfolding step-by-step through a process of *co-crafting*, which included both humans and non-humans. My sense was that action in the Riverfront Crossings District in the months following the council's adoption of the RFC District Master Plan early in 2013 exemplified how co-crafting the unfolding of a city works.

As 2016 approached, several questions needed answering: If, as anticipated, the council elected me as mayor, how would I use my position to lead Iowa City toward becoming a more Just City? How would I engage with people who were part of the growth machine? What unexpected events might divert our attention and efforts? Would we succeed in leading Iowa City toward becoming a more Just City? And would my emerging theory about co-crafting the unfolding of a city prove helpful?

Notes

1 Was this a good decision? I worried that future precipitation and flood events would be more severe than they had been in the past and, therefore, would cause even more flooding than we anticipated. But we lacked valid quantitative projections of global climate change's effect on precipitation and severe weather events in the Iowa City area. In May 2014, the City was awarded a grant that enabled the City's sustainability coordinator to work with her counterparts in other Midwest cities to gather the kind of localized information we needed. I also thought Iowa City needed to join in a worldwide effort to reduce carbon emissions. Influenced by reading a pre-publication draft of Robert Beauregard's 2015 book *Planning Matter* and attending an Energy Cultures in the Age of the Anthropocene symposium at the university, I began thinking of climate change as an "actant" which was influencing the direction in which the city would be unfolding over time.

2 Public benefits identified as warranting height bonuses included: Class A office space, public art, LEED design, high-quality student housing, hotel space, workforce or affordable housing, and elder housing. TDRs were authorized for transfers of public right-of-way, for preserving historic structures, and for providing public open space.

3 A month before this meeting, the city manager informed us that he intended to merge the Department of Housing and Inspections Services and the Department of Planning and Community Development into a new NDS Department. Although I thought this devalued the importance of urban planning, I did not challenge his authority to make organizational changes. At roughly the same time, I was invited to speak at a Beyond Urban Branding forum being held by the University of Washington at Tacoma's Urban Studies Department (Throgmorton, 2014). When I reported back to the council afterwards, I noted the high-quality urban design of that university's campus, especially the adaptive reuse of historic structures in the downtown's old warehouse district, the skillful insertion of new buildings into the ensemble, and the storefront space in which the forum had been held.

4 Karen H.'s presentation can be found at: www.iowa-city.org/WebLink/DocView. aspx?id=1402880&dbid=0&repo=CityofIowaCity&cr=1

5 The FBC focused on physical design and, other than affordable housing, its implications for producing a diverse mix of residents were not at all clear. I wondered, what will happen to the small businesses currently located in the district? Would Hispanic, black, and lower-income residents live in the redesigned neighborhood? When thinking about the narrow set of actors involved in reviewing and commenting on the FBC, I was reminded of urban theorist David Harvey's (2000) comment about utopia: "Utopias of spatial form are typically meant to stabilize and control

the processes that must be mobilized to build them. In the very act of realization, therefore, the historical process takes control of the spatial form that is supposed to control it" (p. 173). To judge by the FBC, local historical processes appeared to be controlling enactment of the RFC District Master Plan.

6 The building was known as Tate Arms. Two African-Americans, Junias and Elizabeth Tate, had operated it as a rooming house, from 1939 to 1963, for African-American University of Iowa students at a time when they were denied the right to live in university dormitories.

7 The economic development director noted one important change had taken place since the RFP was issued. Reductions in state financial support for the university had led the university leadership to plan on increasing student enrollment by 4,500–5,000 students (from a base of about 31,000) within a 5-year period. At that point, the university was already building one new residence hall and it planned to build another one, but, when coupled with the demolition of an older dormitory, there would still be a demand for about 4,000 new off-campus student housing bedrooms.

8 The "gap" refers to the difference between the total cost of the project and the amount of money the developer can generate internally and through borrowing from private lenders. Without a public subsidy filling the gap, the private sector would not invest.

9 The second RFC District topic focused on whether or not to approve a proposed $2 million TIF development agreement for a multi-family housing project on the west side of the river in the southwest corner of the district.

10 The transcript for this work session can be found at: www.iowa-city.org/WebLink/DocView.aspx?dbid=0&id=1445723&page=1&cr=1

11 The transcript for this special formal meeting can be found at: www.iowa-city.org/WebLink/DocView.aspx?dbid=0&id=1446153&page=1&cr=1

12 Minutes of the commission's hearing can be found at: www.iowa-city.org/WebLink/DocView.aspx?dbid=0&id=1449415&page=1&cr=1

13 The City Attorney's memo can be found at: www.iowa-city.org/WebLink/DocView.aspx?dbid=0&id=1447613&page=1&cr=1

14 Minutes of the commission's meeting can be found at: www.iowa-city.org/WebLink/DocView.aspx?dbid=0&id=1450620&page=1&cr=1

15 At that January 20 meeting, we took two other actions concerning developments in the RFC District: we authorized the staff to enter a $16 million "lease-purchase" agreement with a private entity for a new 600-space parking facility that would be built next to MidWestOne Bank's new building. We also approved a development agreement with the same entity to construct almost 30 townhomes lining the exterior of the parking structure. This agreement included a $1 million TIF rebate for the $7 million project. I voted for it.

16 The transcript for this meeting can be found at: www.iowa-city.org/WebLink/DocView.aspx?dbid=0&id=1457069&page=1&cr=1

17 Roughly 10 months later, we conducted a public hearing and first vote on a proposal to rezone the property on which the three working-class cottages had been located. Given that decisions had already been made about removing them, I thought the proposed project would improve the site. The motion carried unanimously.

18 The transcript for this meeting can be found at: www.iowa-city.org/WebLink/DocView.aspx?dbid=0&id=1464649&page=1&cr=1

19 The cluster of four buildings appears in the bottom right of the Clinton Street Promenade view and in the left-center of the Capitol Street Student Housing view.

20 The transcript for this meeting can be found at: www.iowa-city.org/WebLink/DocView.aspx?dbid=0&id=1466614&page=1&cr=1

21 Minutes of this work session can be found at: www.iowa-city.org/WebLink/DocView.aspx?dbid=0&id=1469077&page=1&cr=1

22 Late in July, we unanimously approved the City staff's recommendation to authorize a four-story height bonus for the Hilton Garden Inn. As I said when we had considered the development agreement for the project, I thought this was a perfect location for a tall hotel. My only objection was to the TIF.

23 After negotiating with the developer, the staff recommended late in July that we unanimously approve the development agreement pertaining to the project, now known as "the Rise." According to the agreement, the developer would pay the City $5.5 million for the site; make a $1 million contribution to the City for affordable housing; and construct a $74 million, two-building, mixed-use project. Ten percent of its residential units would be dedicated to affordable housing. Moreover, no TIF subsidy would be required. Roughly 7 weeks later, we authorized a seven-story height bonus for the Rise, primarily because it included a high-quality hotel and professionally managed student housing.

24 In April, we unanimously voted to rezone roughly 4 acres in the 1200 block of Gilbert Street from CI-1 to RFC–SG (South Gilbert). This would enable construction of a five-story mixed-use structure. The project ultimately became part of a multi-structure, mixed-use development.

25 The transcript for this meeting can be found at: www.iowa-city.org/WebLink/DocView.aspx?dbid=0&id=1480326&page=1&cr=1

26 The transcript for this meeting can be found atwww.iowa-city.org/WebLink/DocView.aspx?dbid=0&id=1480717&page=1&cr=1

27 In making these points, the retired law professor was picking up on the continuing controversy over Coralville's very aggressive use of TIFs to finance developments.

28 The transcript for this meeting can be found at: www.iowa-city.org/WebLink/DocView.aspx?dbid=0&id=1414315&page=1&cr=1

29 "Hit rate" refers to instances when illegal items were found as a result of consent searches.

30 I first learned about the importance of discretionary behavior on the part of "street-level bureaucrats" from Lipsky (1980). Policy-making continues all the way down to the street level.

31 The memo and NLC report can be found at: www.iowa-city.org/WebLink/DocView.aspx?dbid=0&id=1429332&page=1&cr=1

32 Seattle's Racial Equity Toolkit delineated a process for assessing the impacts of that city's policies, initiatives, programs, and budgets on racial equity.

33 On July 17, 2014, a New York City police officer killed a 43-year-old black man named Eric Garner by placing him in a choke hold, which led to his death. "I can't breathe," Garner said, 11 times before becoming unconscious and dying. On December 3, a grand jury found "no reasonable cause" to bring charges against the officer.

34 The Center for Worker Justice (with legal assistance from faculty and students in the University of Iowa's Law School) had developed and promoted the Community Identification (ID) card program. Its primary purpose was to enable undocumented residents to obtain identity cards they could use, without threat of deportation, when interacting with local police, other local government departments, and local businesses. Other residents of Johnson County were also invited to sign up for Community ID cards as well. I did so.

35 The transcript for this meeting can be found at: www.iowa-city.org/WebLink/DocView.aspx?dbid=0&id=1457195&page=1&cr=1

36 The resolution adopting this plan can be found at: www.iowa-city.org/WebLink/DocView.aspx?dbid=0&id=1480565&page=1&cr=1

37 The transcript for this meeting can be found at: www.iowa-city.org/WebLink/
DocView.aspx?dbid=0&id=1488490&page=1&cr=1

38 In terms of basic demographics, it showed that, according to the 2009–2013 5-year
American Community Survey, roughly 18 percent of the city's population was
non-white: 7 percent were Asian, 5.5 percent African-American/black, slightly
over 5 percent Hispanic/Latino, and less than 1 percent were either Native American or Native Hawaiian and Pacific Islander. Of all students attending ICCSD
schools located within Iowa City in October 2014, slightly over 35 percent were
non-white: just under 20 percent were black, 8.5 percent were Hispanic, and 7
percent were Asian or Pacific Islander.

39 The two emails can be found at: www.iowa-city.org/WebLink/DocView.
aspx?dbid=0&id=1497484&page=1&cr=1

40 The Joint Cities' inability to act effectively on this regional issue exemplified a
key fact: there was a structural void with regard to acting collaboratively on regional issues (especially land development, transportation, affordable housing, and
climate change) at the regional scale. As a planner, what I saw was implicit reliance
upon *one* projection of future development patterns and trends within the region,
which simply extrapolated past trends into the future as if the trends were natural
and inevitable. My sense was that the School District and the MPOJC's Urbanized
Area Policy Board needed to be assessing the merits of alternative scenarios—e.g.,
a baseline trend analysis, a "grow the same" scenario with more jobs and people,
and a "do things differently" scenario with new land development policies. One
example of assessing alternative scenarios at the regional scale caught my eye at the
time: Northeast Ohio Sustainable Communities Forum (2014).

41 In September, the committee recommended adoption of an inclusionary housing
ordinance. The provision of inclusionary housing would be required: (1) whenever
a project containing residential units received financial support from the City and
(2) whenever a property was being rezoned to a RFC District zone. We directed the
staff to draft an ordinance for the council's consideration early in 2016.

42 "Missing middle" housing types provide diverse housing options, such as duplexes,
fourplexes, and bungalow courts, that fit seamlessly into low-rise walkable neighborhoods and support walkability, locally serving retail, and public transportation
options. See: https://missingmiddlehousing.com/

43 My concerns were heightened after reading Elizabeth Kolbert's (2014) excellent but
unnerving new book about mass extinctions.

44 There was considerable turmoil within our planning staff in 2014 and 2015. To
a significant degree, this turmoil mirrored political conflicts within the city as a
whole. This can be related to ongoing scholarly discussions about the ethical dilemmas that practitioners face with regard to conflicts between the planners' expertise
and democratic legitimacy of political decision-makers. See Campbell (2006) and
Lauria and Long (2019).

45 Had I been writing this speech for a scholarly audience, I would have referred to
the advocates of the "Boomtown" vision as the "growth machine." The full text
of my speech can be found at: https://persuasivestorytelling.wordpress.com/?s=C-
ity+Council+Candidate+Jim+Throgmorton+Wants+Iowa+City+to+be+a+-
Just+City

46 In terms of planning theory, I understood my campaign narrative to be an effort to
shape attention through persuasive storytelling.

47 In plain language grounded in the context of my city at this point in time, I thought
a "just city" would be one in which at least the following four conditions would
exist: (1) every resident would live in good-quality housing they could afford; (2)
there would no major disparities in income, wealth, education, health, and impris-
onment based on race, ethnicity, or sex/gender; (3) the city would be accessible to

all; and (4) the city and the natural ecosystems upon which it depends would be sustainable long into the future.

48 To use urban scholar Andre Sorensen's (2015) term, the 2016 election might have marked a "critical juncture" in Iowa City's unfolding.

49 By this time, I had concluded that Iowa City's version of the growth machine included land development firms, the Iowa City Area Chamber of Commerce, the Iowa City Area Development Group, the Greater Iowa City Area Home Builders Association, the *Corridor Business Journal*, the Iowa City Area Association of Realtors, the Iowa City/Coralville Area Convention and Business Bureau, plus allied banks, building trade unions, and the University of Iowa.

References

Barnum, C. et al. (2014), ICPD Traffic Stop Study; available at: www.iowa-city.org/WebLink/0/doc/1412610/Page1.aspx (last accessed February 4, 2021).

Beauregard, R. A. (2015), *Planning Matter: Acting with Things*, University of Chicago Press, Chicago (IL).

Campbell, H. (2006), "Just planning: The art of situated ethical judgment", *Journal of Planning Education and Research*, v. 26, n. 1, pp. 92–106.

City of Iowa City (2013), IC2030 Comprehensive Plan Update, Iowa City (IA); available at: www8.iowa-city.org/weblink/0/edoc/1965450/Comprehensive%20Plan%20Updated%2010.2020.pdf (last accessed January 3, 2021).

City of Iowa City (2018), Power Point presentation by City planning staff during a council work session on November 6; available at: www.iowa-city.org/WebLink/0/doc/1827755/Page1.aspx (last accessed May 5, 2021).

Fainstein, S. (2010), *The Just City*, Cornell University Press, Ithaca (NY).

Gutsche, R. E. Jr. (2014), *A Transplanted Chicago: Race, Place, and the Press in Iowa City*, McFarland, Jefferson (NC).

Harvey, D. (2000), *Spaces of Hope*. University of California Press, Berkeley (CA).

Hayek, M. (2015), "Iowa city council votes will matter." *Iowa City Press-Citizen* (October 14); available at: www.press-citizen.com/story/opinion/contributors/guest-editorials/2015/10/14/iowa-city-council-votes-matter/73910452/ (last accessed on December 21, 2020).

Hennigan, G. (2014), "Iowa City council opts for smaller 'Gateway' project", *The Gazette* (January 21); available at: www.thegazette.com/2014/01/21/iowa-city-council-opts-for-smaller-gateway-project (last accessed on December 18, 2020).

Jordan, E. (2014), "Protesters unite in Iowa City in support of Ferguson", *The Gazette* (November 25); available at: www.thegazette.com/subject/news/public-safety/protesters-unite-in-iowa-city-in-support-of-ferguson-20141125 (last accessed on December 29, 2020).

Kolbert, E. (2014), *The Sixth Extinction: An Unnatural History*, Henry Holt and Co., New York (NY).

Lauria, M., and Long, M. F. (2019), "Ethical dilemmas in professional planning practice in the United States", *Journal of the American Planning Association*, v. 85, n. 4, pp. 393–404.

Lynch, C. and Murley, S. (2014), October 13 letter to elected officials, Iowa City Community School District, Iowa City (IA).

Lipsky, M. (1980), *Street Level Bureaucracy: Dilemmas of the Individual in Social Services*, Russell Sage Foundation, New York (NY).

Northeast Ohio Sustainable Communities Forum (2014), "Vibrant NEO 2040 Vision Plan and Framework"; available at: http://vibrantneo.org/vibrantneo-2040/vneo-2040-full-report (last accessed on January 5, 2021).

Schmidt, M. (2014), "Voters could vote on local-option sales tax again soon", *The Gazette* (November 5); available at: www.thegazette.com/subject/news/voters-could-vote-on-local-option-sales-tax-again-soon-20141105?template=amphtml (last accessed on December 21, 2020).

Schmidt, M. (2015), "Dozens rally in Iowa City in support of better treatment for black youth." *The Gazette* (July 27); available at: www.thegazette.com/subject/news/government/dozens-rally-in-iowa-city-in-support-of-better-treatment-for-black-youth-20150727 (last accessed on December 21, 2020).

Sorensen, A. (2015), "Taking path dependence seriously: An historical institutionalist research agenda in planning history", *Planning Perspectives*, v. 30, n. 1, pp. 17–38.

Throgmorton, J.A. (2010), "Why storytelling matters: Three stories from the heart of America", Invited presentation at the Department of Urban Studies and Planning, The Massachusetts Institute of Technology, Cambridge (MA) (December 1).

Throgmorton, J.A. (2014), "Branding, storytelling, and urban identity", Invited presentation at the University of Washington at Tacoma's "Beyond Urban Branding: The Promise, The Problem, The Potential." Urban Studies Forum; available at: https://persuasivestorytelling.wordpress.com/2014/02/24/branding-storytelling-and-urban-identity/ (last accessed on December 21, 2020).

Throgmorton, J.A. (2015a), "2 contending visions for Iowa City's future", *Iowa City Press-Citizen*, (April 8), 11A.

Throgmorton, J. A. (2015b), "City crafting in a contested world", presented at the annual conference of the Association of European Schools of Planning, Prague, Czech Republic (July 13–16).

4

CITY CRAFTING AS MAYOR, 2016–2019

The fourth year of my first full term as a council member had ended with a presumption that the council would elect me as mayor coupled with uncertainty about what direction the new council majority and I would lead the city. Most observers expected that the loose coalition called the "Core Four" would try to change several, perhaps many, key City policies and practices. Some residents eagerly looked forward to those changes; others feared them. What those changes would be and how they would affect life in Iowa City would emerge over the next 4 years. If the council elected me mayor, I would have to perform all the duties of a council member while also taking on the additional mayoral duties. In other words, not only would I have to respond to the complexities of each individual topic that came before us, and to the complex interconnections among them, but I would also have to be thinking in terms of the city as a whole and about how, on behalf of City government, I should relate to other mayors, to the state, and to the federal government.

Becoming a Mayor Wanting to Produce a More Just City

One cannot govern without first being elected, and, to be elected, one has to articulate campaign themes that are likely to resonate positively with a majority of voters. I had seen this as a matter of shaping attention through persuasive storytelling. As an incumbent city council member seeking reelection in 2015, I had constructed my campaign around a "Just City" vision: we should build on what is already great about Iowa City and help lead it toward becoming a Just City—that is, a city that is good on the ground for all its residents, both now and in the future (Throgmorton, 2015). But, as I pondered how to enact

DOI: 10.4324/9781003160991-4

the role of mayor, I knew that we four victors faced an exciting opportunity, but also a daunting challenge: we had to shift from campaigning to governing.

The First Steps in Governing

Three difficult challenges confronted the newly elected council members during the first few transitional months. We had to elect a mayor and a mayor pro tem. We had to develop a new strategic plan and modify the preliminary budget to be more consistent with that plan. And we had to respond to the possible departure of the city manager.

According to Iowa City's Charter, the seven council members elect the mayor. Usually one or two interested incumbents gauge their support among other council members, and one emerges as having the strongest backing. That person is elected during the new council's organizational meeting early in January. Susan M., the council member with strong ties to the local development community, had been expecting to be the next mayor, but she had actively opposed the three newly elected members. Consequently, the council elected me mayor early in January 2016 by a 6:1 vote (Susan M. against) after a substantial number of private two-or-three-person conversations.

Election of the mayor pro tem proved more difficult than I had anticipated. Two candidates had emerged: Susan M. and Kingsley B., the young African-American lawyer who had joined the council in 2014. Key leaders in the black community advised me not to choose Kingsley B., but a majority of the council would not vote for Susan M. In order to work our way through the difficulty, I had to orchestrate a considerable number of face-to-face conversations involving the two possible candidates, other council members, and key leaders in the community. With those discussions in mind, I decided to support Kingsley B., and the council subsequently elected him by a 5:2 vote (Susan M. and Terry D. against).

Immediately following that vote, I made a short speech outlining how I expected to perform the role of mayor. This speech emphasized five key points. First, trained as an urban planner, I saw myself as a *pragmatic visionary*. Second, given Iowa City's council-manager form of government, the Strategic Plan was the best way to express our collective vision and short-term priorities. Third, I expected the Strategic Plan would lead Iowa City toward becoming a more "inclusive, just, and sustainable" city.[1] The speech also indicated I thought of myself as a *principled negotiator*, and to negotiate our differences well we would need to listen carefully to one another, focus on the substantive issues at hand, and avoid letting our disagreements become personal. "Last," I said, "we are not completely the masters of our own fate. We will encounter unexpected events. ... When such events occur, I am confident we will work together as a team, doing what our city requires" (Throgmorton, 2016a).

By framing my role this way, I was making a political bet: I thought it would be better to take the time required to make deep changes in some key City policies and codes rather than to make large, immediate breaks with the past. I also decided upon this course because I knew we would have at least a four-person council majority for the next 4 years, unless someone died or quit, and because I knew we faced a fourth daunting challenge: many key members of the growth machine—that is, people who had opposed us in the November election— were definitely not in our corner, at least with regard to economic development priorities.[2] Although our differences were not trivial, I needed to assure them that they were not our enemies. We needed them, and they needed us.

Embedded in my political bet was awareness that existing codes cannot be changed quickly or easily. The new council would have to honor development agreements previously approved by the outgoing council, and we would have to follow existing codes and policies pertaining to land development and the use of TIF until such time as we changed them. The risk was clear: "path dependency" would keep the city on the path of the past while our new council was changing policies and codes incrementally.[3]

At the end of the meeting, we also assigned council members to various committees. As mayor, I automatically became an *ex officio* member of the Iowa City Convention and Visitors Bureau's Board of Directors and co-chair of the City–University Partnership for Alcohol Safety. I recommended, and the council agreed, to appoint Rockne C., Susan M., and me to the council's Economic Development Committee, which was the council's only substantive standing committee. I also understood that part of my job would involve meeting regularly with the president and vice-president of the School Board, with the mayors of Coralville and North Liberty, with the Metro Coalition (mayors of the ten largest cities in Iowa), and, as time passed, with heads of the Iowa City Chamber of Commerce and the Downtown District. No doubt I would also meet periodically with the newly appointed president of the University of Iowa. In an effort to alleviate tensions within the council, I recommended that we appoint Susan M. as chair of the council's Economic Development Committee and, along with me, as liaison to the School Board's leadership.

To identify the council's short-term priorities, we had to develop a new strategic plan. Aided by a facilitator, we held a long work session with key staff and with departing and incoming council members a month before we took office. Prior to taking office, however, the three incoming council members and I had concluded that more than one work session would be required to produce a plan we could call our own. (Although the four winners in the November election had coalesced into a loose coalition, we did not have a unified policy agenda, and I knew that Kingsley B.'s ideas about land development differed in important ways from those of the three incoming members.) This led to a sequence of three very difficult council work sessions after we took office. I tried very hard during these meetings to ensure that every participant, not just those in the majority, had a hand in shaping the final structure, content, and language of the plan.

We had received the City staff's proposed budget and CIP in mid-December. Led by the City manager, Tom M., the staff had proposed a budget that would be slightly more in line with the direction they thought the newly elected council wanted to go. We wanted to put our stamp on the budget, however, so we held a couple of difficult meetings in which the council amended the pre-liminary budget and CIP in light of the Strategic Plan we had developed. This too required extensive discussion and negotiations.

We adopted the new plan, budget, and CIP at our formal meeting in early March on 5:2 votes. Key details of the Strategic Plan and the budget and CIP amendments had appeared in a "State of the City" speech I made in mid-Feb-ruary (Throgmorton, 2016b). When crafting and delivering this speech, I was very conscious of speaking on behalf of City government and the entire council rather than just the winners in November or myself alone. At the heart of the speech was the claim that

> Iowa City is a great place to live but not such a good place for all its res-idents. And because our city is so strong and healthy, we have an oppor-tunity to extend this prosperity to all Iowa Citians and to ensure it lasts well into the future.

With that in mind, our Strategic Plan identified seven priorities for the next 2 years, five of which were modified versions of what had appeared in the previ-ous council's plan. One of the modified priorities called for us to build a vibrant and walkable urban core, whereas the two new priorities were to promote environmental sustainability and to advance social justice and racial equity. I concluded the State of the City speech by saying,

> Though challenging, this is also good work. And we Iowa Citians are up to doing it well. Our city is full of creative and energetic people … who are eager to engage in the great work of incrementally transforming the city we and they love into a place that residents will cherish for genera-tions to come. … And by leading the way for Iowa City, we can lead the way for the region and the state.

I felt very good about how I had facilitated the council's deliberations and led it toward crafting a good strategic plan.

Shortly before the November 2015 election, City manager Tom M. had informed me he was being recruited by other cities. He had, for personal rea-sons, applied to one of those cities a couple of months before the election. Although a couple of the incoming council members were skeptical about re-taining him, I thought he could help us make the transition we were initiating.

I also wanted to avoid having to spend the first 6 months of our term with an acting city manager while we searched for a permanent replacement. And I wanted to avoid the impression that the new council was forcing him out. Later in mid-January, the manager told me he had accepted the new position. From that point on, we had to decide who should fill the position on an interim basis and whether or not to conduct a national search for a permanent replacement. After extensive discussion, we appointed the assistant city manager (Geoff F.) as interim manager and, 3 months later, we unanimously appointed him to the permanent position. Getting to unanimity had required a considerable number of one-on-one conversations.

Putting Our Priorities into Action

The first few months of our term proved rather rocky. Not having conducted council meetings before, I had difficulty managing our first couple of formal meeting agendas. (Does a resolution require a roll call or just a voice vote?) With help from the city clerk, that difficulty soon passed. More painfully, in January, Pauline T. and John T. fell on the ice; she broke her hip, and he broke his glasses. I too stumbled, but on ice of my own making. In early February, we considered a proposal to commit the City to an expensive iconic art project on the Pedestrian Mall. Council member Terry D. was absent that night. After discussion, three council members voted against the proposal while two voted in favor of it. When I realized that, as the last of six people to vote, the motion would be defeated whether I voted for it or not, I decided to vote "yes" as a mark of respect for the members of the Artist Selection Committee and others who had been involved in the process. The resulting tie vote defeated the motion. A week or so later, however, I learned that Terry D. wanted the council to reconsider its decision, and that we would have to do so if a total of three council members agreed. Susan M., Terry D., and Kingsley B. voted to reconsider. When we revisited the topic 2 weeks later, I changed my vote to "no" and explained my mistake. It was an embarrassing error I would not make again.

As much as these occurrences mattered in the moment, they did not hinder our ability to act on the seven priorities laid out in our Strategic Plan. As expected, however, the city manager's departure did. Until we decided whether or not to search for a new city manager, the acting city manager found himself in a caretaker role and felt that he lacked the authority to initiate any major actions on matters directly under his control. Once we appointed him, however, he acted with considerable energy and enthusiasm.

Advancing Social Justice and Racial Equity

To promote social justice and respond to the difficulty residents had in finding housing they could afford, in September we approved a comprehensive

Affordable Housing Action Plan containing 15 specific actions (Davis, 2016). This action plan sought to increase the supply of housing that low-to-moderate-income households can afford, to improve the overall affordability of housing in the city, and to help the School District achieve better socio-economic balance among its schools. Adopting this action plan felt very good, and it signaled to me that our new city manager could get things done.

We adopted the new Inclusionary Housing ordinance for the Riverfront Crossings District, as well as an ordinance which would facilitate establishment of a new "Housing First" facility for chronically homeless individuals. We allocated $500,000 to the Housing Trust Fund of Johnson County for affordable housing projects. As discussed below, we also authorized transition payments to tenants who had been compelled to move out of an apartment complex. In November, following an invitation from the County Board of Supervisors, I travelled with many other local officials to San Antonio, Texas, to learn about their crisis intervention training (CIT) and related programs. One of the speakers told us, "This [CIT] is not 'Hug a Thug'": it seeks to keep mentally troubled people out of jail while diverting them to services that can help improve community relations while ensuring officer safety and saving public money. I was very impressed.

The controversy over the displacement of tenants was difficult but enlightening. In February, the new owner of a housing complex (Dolphin Point) in the southeastern part of Iowa City had informed its tenants that the owners would be renovating the complex substantially and renaming it Rose Oaks. The tenants, most of whom were lower-income, would have to vacate their apartments not later than the expiration dates on their leases. The announcement caught residents by surprise. In some cases, they would have to move within a few days; most had considerably more time. But they all had to move. And few knew where they would go when the citywide vacancy rate for rental units was less than 2 percent. The situation quickly blossomed into a contentious political issue. Friends affiliated with the CWJ immediately intervened on behalf of the tenants and demanded that we stop the evictions.[4] In early August, we decided 5:2 (Susan M. and Terry D. against) to provide all 200 or so households with an opportunity to receive $250 in relocation assistance from the City. I felt very good about facilitating the resolution to this complicated and emotionally stressful topic. The council formally approved the action 2 weeks later, with Susan M. objecting to the process. The experience reminded me why I had sought reelection in the first place.

One unique part of the Rose Oaks controversy especially drew my attention. During our June 5 council meeting, a Congolese man whose family lived at Rose Oaks described their situation. He could not speak English, so we had to find someone who could translate his French into English. A friend of mine in the audience volunteered. The Congolese man told us that he and his family were refugees, and that he walked to work at one of the industrial facilities across U.S. Highway 6. Although he was employed, his family's income was quite low. Their children attended a nearby elementary school. But the owners of Rose Oaks had told him they must move. He had no idea where they would live, whether they would be able to afford the rent, how he would get to his job, and where his children would go to school.[5] His family needed public housing, he said. I knew that the City owned only about 80 public housing units in the entire city and immediately thought, we cannot do what he was asking.[6] Witnessing him speak reminded me why many standard City practices needed to change: many of those long-standing policies and procedures were not designed to facilitate the involvement of lower-income people, people with disabilities, or residents who spoke a language other than English or came from another culture.

To achieve greater racial equity, we initiated use of a Racial and Socioeconomic Equity Toolkit within five City departments on a 1-year trial basis, and we empowered our Human Rights Commission to recommend how to allocate funds contained in the Social Justice and Racial Equity grant program we had created. The Iowa City Police Department hired three black uniformed officers and hired Henri H. (the well-known advocate for black youth) to fill a new community outreach officer position. These actions were designed to increase the department's ability to serve and protect the city's diverse neighborhoods and ensure that our city remained a safe and welcoming place for all its residents. Late in the year, the city manager initiated a search for a new chief of police to replace the chief who soon would be retiring. We also received an updated St. Ambrose study of traffic stops and arrests. It showed improvements over the 2014 study.

Promoting a Strong and Resilient Economy

The city experienced a tremendous amount of new construction. In 2016, almost 800 building permits were issued at a total value of almost $390 million. This reflected a very big jump over 2015, when 645 permits valued at roughly $140 million had been issued. The university opened its new Hancher Auditorium, Voxman Music Building, and Art Building. Construction of the Rise at Linn and Court, the Hilton Garden Inn, several projects in the Riverfront Crossings District, the university's Stead Family Children's Hospital, and many smaller projects was well underway. With Rockne C. and me recusing ourselves, the council approved the City's part of a negotiated settlement of the ongoing court case involving Trinity and the Chauncey, and the council authorized issuance of a $13 million tax increment revenue bond for that project. In a successful effort to preserve a historic church building on the eastern edge of downtown, we rezoned the building's site and adjacent City Hall parking lot, and subsequently resold the lot for new mixed-use development. The School District's new Alexander Elementary School on the far southern edge of the city completed its first full year, and the new Hoover Elementary on the far eastern side was under construction. Detailed engineering design for construction of the Gateway Project was well underway. And we modified the City's economic development policy to require that 15 percent of residential units must be affordable in any new residential or mixed-use project that requested TIF support.

Building a Vibrant and Walkable Urban Core and Fostering Healthy Neighborhoods throughout the City

We hosted nationally recognized experts Jeff Speck and Jay Walljasper to enlighten us about best practices for community design and walkable cities, as well as noted urban scholar Robin Hambleton (2014) to present his ideas about governing the inclusive city. And we hired a nationally respected urban design firm (Opticos Inc.) to help us prepare new "missing middle" development standards for the historic Northside neighborhood near downtown and for the South District around the new Alexander Elementary School.[7] We set a goal of raising our League of American Bicyclists' bike-friendly status from silver to gold by the end of the year with an ultimate ambition of achieving platinum status. To help us achieve those goals, a consultant began updating the City's Bicycle Master Plan. To foster healthy neighborhoods throughout the city, we also made major investments in our neighborhood and community parks.

Enhancing Community Engagement and Intergovernmental Relations

We tried very hard to improve relationships with other local governments and to improve or strengthen the City government's connections with diverse parts of the Iowa City community. As part of this effort, council members conducted five listening posts in diverse parts of the city, and I initiated a new Mayor's Walks program and conducted five such walks through our city's neighborhoods. City staff improved the City's public outreach efforts through Cable Channel 4 and other media, including televising council work sessions and Economic Development Committee meetings. Needless to say, I frequently was interviewed by reporters affiliated with local newspapers and television stations, and, once every 7 weeks or so, individual council members (myself included) were interviewed on KXIC Radio. I made invited speeches to the Rotary Club, the United Nations Association, the Chamber of Commerce's Local Government Affairs Committee, students at Kirkwood Community College, and many other venues.

On my first Mayor's Walk in late April, a TV reporter accompanied me as I climbed aboard a City bus to talk with lower-income riders while travelling to one of our eastside neighborhoods. I introduced myself to the driver and gained his permission to speak to riders. Standing at the front of the bus, I said, "Hi.

I'm Jim Throgmorton, the mayor of Iowa City. If there is anything you would like to talk about pertaining to the city, please let me know." A passenger sitting in a seat immediately to my right said (with evident surprise), "What? You're the mayor?" I then proceeded to talk with him and a few other passengers. Once off the bus, the reporter and I moved from door to door. When residents were home and willing to speak to an unexpected visitor, I would introduce myself and tell them I was there to learn how things were going in the neighborhood and the city as a whole. Many months later, when speaking with visitors from Ukraine and other countries, I told them that story. They responded with amazement. Their elected officials would never do such a thing!

Promoting Environmental Sustainability

We initiated an ambitious climate action planning effort. When first conceiving of this effort, I thought that we had to proceed step-by-step toward building a solid, locally grounded knowledge base while also expanding the local political constituency for climate action. Building that constituency included fostering solid support within the council. Our initial efforts involved three steps: first, we adopted the challenging Paris Accord goals of reducing carbon emissions 26 percent by 2026 and 80 percent by 2050; second, we created a Climate Action Plan Steering Committee, which would play a major role in expanding community support for key climate-related actions; and third, City staff prepared a request for proposals (RFP) for a consultant to provide technical advice about how to achieve those goals. To my disappointment, however, the turnover in city managers significantly delayed issuance of the RFP. In early October, we adopted a long-desired waste reduction and recycling ordinance requiring recycling facilities in multi-family structures.

Managing the Conflict between "Boomtown" and "Just City" Advocates

For the first 6–9 months of our term, leaders of the local growth machine consistently opposed many of the new council's actions and expressed fears about the council being "anti-growth." As mayor, I consistently tried to find ways to defuse their fears and take their interests into account while promoting changes in City codes that would bend the city toward justice and sustainability. Not surprisingly, much of this anti-growth talk was driven by disagreement between property owners, businesses, and developers who wanted to densify the downtown and residents who wanted to preserve the downtown's historic character and identity. In early June, we rejected a developer's proposal to build a 14-story building downtown. This eventually resulted in a more contextually sensitive seven-story structure. But, in the short run, our rejection of the taller structure caused many developers and their allies to roundly condemn us. This led me to distribute in mid-August a proposed strategy for preserving, renovating, and developing downtown (Throgmorton, 2016c). I was trying to create conditions which would lead developers to recognize the value of (1) preserving historic buildings and streetscapes and (2) designing new buildings that would sustain the historic character of the entire downtown. This proposed strategy became a topic of public conversation for several months, especially among downtown property and business owners (Iowa City Downtown District Board, 2016). During a work session early in August, Susan M. condemned me for trying to impose my will on the council by circulating the proposed strategy, which I found absurd as everything in the proposal was simply that, a proposal. But what surprised me is that Mayor Pro Tem Kingsley B. supported her. This caught me off guard, and so I had to talk with him about it later. As time went by, this conflict reoriented around the council's efforts to amend the City's policy regarding the use of TIF. I was determined to ensure that our TIF policy would require any TIF-supported projects downtown to help us achieve what our Comprehensive Plan called for, namely: "to preserve and enhance the historic buildings and character of Downtown, while encouraging appropriate infill redevelopment with a mix of building uses" (City of Iowa City, 2013, p. 18).

Encountering Unexpected Events

While we were making progress on converting our Strategic Plan priorities into new policies, plans, codes, and practices, we also had to deal with several unexpected conflicts. In addition to the very heated conflict over the Rose Oaks apartment complex, three other unanticipated clashes involved, first, a possible development (Forest View) that might result in the eviction of roughly 140 mostly Hispanic, lower-income households from a trailer court; second, a surprise announcement that a large and controversial building (the Kinnick House), designed to look like the University of Iowa's football stadium, would be constructed in one of the city's older and wealthier residential neighborhoods; and, third, brief anxiety over an alleged hate crime against an African-American student. Moreover, our long-time city clerk announced she would be retiring near the end of the year.

Making Good Progress in 2017, but …

All in all, I was satisfied with what we had accomplished in 2016 and, until early November, was eagerly looking forward to the next year. But the November elections of Donald Trump as president and Republican Party majorities in the U.S. Congress and Iowa legislature felt like a crushing blow which placed many our initiatives at risk. Most of the people I knew were shocked and grief-stricken. On November 11, more than 200 City High students marched downtown and back to protest what the new president stood for; another 100 or so young people marched north from downtown, along Dubuque Street, and onto Interstate-80, where they blocked traffic for half an hour as a way of protesting (Davis and Hines, 2016). And, near the end of December, we started receiving a flurry of hostile and angry emails and phone calls from people who were upset that we had discussed (in our last work session of the year) the possibility that we might declare Iowa City a "sanctuary city."

These events were on my mind as I made another State of the City speech (Throgmorton, 2017a) in February 2017. The speech juxtaposed our achievements with the statements, actions, and policies of the new state and federal regimes. Let me just give a hint about the rhetorical tone of that speech:

> "It was the best of times, it was the worst of times, it was the age of wisdom, it was the age of foolishness, it was the epoch of belief, it was the epoch of incredulity, it was the season of Light, it was the season of Darkness, it was the spring of hope, it was the winter of despair, we had everything before us, we had nothing before us, we were all going direct to heaven, we were all going direct the other way."

> Although Charles Dickens wrote those words for a different place and time, they resonate with our experience in 2016. We had a year filled with good news and great progress, but also a year that ended with an array of traumatic challenges.

As these words suggest, it felt as though we were acting in two parallel worlds throughout 2017. One was the world in which we monitored City staff's efforts to carry out our new policies. The other was the alternative world being created by the new regimes in Washington and Iowa's capitol, Des Moines.

Converting Policies into Actions

With regard to the first world, my task was twofold. One might think of it as an "inside/outside" game. Inside City government, I had to work closely with the new city manager to ensure that City staff was acting on our priorities, while also responding to issues and possible actions that he brought to my attention. I also had to improve relations and negotiate political differences with council members, both during and outside our council meetings. And I wanted to improve connections with City employees and learn more about what they did day in and day out. Outside City government, I had to coordinate with leaders of the major governmental entities and nongovernmental organizations, and to meet with the diverse groups of residents in a wide variety of circumstances.

I felt like I was learning something new every step of the way.

Much as I loved what I was learning, I also found the routine mayoral work to be daunting. In the last half of February, for example, I met with the director the local Chamber of Commerce, met with public sector union members before they travelled to the state capitol to oppose a bill concerning collective bargaining, and attended neighborhood workshops concerning possible form-based codes for the Northside neighborhood and the South District. I also participated in a Convention and Visitors Bureau Board meeting, was interviewed on KXIC Radio, and went to the Chamber of Commerce's annual banquet but caused a minor stir by departing early in order to attend the City Federation of Labor's annual chili supper. In addition, I met with officials at the Veterans Administration Hospital to discuss the proposed Behavioral Health Access Center, attended a Fire Department promotion ceremony, and spoke in a couple of Kirkwood Community College classes about the immigrant/refugee situation. I met with Susan M. and City staff to discuss possible renovations at an older elementary school in the Northside neighborhood, met with Hispanic mothers who feared the new president's aggressive policy toward undocumented residents, and did a ride-along through the landfill with City staff. In the midst of all these meetings (and more), the city manager and I conducted our regular weekly meeting, I prepared for and chaired a council work session and formal meeting, and I chaired a meeting of the City Conference Board. During the council meeting, I recommended that we initiate two climate actions, both of which were designed to inspire and motivate people and would be announced on Earth Day.

I thought we were making good progress in 2017, but definitely not so much as I had hoped. In some cases, I sensed there was a disconnect between specific components of our Strategic Plan and what the staff did in response to them. For example, the public works staff was committed to completing projects that had been approved previously (such as the Washington Street renovation part of the Downtown Streetscape Plan), and they got a slow start on other projects we had prioritized (such as a four-to-three-lane conversion on a major street downtown). Consequently, a few projects were delayed owing to the lack of contractor availability or a desire to have more favorable weather conditions. More important, much of my time and energy became focused on responding to unexpected events at the national and state level. Largely as a result of the state's actions (see below), our planning staff became overloaded with unanticipated work during the second half of the year. Even so, we took some important steps on our priorities.

Advancing Social Justice and Racial Equity

With regard to the Affordable Housing Action Plan we had adopted in 2016, the most important step was to allocate $650,000 of the FY 2017–2018 budget to the City's affordable housing fund. The Johnson County Housing Trust Fund would use much of the allocation to leverage additional public and private dollars for building new affordable units in Iowa City. In response to the Rose

Oaks controversy, we amended the Comprehensive Plan and the zoning code to mitigate the impact of redevelopment on occupants of proposed projects involving the remodeling or reconstruction of existing multi-family residential dwellings. And we amended the Affordable Housing Location Model to increase the number of sites eligible for City financial assistance. But we also started feeling pressure from University of Iowa students and other residents about the high cost of off-campus student housing.

To improve racial equity and social justice, we collaborated with the county, the university, and other governmental entities to provide our public safety officers with crisis intervention training and to move the proposed Behavioral Health Access Center closer to construction. (Action on the center moved quite slowly owing to the significant amount of intergovernmental coordination involved.) We funded five organizations through our new Social Justice and Racial Equity grant program. We significantly improved relationships between City government and leaders of Iowa City's minority communities, partly because our new city manager hired an outstanding new chief of police (Jodi M.). Guided by the new chief, the Police Department developed a strategic plan to effectively address disproportionate minority contact issues. City staff successfully completed the pilot program for using the Racial and Socioeconomic Equity Toolkit and planned on extending it to other departments. I did more Mayor's Walks but, alas, had to stop doing them after mid-summer owing to declining health and competing demands on my time. But I did begin meeting periodically with leaders of the Congolese and Sudanese communities.

Building a Vibrant and Walkable Urban Core and Fostering Healthy Neighborhoods throughout the City

Opticos completed its preliminary assessment of possible form-based codes and the use of missing middle housing for the Northside and Alexander Elementary neighborhoods. In the middle of the year, we rejected (rightly, I thought) a developer's request to rezone about 38 acres to make way for 600–1,000 multi-family apartment units on the far southern edge of the city and beyond the reach of public transit. Conversely, we rezoned a site immediately north of downtown from CB-2 to CB-5. (This greatly disappointed councilman John T. In his view, the resulting building would be out of scale with nearby two- and three-story buildings.) And we amended the Comprehensive Plan to enable subsequent rezoning for the proposed Forest View development near the intersection of I-80 and Dubuque Street. This would be a very large project, but we made it very clear from the outset that the project would not be approved unless it included high-quality affordable housing for the lower-income, mostly Hispanic residents of the existing trailer court on the site.

Enhancing Community Engagement and Intergovernmental Relations

We collaborated with the School Board to enable passage of the bond referendum funding the remaining portions of the district's facilities master plan at a total cost not to exceed roughly $192 million. I was especially pleased that this would fund major improvements in all but one of our older schools. The vote was decisive, but, to my surprise, the debate leading up to it proved to be more complicated politically than I had anticipated; some of our political allies criticized me and other council members for supporting it.

Promoting a Strong and Resilient Economy

The city continued to experience very strong growth in construction. We approved development agreements for two major projects in the downtown area. One of them (Augusta Place) included a TIF for construction of townhouses and apartments in return for preservation of the historic church near City Hall, along with construction of a new parking facility for City vehicles. The other (Hieronymus Square) included a TIF which enabled construction of a pair of seven-story buildings at a key intersection immediately southwest of downtown. The site had been vacant for almost two decades, and I enthusiastically supported the project. Reconstruction of Washington Street downtown was mostly completed, and we budgeted funds for renovation and reconstruction of the Pedestrian Mall. And, with the assistance of an engineering consulting firm, we finally initiated construction on the Gateway Project.

Promoting Environmental Sustainability

With regard to environmental sustainability, we appointed an outstanding group of people onto our new Climate Action Steering Committee, hired a consulting firm to provide technical advice, and set the team to work on developing our Climate Action and Adaption Plan. Not long after Earth Day, we created a Community Partnerships for Climate Action Grants program, which would provide seed grants for small community-based projects or events designed to inspire additional community-based action. With the assistance of various consulting firms, we completed the Bicycle Master Plan, a new Master Parks Plan, and the first phases of a new 17-acre Riverfront Crossings park where the flood-damaged North Wastewater Treatment Plant had once stood. We instructed staff to assess the potential of converting a major southern entryway to downtown from four to three lanes with a bike lane. Likewise, we authorized a similar conversion for another main street intersecting the downtown.

We accomplished all of the actions described above while (1) continuing to provide normal city services effectively and efficiently, (2) reducing the City's property tax levy for the fifth straight year, (3) continuing City government's long history of receiving a Triple-A Moody's bond rating, and (4) adopting fiscally sound budgets. And, after roughly 15 months of extensive stakeholder participation and vigorous debate, we embedded our values in an amended TIF policy.

Amending the TIF policy proved to be time-consuming but rewarding. Our 2016–2017 Strategic Plan had indicated we would review and consider amending the City's TIF policy, and it did so partly because of our desire to ensure new developments would not undermine the historic character of the downtown. The council's three-person Economic Development Committee initiated the process of considering amendments to the policy by (1) reviewing the existing TIF policy, (2) having a key staff member prepare a video presentation informing the public about how TIFs work, and then (3) having City staff conduct focus group meetings with nine different stakeholder groups. Influenced by the information collected during those focus groups, the committee (with staff assistance) began crafting amendments. In seven meetings over an 8-month period, the committee proposed and refined amendments, considered written commentary received from diverse stakeholders, debated various detailed modifications, and finally, in mid-October, recommended council approval of the amendments. (The amended policy was designed to ensure that any new TIF-supported project would comply with the downtown portion of the Downtown and Riverfront Crossings District Master Plan. Heights of new buildings could deviate from that plan only if they produced "exceptional public benefits"—for example, by being carbon-neutral or achieving LEED Gold or higher.) Moreover, for a proposed project which would be located on a street containing a substantial number of buildings eligible for historic landmark designation, the tallest portion of the project had to be stepped back from its street frontages far enough to produce "no significant impact" on the existing historic character of the street fronts when seen from the public right-of-way. All of the committee's meetings were held in the council chambers, were televised live on Cable Channel 4, and subsequently made available through online streaming. The council passed the amendments during our November 21 meeting by a 4:3 vote, with Susan M., Terry D., and (to my disappointment) Kingsley B. against. I felt very good about the process and result.

Encountering a "Tidal Wave" of Unexpected Actions

When considering the actions described above, I felt good about what they meant for the city's unfolding. But, in the first few months of 2017, we also encountered what felt like a tidal wave of executive orders and proposed legislation coming from the new president, the U.S. Congress, and the Iowa legislature. The president's campaign speeches and especially his inaugural address sounded the siren for this tidal wave: "American carnage stops right here and stops right now," he said. "From this day forward, a new vision will govern our land. From this moment on, it's going to be America First. … The time for empty talk is over. Now arrives the hour of action." Together, he said, we will make America strong, wealthy, proud, and safe again. "And, Yes, Together, We Will Make America Great Again" (Trump, 2016).

Immediately after being inaugurated, the new president began issuing "shock and awe" executive orders cracking down on sanctuary cities and banning travel from six predominantly Muslim countries.[8] Both of these orders greatly heightened existing anxiety and fear among our Hispanic, Muslim, and other immigrant or refugee communities. The new president's budget proposed to eliminate or dramatically reduce funding for environmental programs, climate-related data collection and research, and a wide range of programs serving lower-income people, while also dramatically increasing funding for the military and reducing taxes for the rich. The U.S. House of Representatives approved a bill which threatened to decrease the number of people, including Iowa Citians, covered by health insurance and increase the cost of insurance for older, less healthy, and lower-income people—some of whom live in Iowa City—while simultaneously reducing taxes for wealthy people.[9] And, very late in 2017, the Republican Congress enacted a $1.7 trillion Tax Cuts and Jobs Act, which cut the corporate tax rate from the existing 35 percent to 21 percent and cut tax rates for individuals (although the cuts would expire in 2025). It also doubled the size of inheritances shielded from estate taxation to $22 million for married couples. Additionally, it struck at a key element of the Affordable Care Act by eliminating the requirement that most people must have health coverage or else pay a penalty. And it would open the Arctic National Wildlife Refuge in Alaska to oil and gas drilling, which would only worsen the global climate crisis.

Almost everybody I knew in Iowa City thought the president's speech and subsequent actions expressed a dangerous fundamentalist Christian, ethno-nationalist agenda that disparaged facts, scientists, and scholars; demonized Hispanic and Muslim immigrants, women, and lower-income African-Americans; and claimed to be "transferring power from Washington, D.C. and giving it back to you, the American People," while obfuscating its intent to transfer wealth to the wealthiest people in American society. At the very least, most Iowa Citians I knew thought the president's words and actions concerning immigration and refugees were completely antithetical to the values that had made Iowa City such a great place to live. As the months passed, especially with the passage of the package of tax cuts late in 2017, it seemed clear to many that the president's statements of support for working-class people were similar to the actions of magicians who divert their audience's attention away from where the real action is.

In normal times, I would have said, "Well, so it goes. A new administration gets elected and has a right to enact the policies it favors." But we were not living in normal times. As a prominent writer (Frum, 2017) observed,

> We are living through the most dangerous challenge to the free govern-ment of the United States that anyone alive has encountered. What hap-pens next is up to you and me. Don't be afraid. This moment of danger can also be your finest hour as a citizen and an American.

In my judgment, the context called upon mayors like me to display moral clarity, courage, and an ability to strengthen bonds of community across racial, ethnic, religious, and political divides. To my great surprise and pleasure, the new president's election seemed to reduce tensions between Susan M. and the four members who had been elected in 2015.

Our sanctuary city process in late 2016 and early 2017 concisely revealed the magnitude of the gap between the new president's agenda and the "inclusive, just, and sustainable" city we were trying to build. Shortly after the new president was elected, we started receiving a large number of emails urging us to declare Iowa City a "sanctuary city." This led me to ask my fellow council members during a work session early in December whether we should place the question on our Jan-uary 3 work session agenda. My personal sense was—given that Iowa City was a "blue" city in a "red" state—that formally designating Iowa City a "sanctuary city" might make us a target and have the ironic result of worsening the situation for our Hispanic residents. But we decided to consider the public's request.

Subsequent to that decision, on December 28, the City clerk's office began receiving a flood of emails, phone calls, and letters condemning us for even preliminarily discussing the possibility. By far the largest proportion of the objecting emails and phone calls were stimulated by "robo calls" that had come from a Des Moines-based organization, Priorities for Iowa Inc. The objectors, many of whom did not live in Iowa City or the state of Iowa, systematically repeated claims that were not true. And some of the objectors condemned us in very harsh and sometimes personally threatening language. One person's email said, "[I]llegal aliens … [A]re you out of your freaking minds?"

> [T]hese people … will place undue burden on the tax-payer, will tax the medical and law-enforcement infrastructure beyond the breaking point, and Iowa City, as a whole, will become nothing more than a cesspool of crime, filth, and drugs. This is NOT conjecture, it is proven fact in sanc-tuary city after sanctuary cities.

Another said,

> Well, I hope you all are proud of the fact that you no longer recognize the rule of law. This is SO against everything that anyone who believes

in the US Constitution stands for. We are either a nation of laws, or we are a lawless nation. The fact that you would even consider this makes you anti-patriots, and against the very values that this nation was founded on. You are despicable.

Late in the evening of January 9, I received a threatening "no caller ID" phone message from a man who did not identify himself, his place of residence, or his phone number. His message basically said, "The Trump Train is going to run all over you. You will receive a visit … when you're least expecting it." (The tenor of the call reminded me that I might need to update my will.) I reported it to the Police Department the next day and gave them a digital copy of his message. The same man phoned me a few weeks later, and I immediately said, "I know who you are, and I have spoken to the police about you." The coward hung up. I also received another phone call from a woman who seemed quite polite at the start, gradually became angrier and angrier as she spoke, and ended by telling me she hoped I would burn in hell. And a man emailed me to say,

> Allowing Iowa City to be a sanctuary city for criminal illegals is breaking federal law. Therefore you are a criminal. I truly hope one of the criminal illegals find your kids before they kill mine! I spit on you. You are a fuckin coward!

The objectors made several claims concerning what they thought we were intending to do, but the main ones were: we would be designating Iowa City a "sanctuary city," we would be harboring (or "aiding and abetting") dangerous criminals, we would be violating federal law, we had been following an undemocratic process, and we would be exposing Iowa City to a loss of federal and state funding. None of these claims were correct.[10]

We did, in fact, discuss on January 3 whether or not we wanted to declare Iowa City a sanctuary city. My general sense was that most of the people who had communicated their opposition to our possible actions thought that undocumented residents meant illegal aliens, which meant dangerous criminals on federal welfare, which meant ruin for Iowa City, the State of Iowa, and the U.S. But the Hispanic immigrants I knew in Iowa City were not dangerous criminals; they were good, hard-working people who paid income taxes and had families whose children attended our schools. Moreover, I was aware of no evidence that our Hispanic residents were more dangerous than non-Hispanic ones. But I knew very little about federal immigration law and relevant court cases, which meant that I had to have several conversations with our city attorney. Those conversations helped me enormously. During our January 3 work session, she told us the proposed policy would not violate the law because no state or federal law required local municipalities to aid in immigration enforcement. After a lengthy discussion that night, we instructed her to craft a proposed resolution affirming that local resources were to be used for public safety and not for the enforcement of federal immigration law. Working closely with the Police Department, she drafted a resolution as requested. She and I jointly crafted the title for it: "Reaffirming the Public Safety Functions of Local Law Enforcement."

When we considered adopting the resolution on January 17, many dozens more people had communicated with us to express their support or opposition. Most of the opponents lived outside Iowa City, and most of the Iowa City residents who expressed their views favored adoption. Fifteen people spoke to us during the meeting; none of them opposed adoption. The resolution reaffirmed that the focus of our law enforcement efforts was on protecting the safety of our residents and visitors, and that—except as necessary for public safety or as otherwise required by state or federal law—the city's law enforcement resources would not be used for immigration enforcement. Put in less legal language, we affirmed that Iowa City was, and would continue to be, a safe and welcoming city for all its residents and visitors. Our vote in favor of adopting the resolution was unanimous (Arnold, 2017).

We were not the only city to take this kind of action. Later in January, the new president issued an executive order to restrict federal funding to cities and counties that had adopted "sanctuary city" policies. This led to lengthy court actions, some of which we participated in by joining the U.S. Conference of Mayors and many other cities in filing *amicus curiae* briefs.

More significantly for Iowa City, a member of the Republican majority in the Iowa Senate filed Senate File 481, which would, among other things, prohibit local governments from discouraging local law enforcement from enforcing federal immigration laws, and it would require law enforcement agencies to comply with federal immigration "detainer requests" for persons in their custody. Sanctions would include the loss of state funding. We believed this bill, if passed, would make Iowa City less safe for all our residents. If Hispanic residents thought that engaging with our police might lead to friends or loved ones being deported, they would be less likely to report to the police crimes they observed or had committed against them. In the end, the Iowa Senate approved SF481, but its companion bill in the House (HF265) did not receive a committee vote or make it to the floor of the House. However, SF481 would be "funnel-proof" in the 2018 session and, therefore, would probably be adopted in the 2018 session.

As the state legislature's adoption of SF481 exemplified, the situation at the state level also proved to be profoundly concerning. Proposed changes in Iowa state law came at furious pace during the January through April 2017 legislative session. Fully controlled by the Republican Party, the legislature sharply constrained collective bargaining by public labor unions. It preempted local governments' ability to establish minimum wages in their jurisdictions. It dramatically expanded access to guns, authorized people who felt threatened to shoot and kill the allegedly threatening person, and allowed people to bring guns into city council meetings.[11] It established new barriers which would make voting more difficult for people who frequently have to move—for example, renters and students. The legislature also undermined our ability to sustain the viability of neighborhoods which are located near the university by preempting cities' authority to use a regulatory tool we had relied upon for many years. In response to the legislature's preemption, we had to divert a substantial amount of our staff's time over a 6-month period toward developing a new "rental cap" ordinance and taking other actions to protect those neighborhoods.[12] It was impossible for me and others not to notice how this and other state legislative action to put further constraints on local home rule completely contradicted the president's and the Republican Party's claim to be, in the president's words, "transferring power from Washington, D.C. and giving it back to you, the American People."[13]

Again, in normal times, one might say, "Well, so it goes. A new administration gets elected and has a right to enact the policies it favors And, don't forget, cities are but creatures of the state." But we were not living in normal times. Many of the legislature's new laws were adopted very quickly, with little or no opportunity for public debate or for the minority (even a very large one) to influence the outcome. This was the antithesis of democracy as I understood it.

In response to this tidal wave of executive orders, policies, and legislation, I found myself making many speeches; writing guest opinions for newspapers; being interviewed by radio, television, and print media reporters; and issuing a number of public proclamations and resolutions concerning the new president's executive orders and some of the Iowa legislature's proposed or enacted legislation. For example, I made a short but hopefully inspiring speech on January 20 shortly before 110 Iowa City women climbed on buses to join half a million other women at the Women's March in Washington, D.C.

I felt like I was being called to become a new or larger self.

Not for a second had I ever imagined that Iowa City and I would be treated as an enemy by the president and other powerful leaders at the national and state levels. For guidance and support, I looked for good new scholarly work that would help me make sense out of this abnormal situation. This included reading historian Timothy Snyder's (2017) *On Tyranny* and historian Nancy MacLean's (2017) *Democracy in Chains*. I also turned to other mayors and joined with them in expressing views and concerns shared by millions of people in the U.S. and around the world.[14] This included joining the U.S. Conference of Mayors and the Global Covenant of Mayors, attending meetings of the National League of Cities and the Mayors' Innovation Project, and being invited to speak at a Mayors Institute on City Design event (Throgmorton, 2017d).[15] In the middle of the year, I participated in the annual meeting of the Association of European Schools of Planning in Lisbon, Portugal (Throgmorton, 2017b).

Near the end of 2017, I organized and moderated a public panel discussion involving mayors from Cedar Rapids and Waterloo (Iowa), Madison (Wisconsin), and myself.

In March, I was surprised to learn that Mayor Thikra Alwash of Baghdad, Iraq, and the director of that city's City of Literature program had invited the director of the University of Iowa's International Writing Program and me to attend Baghdad's Festival of Flowers late in May. We accepted as representatives of Iowa City's City of Literature, and the visit proved to be an extraordinary experience. Put simply, it was one of the highlights of my life. Unquestionably, for me, the high point of our visit was attending the festival's opening ceremony in the Garden of Ridvan on the banks of the Tigris River. There—surrounded by the wreckage of war—we joined a few thousand Baghdadis (including small children) in walking around, hearing music, seeing fireworks, admiring beautifully designed flower gardens, and visiting an array of booths in which various kinds of handmade art were displayed. Shortly after returning, I reported what I had seen and learned in a guest opinion for the *Iowa City Press-Citizen* (Throgmorton, 2017c).

A Year Marked by Progress and Conflict

In November 2017, another city council election took place. There were only three candidates for two at-large positions: incumbent Kingsley B. and two challengers, Angela W. (a young employee of the Downtown District) and Mazahir S., a Muslim Sudanese-American woman with a strong base in the Center for Worker Justice. Named on 78 percent of the ballots, Kingsley B. was reelected. Mazahir S. finished a very strong second, just a point behind him. Two people ran for the District B seat: incumbent Susan M., who had become a candidate for the district seat after Terry D. had announced he would not seek reelection, and Ryan H., a politically active student who was serving on the City's Board of Adjustment. Susan M. defeated Ryan H. by 59 to 41 percent and thereby won her third term on the council.

In January 2018, after a substantial number of private face-to-face conversations, the new council elected me to a second 2-year term as mayor and supported Pauline T. (the councilwoman with a strong labor background) as mayor pro tem. This greatly disappointed Susan M., who had just been reelected. I think it is fair to say she felt far better prepared than Pauline T. to occupy the role and to step in as mayor should my health decline precipitously.

With council leadership in place, we started the Strategic Plan, budget, and CIP cycle all over again. The new Strategic Plan, which we eventually adopted in March, retained the general structure of the previous one and focused primarily on fulfilling the ambitions of our major plans, especially with regard to affordable housing, climate action, and racial equity. But it also contained several new or modified sub-elements.

Although chaos and polarization continued to rule national politics, 2018 felt much less frenzied to me. Instead of feeling inundated with new presidential executive orders, I tried, partly for health reasons, to pace myself better and spend most of my time ensuring the City staff was following through on our prior initiatives, exploring ways to improve upon some of those initiatives, responding to unexpected events, and privately supporting good candidates for state and federal offices.

Early in February, I delivered my third State of the City speech (Throgmorton, 2018a). After celebrating what had been accomplished in 2017 and after praising a variety of people, both within and outside City government, I ended the speech with the following words:

> These are not normal times. This is no time for fighting among ourselves. Yes, we should passionately debate about local issues, but the moment we are living through demands moral clarity, courage, and an ability to strengthen bonds of community across racial, ethnic, religious, and political divides. This *is* a time for us to love one another, to care for one another, to help one another. It *is* a time to stand strong together—men and women, blacks and whites, gays and straights, disabled and abled, Latinos and Asians, union laborers and scholars, Muslims, Jews, Christians, and others—stand together in solidarity with everyone who is at risk.
>
> Standing together, we can take our cue from the Oakdale Prison Community Choir and its recent performance in this room. Let us "lead with love" and, by leading with love, help build the Reverend Martin Luther King, Jr.'s "beloved community" right here in Iowa City.

Making Progress on Our Initiatives

We took many significant steps in 2018 toward making Iowa City a more inclusive, just, and sustainable city. But those steps were accompanied by some intense complaints, critiques, and conflict.

Promoting Environmental Sustainability

In mid-September, we adopted the long-awaited Climate Action and Adaptation Plan. It laid out a means by which we could reduce greenhouse gases emitted from activities within Iowa City by almost 30 percent by 2025 and 80 percent by 2050. In my view, the plan offered a way to turn the threats posed by global climate change into an opportunity to build an economy and community that would sustain us and other living creatures long into the future. As we desired, the plan also paid considerable attention to social equity and collaborative partnerships among our city's many diverse communities, organizations, and interests. The plan was also tightly connected with other plans we had recently adopted, or were close to adopting, especially the Bicycle Master Plan, the Master Parks Plan, and the new FBC efforts. Early in the year, we commissioned a solar feasibility study of City-owned properties, and we received a complicated consultant's report early in December. This report revealed tremendous potential for generating electric power at several of the sites. We eventually decided to proceed with a photovoltaic (PV) array on the roof of a planned new public works facility, and we instructed City staff to install a companion PV facility at a large City-owned park nearby and to include educational components at both sites.

Seven community groups received funding from the new Community Partnerships for Climate Action Grants program. One of them, the Pedals for People project, exemplified the kind of cross-group, community-building collaborations we had hoped to inspire. Co-sponsored by the United Nations Association of Johnson County, the Immigrant and Refugee Association, Bicyclists of Iowa City, the University of Iowa College of Public Health, and the Iowa City Bicycle Library, this project would provide lower-income residents with bicycles, safety equipment, and a short course about basic bicycle maintenance and bike safety.

And, consistent with our 2018–2019 Strategic Plan, the city manager presented us with a bold and exciting vision for the City's public transit system in mid-October.[16] According to it,

> Iowa City Transit is [will be] a sustainable, reliable and safe transportation option that welcomes and connects all riders with economic and community opportunities seven days a week. Iowa City Transit will double 2018 ridership levels by 2028 through policy and investments that target and expand our level of service and eliminate barriers to access, potentially including the elimination of fares. As new buses are procured, Iowa City Transit will begin the conversion to an all-electric fleet.

We would need to hire a consultant to help us plan how to bring that vision to life.

Enhancing Community Engagement and Intergovernmental Relations

With regard to intergovernmental relations, I was extremely happy to participate in a late-summer ribbon cutting for a major renovation and addition at an elementary school located in an older eastside neighborhood. We also amended the Comprehensive Plan to include an affordable housing requirement for voluntary annexations involving proposed residential developments. We collaborated with Coralville and the university to fund a housing study which could help us devise a long-term strategy for responding more effectively to the demand for off-campus student housing. The consultant we jointly hired completed the study early in 2018. And we rezoned almost 6 acres to make space for the county's planned Behavioral Health Urgent Care Center.

Building a Vibrant and Walkable Urban Core and Fostering Healthy Neighborhoods throughout the City

Seeking to foster more sustainable urban development, we had hoped that Opticos would have prepared new FBCs for the Northside and the South District; however, the cost of this work proved to be higher than the council was willing to pay. Consequently, we had to choose one area over the other. In the end, and to council member John T.'s chagrin (his district included the Northside), we settled on the South District. For two major roadway projects located near the two newest schools, however, he and I successfully pushed the staff to ensure the roadway designs would signal to drivers that they should drive at a speed (25 m.p.h.) which was consistent with walkable neighborhoods.[17] And we rezoned approximately 50 acres of property located immediately south of I-80 and east of Dubuque Street to make space for the proposed Forest View development. Most residents of the existing trailer court were very happy about the rezoning being approved. A compelling story could be told about the residents' involvement in the project. The short version is this: they told us (mostly in Spanish) deeply moving stories about what had brought them to Iowa City, how hard they had been working, how much they wanted to stick together as a community in better housing, and how, with assistance from allied organizations and individuals, they had been collaborating with the property owner and developer as co-applicants for the rezoning.

Seeking to avoid a replay of the "three cottages" conflict and to sustain the historic character of the city's core, we approved numerous historic land-mark designations. Unfortunately, we were unable to do so for two specific buildings owing to our inability to obtain the state-required super-majority vote by the council. Stimulated by the Historic Preservation Commission, we also initiated efforts to collaborate with the university and a local church to preserve the oldest surviving building within Iowa City's original city limits. And, in mid-October, we received a consultant's report concerning historic properties downtown. To a degree, the fact that we had commissioned this study derived from my earlier policy memo about the downtown and from the historic preservation elements of our new TIF policy. The report identi-fied properties eligible for listing in the National Register of Historic Places, key historic buildings in the downtown, and two potential National Register Historic District boundaries, and it offered the consultant's recommendations about what to do next.

Promoting a Strong and Resilient Economy

With regard to major construction projects, contractors finished rebuilding and renovating Washington Street downtown, and other contractors moved the Gateway Project closer to completion. The City staff and a construction firm initiated a 2-year-long, $7 million Pedestrian Mall reconstruction project as called for in the Downtown Streetscape Plan. Late in October, I helped celebrate the grand opening of a Hyatt Place Hotel, which was part of the Rise project at Court and Linn Streets. And we approved a couple of rezonings near the middle of the Riverfront Crossings District to make space for two separate four-story apartment buildings. To my disappointment, one of the rezonings would eliminate the possibility of having a station plaza as called for in the RFC District Master Plan. I really did not want the plaza possibility to disappear, largely because it would be gone for good, even if the plan's railroad ambitions were fulfilled at some point in the future. But what we confronted was a choice between development consistent with existing zoning or redevelopment consistent with the new Riverfront Crossings District zone. I preferred the latter.

Advancing Social Justice and Racial Equity

With regard to affordable housing, we increased the proposed FY 2018–2019 budget funding for the Affordable Housing Fund from $650,000 to $1 million. To a significant degree, this increase resulted from council member Mazahir S.'s passionate and relentless advocacy, I initially supported increasing it to $750,000, but shifted to the larger amount as a marker of my support for her as a new member of the council. In April, Shelter House broke ground on its new 24-unit Housing First facility for chronically homeless individuals; it was partially funded by a pass-through of dollars from our Affordable Housing Fund. We also used a unique type of TIF to facilitate construction of a road in the north-central part of the city. The tax increment would derive from taxes that would be paid by a new multi-unit housing complex, and 45 percent of the increment ($2 million–$3 million over its 10-year life span) could be used to fund additional low-to-moderate income housing anywhere in the city. During 2018, we completed a variety of agreements that resulted in construction of a housing project in the RFC District which would include almost 30 rental units affordable (for 30 years) to households at or below 60 percent of areawide median income and would be managed by a local not-for-profit entity. Even so, we experienced blistering criticism from Mazahir S. and others for not doing anything about the affordable housing situation. Although I was really unhappy with the critics' unwillingness to acknowledge the good work we had done, I agreed that we needed to do more. This led me to present some ideas to the Affordable Housing Coalition in mid-September about how a much larger number of affordable units could be built. Early in October, a staff member reported to us that the City had provided almost $8 million for affordable housing projects from FY 2015 through FY 2018. This had created or would create almost 400 assisted units of affordable housing in the city. Nearly half of the funds had gone toward developing new rental units. Another one-fifth of these funds had gone toward rehabilitating existing owner-occupied units.

In addition to these efforts, we increased funding for the Social Justice and Racial Equity grant program from $25,000 to $75,000 per year. In August, the city manager appointed a highly respected and locally well-known black woman as director of the City's Senior Center. And, early in November, we began considering a Home Investment Partnership Program for the South District. This program would have the City renovate two older duplex structures and then, as urged by the Black Voices Project, make them available for purchase by lower-income renters who lived in the immediate neighborhood.

Mayor Pro Tem Pauline T. and I also met with ten or so parents of black youth early in February. I had invited the parents (all but one of them were mothers) in response to a conversation I had had with Henri H. (the Police Department's community outreach officer). I had asked him to meet with me, explain why he felt progress had been slipping backwards over the preceding few months, and share his ideas about what we could do to turn things back around. The mothers made numerous observations and recommendations, four of which struck Pauline and me as being most important. First, there is not much for kids to do in Iowa City to stay out of trouble, regardless of color. The City could provide a place black youth could go for structured activities other than the City's two large recreation centers. Second, the place and activities would have to be well managed, with on-site guidance and leadership being provided by African-American residents who would be part-time employees of the City. Third, the City could work with leaders in the black community and faculty at the university and Kirkwood Community College to help black youth gain a deeper understanding of African-American history. And fourth, the City could help small or new community organizations learn how to write successful grant applications. Council members discussed these ideas during our first work session in May, but, much to my disappointment, I could not persuade a majority of the council to do anything more than have the City's recreation staff generate some options for the council to consider. I felt as though I had let the black parents down.

Early in July, we received an annual report from the Police Department for 2017. Police Chief Jodi M.'s introduction to that report stated that the ICPD had enhanced its efforts to reduce disproportionality in minority contacts. Its objectives were: (1) to enhance training in cultural competency and implicit bias, (2) deploy resources to address crime trends without targeting whole communities, particularly communities of color, and (3) increase the ICPD's community outreach programs. The chief also reported there had been an 11 percent decline in violent crime (including murder, sexual assault, robbery, and aggravated assault) and less than a 1 percent increase in crime overall. However, there had also been four homicides in 2017, whereas, in the previous 4 years, there had been only one. In late August, we received another oral and written report about the St. Ambrose traffic study, this time using 2016 and 2017 data. A memo from the police chief indicated disproportionality in traffic stop *outcomes* (such as citations and searches) had been reduced significantly, but there was still more work to be done with regard to reducing disproportionality in traffic *stops* themselves.

We also considered the possibility of immediately increasing hourly wages for all City employees to a minimum of $15 per hour within 2 years. Mazahir S. first proposed the idea early in September. At that moment, the lowest starting wage for full-time City employees was slightly more than $17.50 per hour, but the City also had approximately 370 temporary hourly employees (including seasonal part-time employees) who were earning between $10 and $15 per hour. City staff estimated that raising temporary hourly employees' wages to $15 per hour would require $900,000–$1 million annually. I was very leery of increasing the minimum wage for all hourly employees to $15 per hour within 1 or 2 years without having better information about possible adverse consequences for other council priorities. After contentious discussions during two September work sessions, we decided to start with $11.50 in July 2019, to revisit the topic during our January budget discussions, and to have an intention of getting to $15 per hour by July 2021.

While we were taking the many steps just described, several new clashes were occurring. Climate activists condemned us for doing nothing to reduce the city's carbon emissions. Drivers on the west side of town complained about our proposed four-to-three-lane conversion (with bike lanes) on a major north–south street. A developer proposed a massive new student-housing project for the Riverfront Crossings District just southwest of downtown. And unexpected clashes took place among council members. As the year proceeded, those clashes led me to conclude that there was no longer a consistent 5:2 or even 4:3 majority on the council. Instead, the council was dividing in more complicated ways on particular topics. I felt the best way I could lead in that altered context was to facilitate thoughtful and informed discussions by the council.

An Inspiring Civil Rights Tour

The highlight of the year for me was joining 50 or so other people (including council member Rockne C. and my wife and daughter) on a mid-June tour of historically black colleges and universities, museums, and sites of important events in civil rights history. Organized and conducted by Henri H., with considerable help from Teamsters Local 728, the tour included visits to major sites in Memphis (Tennessee), Birmingham and Selma (Alabama), and Montgomery and Atlanta (Georgia).[18] Roughly half of the people on the tour were black youth from Iowa City, and many of their parents were involved as well. I greatly enjoyed being with them and hearing the students react to what they saw and learned. And I hoped that Rockne C.'s and my presence on the tour would send a powerful signal about the City government's commitment to improving racial equity in Iowa City. As I had done for the trip to Baghdad, I reported about the tour in a guest opinion for our local newspaper (Throgmorton, 2018b). I ended the trip thinking that every American would benefit from visiting the sites and sharing what they learned with friends.[19] Alas, I also damaged my right ankle in a pick-up basketball game on the last night of the tour. ("There's only one rule in this game," I said to the three other players before starting: "Don't hurt the mayor." So much for rules from authority figures.) The injury greatly limited my mobility and forced me to begin seeing a physical therapist.

Inspired by a youth center we visited in Birmingham, Rockne C. and I came back advocating the creation of a similar but smaller center for black teens in Iowa City. Regrettably, as had been the case with the recommendations black mothers had given Pauline T. and me, we were unable to do any more than to direct the staff to investigate the possibility further.

Encountering More Unexpected Events

Not surprisingly, several unexpected events occurred in 2018, including: (1) an announcement by a large transnational corporation (Procter & Gamble) that it would be phasing out 500 jobs at one of its plants in the city; (2) an emerald ash borer infestation, which threatened to kill all our ash trees and greatly undermine many of our older neighborhoods; and (3) a significant increase in the number of deer, which, absent any natural predators, threatened public health and safety. Moreover, heavy rainfall produced another major flood in the fall, just as we were preparing to celebrate completion of the Gateway Project. We had to delay the big celebration owing to high water, but, in the end, the completed project worked just as planned. In late September, a middle-aged friend on the County Board of Supervisors died unexpectedly from unknown causes. He had been pouring his energy into a job he truly loved. His death caused me to ask myself many "what if?" and "if only?" kinds of questions.[20]

But the biggest surprise occurred on July 17 when, at the end of one of our council work sessions, Kingsley B. told us that he would be resigning and taking a new job with the School District in Waterloo, Iowa. I liked Kingsley B. a lot and I thought he had considerable potential, but I was very disappointed that he did not discuss his plans with me prior to making his announcement. His resignation forced us to decide very quickly whether to appoint a replacement for him or schedule a special election. At first, I thought we would not have time to hold an election prior to January, and I spoke with several people who might be interested in serving as an appointee. But, once I realized we could call for a special election in early October, I scheduled a special council meeting for August 1 to discuss the matter. During that meeting, we quickly decided that scheduling an early October election was the best of the limited set of choices available to us owing to constraints and requirements imposed by state law. Five candidates filed nomination papers. This necessitated a primary, which took place on September 4. My sense was that all of the candidates had meritorious qualities, but only one of them understood how City government works and how to get things done, and none of them seemed to know much about what our council had been doing over the preceding 3 years. When the primary took place, Ann F. (long-time chair of the P&Z Commission) and Bruce T. (owner of a small business who happened to be a gay black man) moved on to the general election. On October 2, Bruce T. emerged victorious, 54 to 45 percent. He immediately began serving on the council.

If Kingsley B.'s resignation was the biggest surprise for me, the most troubling one concerned our newest council member, Mazahir S. I knew her fairly well through the CWJ, liked her, and admired her passionate commitment to social justice; she knew what she and her constituents experienced on the ground. However, over months of meetings, I gradually realized that she had very rigid views and tended to monopolize council discussions about the topics she cared about. Moreover, she often spoke very critically in public about City staff and other council members. Furthermore, like most new council members, she often went awry whenever she spoke about what City government had been doing. During our first council meeting in October, she personally attacked me for treating her differently than other council members, for not appointing her to the council's Economic Development Committee at the start of her first year on the council, and for monopolizing work session discussions. And she accused the City staff of displaying racial bias in how they had applied the Racial Equity Toolkit to the South District Home Investment Partnership Program. The situation deeply troubled me, and I struggled to think of a good way to turn it in a better direction.

Conflict over a Project at 12 Court Street

Our council also became immersed in a heated conflict over a proposed rezoning of property located near downtown in the northwest corner of the RFC District. I first learned about the project by opening the agenda packet for our May 1 formal meeting and finding an item setting a May 15 public hearing and first vote on the rezoning.

The staff report on the proposed rezoning conveyed many relevant facts. The site was zoned RM-44 (the highest density permitted under the City's zoning code) and was currently the site of the four-building, 96-unit Pentacrest

Garden Apartment complex. The site would be rezoned to RFC–SD (South Downtown), which was intended for high-intensity mixed-use development. Pursuant to the FBC we had adopted in 2014, the maximum permissible height for buildings in the subdistrict was eight stories plus a possible seven-story height bonus. The project would also have to comply with our recently adopted "inclusionary housing" requirement. The staff report also noted that the RFC District Master Plan called for the extension of a street through the center of the site to connect two east–west streets, and it indicated that this area was an appropriate site for student housing owing to its proximity to the University of Iowa's campus and its student recreation center. The staff report acknowledged that the RFC District Master Plan had envisioned that the property would be combined with others in the area and redeveloped into a cluster of apartment buildings surrounding an internal courtyard. (See Figure 3.3.) Because part of the block (316 Madison Street) was already in the process of being redeveloped, however, arranging buildings around an internal courtyard was no longer feasible. The staff report included a very rough site plan, which showed only the footprint of the proposed project. As a condition of the rezoning, the applicant had agreed to transfer right-of-way for the street to the City as called for in the Master Plan.

From the moment I read the staff report and saw the site plan, I thought, oh no, this is a really dreadful idea. I had known that somebody would eventually take advantage of the FBC's density and height bonus provisions, but I had not known this specific project would be coming our way at this particular moment. And, as I told the city manager near the end of April, I thought the staff report was astonishingly thin for a project of this magnitude. By approving this rezoning, we would be authorizing an unknown number of residences in perhaps just two very large buildings. My sense was that the rezoning would be the council's only opportunity to influence the project significantly; to wait for the moment when we reviewed the final design for bonus approval would be far too late.

This initiated a process that, for diverse reasons, lasted for the next 8 months. After receiving the staff report and scheduling the May 15 public hearing, the process involved at least nine steps, plus some surprises.

- Step 1: During the May 15 public hearing on the proposed rezoning, I argued that we needed to have more specific understanding of what the developer had in mind. After considerable discussion, we voted 5:2 (Susan M. and Kingsley B. against) to continue the public hearing to May 29 so the developer could clarify his intentions. The developer agreed to do this.
- Step 2: During the public hearing on May 29, the developer's consultant told us the applicant envisioned four 15-story buildings, which would contain a total of 800–1,000 residential student-oriented units plus first floor retail. Except for the heights of the buildings, the bird's-eye-view

image the developer provided appeared to be very similar to what was recommended in the Master Plan (see Figure 4.1). Only two members of the general public spoke during the public hearing. During council discussion, Susan M. argued that there was no reason to delay the rezoning, and that details would be resolved during the FBC design review process. However, I strongly believed the council should propose conditions for the rezoning as a way of signaling clearly what it expected from the developer, rather have the developer spend a lot of money designing the buildings only to risk having the council deny the bonuses. Consequently, I argued we needed more time to identify and discuss possible conditions on the rezoning and I emphasized that the council had a legal right to propose such conditions. I also wanted to learn from P&Z commissioners why they voted unanimously to support the proposed rezoning. This quickly led to a stalemate: Susan M., Kingsley B., and Rockne C. said they were inclined to support the P&Z Commission recommendation to approve, while John T., Pauline T., and I were not, and Mazahir S. was absent for personal reasons. This meant we were required to offer to consult with the commission and continue our public hearing.

In the days after that meeting, I learned that perhaps as many as 2,000 residents would be housed in the proposed development. The development would be equivalent to four buildings the size of the Rise at Court and Linn Street and would be, in my judgment, significantly out of scale with surrounding structures. Susan M. made a forceful counter-argument in a guest opinion published in a local news weekly, *Little Village*. In her view, the proposed rezoning was

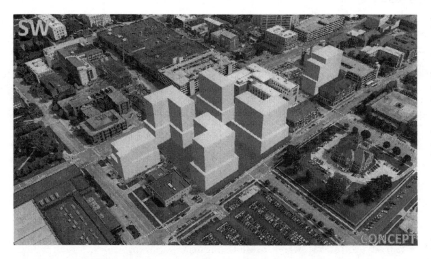

FIGURE 4.1   Bird's eye view of 12 Court Street (Pentacrest Gardens).
Source: City of Iowa City, 2018.

consistent with the RFC District Master Plan, and the three of us who opposed the rezoning simply opposed tall buildings (Mims, 2018).

- Step 3: Owing to scheduling difficulties, we were unable to consult with the P&Z Commission until July 3. A few days prior to that meeting, I shared a memo with the council which provided some background information and recommended several specific conditions for the proposed rezoning (Throgmorton, 2018c). In brief, the conditions sought to ensure the development would be more consistent with the RFC District Master Plan and demonstrate high-quality urban design.
- Step 4: On July 3, we consulted with the P&Z Commission. Immediately afterwards, the development team asked us to defer our first vote until the August 7 council meeting. Consequently, we re-opened the continued public hearing, heard from seven members of the general public, and then continued the hearing and deferred our first vote to August 7.

It was at this point (mid-July) that Kingsley B. surprised everyone by announcing his resignation. This shrank the council to six members pending the selection of a replacement either by appointment or by special election

- Step 5: At our August 7 meeting, the developer submitted a substantial amount of new information. Only five members of the general public expressed their views. With Kingsley B. (who had supported the original rezoning proposal) no longer on the council, we had two possible courses of action: (1) to continue the public hearing and defer first consideration to August 21 or (2) to vote on the motion to approve the proposed rezoning knowing that a 3:3 split on the council would defeat the rezoning. As the council discussion proceeded, I acknowledged that I could see a majority of the council would not agree to my proposed conditions pertaining to building height. But other conditions pertaining to urban design remained. After extensive discussion, it became clear that three members favored deferral, and three (Susan M., Rockne C., and Mazahir S.) opposed it. Mazahir S.'s opposition really surprised me because I had spoken with her the day before the meeting and understood she would be supporting deferral. After lengthy and increasingly heated discussion, we remained at a 3:3 impasse. I was on the verge of voting against deferral just to break the log jam and get on with voting on the rezoning when the city manager, Geoff F., suggested we defer, instruct him to discuss the proposed modified conditions with the developer, and perhaps return with something mutually agreeable at our next meeting on August 21. That sounded acceptable to me. Eventually, others agreed, and we voted 6:0 to defer.
- Step 6: A little over a week later, the city manager reported that staff had negotiated amended language and that the staff recommended its approval.

Staff also recommended, as discussed in the previous meeting, that we collapse the second and third readings of the proposed rezoning ordinance. The amendments looked okay to me. The council subsequently voted in favor of the rezoning on August 21 and then unanimously supported condensing the second and third readings on September 4. Even though we unanimously approved the rezoning that night, we remained closely divided over whether to support the height bonuses required to achieve the developer's ambitions.

Partly because of the council's conflict over the 12 Court Street project, and partly because we still had not yet approved our Climate Action Plan, I was feeling that I was faltering in my role as mayor. In mid-August, however, my wife, daughter, and I made a wonderful 8-day trip to Helsinki, Finland, where I had been invited to make a keynote presentation to a group of scholars at Aalto University (Throgmorton, 2018d). Shortly thereafter, I attended the Mayors Innovation Project's annual meeting in Grand Rapids, Michigan. The trip to Helsinki and the presentations and conversations with other mayors revived my spirits.

- Step 7: On November 6, we discussed possible height bonuses for the project, now known as Pentacrest Gardens. By this time, Bruce T. had been elected to replace Kingsley B. on the council. To help him and the public understand what was at stake, I asked the City planning staff to provide an overview of the RFC District Master Plan, its FBC, the height bonuses, and how they applied to the 12 Court Street site (see Figure 3.1). After the staff presented this information, four council members (including Bruce T.) indicated they were tentatively willing to approve a seven-story height bonus. Rockne C. supported the project because it would produce a large number of good construction jobs, would greatly increase the tax base, would increase funding for affordable housing, and had generated no substantial opposition from the general public. As she had done ever since returning from a lengthy trip to Sudan, Mazahir S. said she would support the project so long as the developer met the affordable housing requirement by making a payment in lieu of providing affordable units on site. However, Bruce T. continued to sound quite ambivalent and tentative when expressing his support.
- Step 8: In a subsequent memo to the council (Throgmorton, 2018e), I indicated that the maximum pre-bonus height permitted in the RFC-SD was appropriate in scale and sufficient in density. Even so, I recognized there were good reasons to provide some height bonuses. In my view, however, permitting the maximum permissible bonus would be a serious mistake: it would result in a project that would be excessive in scale and unnecessarily risky for both the developer and the city. In my judgment,

the development needed to be scaled down and stretched out over time. I offered six reasons, which I will not belabor here except to say that I emphasized risks to the developer and the city, namely: that the project would undermine other rental housing complexes or fail owing to the possibility that enrollments at the university would decline and/or University of Iowa leadership would decide to require second-year students to live on campus. Trying to forge a unanimous vote by the council, I advocated authorizing bonuses resulting in an average maximum building height of 11–12 stories.

- Step 9: We discussed possible height bonuses again during our December 4 work session. I thought it would be especially important to give Bruce T. an ample opportunity to ask questions and become comfortable in making his decision.[21] I had spoken with him a couple of times beforehand, but never tried to pressure him into voting as I would prefer. Council discussion that night revealed that Bruce T. was likely to end up supporting the developer's requested bonuses and, therefore, that four council members favored permitting the maximum height bonus. The developer indicated it would take many months to develop a formal application.

By the time this 8-month process ended, I could see that I had erred in voting for the RFC District FBC's excessive height bonuses back in 2014. Although voting differently then would not have affected the council's passage of the FBC, my vote did make it harder for me to justify objecting to future height bonuses. The council's adoption of those bonuses established a path that would be very hard for any future council to deviate from. Moreover, I realized that adoption of the FBC had effectively eliminated the possibility that the general public could influence the council's decisions. In the end, my view did not carry the day. But I think I was right and I do not regret the effort I made.

Navigating Conflict with the State and National Administrations

To state the obvious: what happens at the national level can have important ramifications at the local scale. From my point of view as the mayor of a minor city in the Midwest of the U.S., it appeared as though incompetence, bad policy-making, and chaos reigned in Washington, D.C., or at least in the White House. Cabinet-level officials turned over at a record-breaking pace. The investigation led by Special Counsel Robert Mueller into possible collusion between Russia and the Trump campaign during the 2016 presidential election yielded dozens of indictments. The president briefly shut down the federal government over an Obama-era program deferring deportation for immigrants brought illegally to the United States as children. And, for 35 days at the end of 2018 and start of 2019, the president imposed a partial shutdown of the federal government in an unsuccessful effort to pressure the Democratic members of

Congress to accept his demand to provide $5.5 billion to build his signature campaign promise: a wall.

If shutting down the federal government failed to produce the funds the president wanted for his wall, he did succeed in fulfilling at least one major campaign promise: in July, the president nominated a judge to fill a vacancy on the U.S. Supreme Court. In September, the U.S. Senate had a horribly partisan battle over his nomination. I found the Senate committee hearings on his nomination traumatic to watch.

Continuing the 2017 pattern of one-party rule, the Iowa legislature adopted more legislation that ran counter to the preferences of most Iowa Citians in 2018. It de-appropriated funds in the middle of the budget year, which resulted in a large mid-year cut in funding for public universities. It cut state taxes by $2 billion over the next 6 years, with the greatest benefits going to the wealthiest taxpayers. It banned abortions after a fetal heartbeat was detected (roughly 6 weeks after conception). It significantly reduced energy-efficiency programs and allowed municipal utilities to discriminate against solar energy customers. And, in an explicit response to the resolution our council adopted early in 2017, it adopted a slightly modified version of its "anti-sanctuary cities" bill, SF481.

I had decided to lay low while the state legislature considered modifications to SF481. However, with help from an ICPD captain, on March 19 I did participate in Iowa Public Radio's "River to River" talk show along with Storm Lake's Police Chief Mark P., Monica R. of DREAM Iowa, Republican Representative Steve H., Republican Senator Julian G., and Democratic Representative Wes B. The interview proved to be testy but hopefully enlightening for its listeners. Other than that, we relied heavily on testimony from police chiefs (including ours) and our lobbyists. Their testimony persuaded the legislature to modify the bill somewhat, but even the modified version would revoke state funding for communities that, in the legislature's opinion, circumvented federal immigration laws. It specifically indicated local entities could not prohibit or discourage law enforcement officers or other employees from assisting or cooperating with a federal immigration officer as reasonable or necessary, including providing enforcement assistance. Moreover, local entities could not prohibit or discourage law enforcement or other officials from: (1) inquiring about the immigration status of a person who was under arrest, (2) sharing that information with other authorities, or (3) assisting federal immigration officers as reasonable or necessary. To justify adoption of this bill, Republican legislators pointed to the death of one person, a 22-year-old Council Bluffs (Iowa) woman who had been killed in Omaha (Nebraska) in a January 2016 car accident involving an undocumented immigrant, and they said the bill was designed to avoid similar crimes in the future (Petroski and Pfannenstiel, 2018). Conversely, the legislators disregarded the fact that violent and property crime rates had been declining dramatically in the U.S. since the early 1990s (Gramlich, 2020). To my way of thinking, the bill was a politically symbolic act designed to appease the ethno-nationalist base of the Republican Party. I was growing increasingly fearful that the country was teetering on the brink of a civil war, and I was profoundly dismayed that none of the leaders of either political party was trying to de-escalate the situation and talk their constituents back from that precipice.

I needed to act out of hope rather than fear. Throughout the last two-thirds of 2018, I joined many other Iowa City residents in supporting efforts to elect a new governor, new representatives to the Iowa legislature, and new representatives to the U.S. House of Representatives. Given the nonpartisan nature of my mayoral position, I had to be careful to act not as the mayor of Iowa City, but as a private individual. On November 6, voters gave the president and his party a resounding defeat, especially in elections to the U.S. House, where the Democratic Party swept into control by flipping more than 40 seats, two of them in Iowa. At the state level, the Republican Party lost five seats but still narrowly retained control of the House. It also retained control of the Iowa Senate and, most important, narrowly won the gubernatorial race. Although most Iowa Citians I knew were ecstatic about the national results, I found it impossible not to feel very anxious about the coming year.

And then there was the November 2019 council election to think about. Shortly after the start of 2019, people began asking whether the four people elected in November 2016, myself included, would seek reelection. If some or all of us decided not to run again, it would be important to recruit candidates who would continue and improve upon the changes we had initiated. If that did not happen, then many of our policy initiatives might be overturned or not completed. It would be a hard decision for me to make.

Accepting Limits in My Fourth Year

Over the previous 7 years, I had grown accustomed to the annual rhythm of city council activities punctuated by (1) actions explicitly designed to fulfill the council's priorities and (2) an irregular drumbeat of unanticipated events and challenges. Moreover, I had grown more capable of seeing how our efforts to transform policies into action revealed key linkages (that is, aspects of the city's organized complexity) which had scarcely been considered when the policies were first being adopted.[22]

With that as background, the fourth year of my term was marked by making great strides toward converting our policies into action, navigating nontrivial interpersonal conflicts on the council, responding to additional preemptions by the state legislature, preparing for the next round of council elections, and being affected by the nationwide debates over the president's behavior and the forthcoming November 2020 elections. At a more personal level, I found myself forced to recognize and respond to personal limits on my time, health, and energy; limits on the power of Iowa City's mayor; and limits on the authority of Iowa City's government as a whole.

Dealing with the Annual Rhythm

A key part of the annual rhythm of governance in Iowa City is the wintertime process of reviewing, amending, and approving City government's annual budget, 3-year financial plan, and Capital Improvements Plan (CIP). This would be our fourth budget, so by now we should have been seeing our priorities clearly reflected in the city manager's proposed budget. And we did. For example, his draft budget included the following five items: (1) allocating a significant amount of funding for the first steps in our Master Parks Plan, (2) putting another $650,000 into the Affordable Housing Fund, (3) committing $2.5 million in capital funds for the planned Behavioral Health Access Center, (4) including roughly $700,000 for a large solar array on our soon-to-be-built public works facility, and (5) increasing the minimum wage for hourly staff to $11.50 per hour. The draft budget also proposed to continue funding our Social Justice and Racial Equity and Climate Action Small Grants programs, to provide CIP funding for urban forest management (including trying to save the healthiest of our infected ash trees), and to make several pedestrian- and bike-friendly roadway improvements consistent with our recently adopted Bicycle Master Plan. And the city manager proposed to reduce the City's property tax levy for the seventh consecutive year. During council discussions about the draft budget, we chose to allocate an additional $100,000 for a solar installation in one of our newest parks and to provide funds for the new South District Homeownership Program.

But this year's budget discussion felt far more challenging emotionally for me than the preceding two had been, primarily because it involved further interpersonal conflicts among council members. In addition to actions we discussed in the latter half of 2018, council member Mazahir S. demanded that we convert some or all of City hourly staff positions to permanent positions with standard employee benefits. After a few testy conversations, we directed the staff to analyze the feasibility of converting hourly staff positions to full-time with benefits. From Mazahir S.'s point of view, this was insufficient. She wanted more immediate action and she appeared to become quite upset with me and some other council members during our televised council meetings. I discuss this further in Chapter 5 below.

Delivering the State of the City speech is another part of the annual rhythm. In this year's speech, I sought to focus the public's attention on the many specific actions we had taken over the preceding 3 years (Throgmorton, 2019). I also tried to make my oral presentation livelier and more interesting by adding quite a few photographs of places and activities mentioned in the speech, especially at the end when I showed a dozen or so photographs of residents participating in events that had been strengthening bonds of community across racial, ethnic, religious, and political divides (see Figure 4.2).

And a third key moment in the annual rhythm is trying to influence or simply respond to actions taken by the state legislature during its legislative session

FIGURE 4.2 Black youth dance troupe in southeastern Iowa City's Wetherby Park. *Source*: Photo by author, June 29, 2017.

from January through April. As it had done in the 2 preceding years, the state legislature considered several bills that would undermine what we had been doing in Iowa City. One of the proposed bills would have imposed a cap on property tax revenues and significantly altered the process by which City budgets could be approved. We joined most other cities in the state to push back hard on the initial proposal. A revised bill was ultimately adopted, but it was far less onerous than we initially feared it would be.

Another bill, which basically applied only to the two cities (Ames and Iowa City) that host large public universities, would ban the kind of "rental cap" ordinance we had adopted late in 2017. This bill, which apparently was pushed by realtors in the two cities, was introduced with no notice and immediately passed by a Senate subcommittee and committee. In the House, I had an eye-opening opportunity to witness state legislators in action, when our city manager, our lobbyists, the mayor of Ames, and I met with the Republican floor manager of the bill and lots of realtors and their lobbyists in a small meeting room of the State Capitol building. Although the floor manager invited people to make their cases, listened attentively, and generally treated us fairly, the compromise language he ultimately devised would have been worse for us than the original bill. We offered amendments responding to most of the realtors' concerns but without any positive effect. The state legislature passed the original bill banning rental caps.

This new legislation led us to hold a special council meeting at the start of May to consider establishing a 10-month moratorium on converting single-family houses and duplexes to rentals in designated parts of the city. The moratorium would give our staff time to assess possible responses to the disappearance of this key tool. In the public comment period of that meeting, a large crowd of realtors roundly criticized us. Many of them claimed that property should be put to "the highest and best use," and that we were taking private property by not letting owners sell their property to the highest bidder. Regrettably, those who wrote and spoke to us often appeared to be badly informed about what our rental cap ordinance actually did and what exceptions it authorized. Before voting on the moratorium, which we unanimously approved in mid-May, I pushed back and said—in the spirit of engaging the realtors in dialogue—their claim about "highest and best use" misunderstood the relationship between private property owners and governmental entities like ours. There is no such thing as a perfectly free market for residential housing, I said. The market for housing is always shaped by the rules set by local governments.

Acting on the Council's Priorities

The annual rhythm is punctuated by actions intentionally undertaken to advance the council's policies and initiatives. We dealt with several such actions during the year. Some of our responses felt good to me, others not so much. The actions that felt good pertained to the FBC for the South District, historic preservation downtown, and the city manager's bold public transit initiative. The more problematic actions pertained to the 12 Court Street project, the Forest View project, and our 2018 Climate Action Plan.

I was very pleased when we approved the hiring of Opticos to develop, by the end of the year, the FBC for the South District area around the new Alexander Elementary School. Later, just as Opticos was beginning its work, I learned that, perhaps as a result of pushback from developers and some residents of the area, some key staff seemed not to understand the critical relationship between the design of missing middle neighborhoods and the design of a new boulevard that would run through the neighborhood's proposed mixed-use center. After I drew the city manager's attention to this concern, the staff came back to us with a boulevard design that would fit well with Opticos's neighborhood design. This displeased council member Susan M., and she stressed that the City had long been planning for the roadway to be a 45 m.p.h. belt road around the southeastern part of the city. You're right, I said, but we are changing that. Late in the year, City staff briefed us about the status of Opticos's work. The draft FBC and regulating plan had been submitted and were being reviewed by the staff, and the staff expected a final version to be submitted to the council for approval by late winter. I felt very pleased; getting this done had been a long, hard slog, but it now looked as though we would be able to move new development on part of the city's periphery in a much more sustainable direction.

We also took several actions pertaining to historic preservation. I was especially pleased when we authorized hiring a consultant to prepare the nomination forms for listing our downtown on the National Register of Historic Places, and, in a parallel action, when the City's Historic Preservation Commission began engaging stakeholders about the possibility of designating part of downtown as a local historic preservation district. We also designated several buildings as historic landmarks; however, we failed to preserve a historic building located three blocks north of downtown, primarily because the owner had objected to the necessary rezoning. Once again, this invoked a super-majority requirement, and, despite a council majority in favor of rezoning, the motion failed. Contrary to my own recommendation, this led us to instruct the planning staff to craft a transfer of development rights (TDR) ordinance as a way of preserving historic buildings.[23] The staff came back to us 6 months later with a well-crafted TDR ordinance backed by excellent research, but a majority of the council (myself included) decided it would, in fact, be too complicated to administer.

Although that preservation effort fell through, we engaged in conversations with University of Iowa leadership about not demolishing an 1840s-era house located a couple of blocks north of downtown. During this conversation, we also discussed the possibility the university might soon be requiring second-year students to live on campus and building two new residence halls to accommodate them. The last two actions would, as best I could judge, have enormous implications for the viability of the 12 Court Street project.

And, in August, we followed through on the city manager's bold public transit initiative by approving an agreement with a nationally known consulting firm to conduct a comprehensive analysis of our public transit operations. Funded in collaboration with the university and the City of Coralville and designed with our climate action goals in mind, this study would include taking a close look at transit routes and schedules, as well as (in Iowa City's case) investigating the possibility of converting our fleet from diesel-powered to all-electric buses and assessing the viability of doubling Iowa City's 2018 bus ridership by 2028.

Our efforts pertaining to 12 Court Street, Forest View, and climate action proved less satisfying. In mid-February, we learned that the developer of 12 Court Street had firmly decided to apply for a seven-story height bonus, to build four 15-story buildings, and to meet the affordable housing requirement entirely by making "fee-in-lieu-of" payments. Applying for the bonus would require the owner to develop detailed plans for the project. In my view, this was a risky decision. The owner was fully aware that three members of the council opposed the seven-story height bonus he had requested. He also knew that council member Bruce T. was still very new and not yet well informed.

In private conversations with the developer, I suggested he had three choices: (1) to prepare the detailed application and risk having the request for bonuses denied, (2) to ensure majority support from the council by scaling back the project and building it incrementally over time, or (3) to wait for the election of a new council. He chose the first path. Unsure of who might be on the council beginning in 2020, he pushed hard to ensure his application for height bonuses would go to the council before our last meeting in December.[24] However, much to my surprise, the application did not come to us by then.

Early in April, we amended the North District part of the Comprehensive Plan to enable development of the Forest View project near the intersection of Interstate-80 and North Dubuque Road. Immediately after this decision, we held a very long public hearing on its proposed rezoning. The hearing was marked primarily by comments made by residents of the Forest View trailer court (most of whom were lower-income Hispanic residents and their allies in the CWJ and the local labor movement). These were political allies and residents with whom several council members and I had worked closely over the past few years. But the rezoning turned out to be agonizingly complicated. It involved not just treating the lower-income residents well, but also dealing with at least seven complications associated with the development. First, storm water runoff from the project might adversely affect Idyllwild condominiums downhill from Forest View. Second, the project would include a new road that would provide secondary access to residential areas which had been isolated during the 2008 flood. Third, it might involve the removal of a large number of trees that lined the most scenic entryway to the city. Fourth, the project would adversely affect a large swath of woodland and wildlife. Fifth, it would significantly transform the landscape near two neighboring residential areas. And, last, the project would greatly increase the volume of motor vehicle traffic on North Dubuque Street and, consequently, require that street to be widened and make the reconstruction of the interchange of the street with I-80 more necessary.

After the public hearing, I stated that the project was much bigger than I had expected, had huge traffic implications, and was a very big step in the wrong direction from a climate action and adaptation point of view. But two council members (Rockne C. and Mazahir S.) and my friends and allies in the CWJ and the local labor movement reduced the issue to one thing: providing better housing for the trailer court's residents. What was I to do? Luckily, for me at least, neighbors of the proposed project had filed a petition opposing the rezoning, and staff had not yet had time to determine whether the petition was sufficient to invoke the super-majority requirement. Consequently, we continued the public hearing to our next meeting in April.

I felt terrible after the first meeting. If we approved the development without making any significant changes, it would, for me at least, be almost as big a failure as 12 Court Street. Prior to our council meeting in late April, I shared a memo with the council proposing a few new conditions, the key parts of which were (1) to require major reductions in the expected traffic volumes, (2) to ensure the City's public transit system would serve the area, and (3) to incorporate electric-vehicle recharging stations and energy-efficient lighting on the streets and parking lots. The city manager suggested that I could simply call for deletion of a proposed gas station/convenience store: it alone accounted for more than one-third of all the traffic expected to be generated by the development. Between that April meeting and our next one early in May, the developer agreed to delete the gas station. With that hurdle overcome, at our first meeting in June, we condensed the second and third readings and unanimously approved the rezoning with conditions. Much to my surprise, however, later in August, the development team asked us to approve a TIF slightly in excess of $1 million to cover the cost of installing manufactured homes wider than the ones initially planned. Feeling blindsided, manipulated, and very unhappy, I tried to rectify the situation by meeting with some of the people who had made the request. This proved fruitful; however, action seemed to stop for reasons I did not fully understand, but might have been a consequence of the developer encountering cash flow challenges. I heard nothing more about the project for the remainder of the year.

In March and April, the council, city manager, and I started getting hammered by student "climate strikers" and a few of their adult allies for having adopted in 2018 what was, in their view, a woefully inadequate Climate Action Plan. I too had had concerns about our plan, which relied very heavily on large carbon emission reductions by Iowa City's major energy supplier (MidAmerican Energy) and the University of Iowa.[25] Moreover, we had adopted the plan just a week or two before the Intergovernmental Panel on Climate Change (2018) published a new report indicating that climate change was occurring more rapidly than expected just a few years ago. The pressure continued through May and June as the climate strikers (who were acting as part of a global-scale social media-based movement) held a couple demonstrations (which I attended) and demanded that we (1) proclaim a "climate emergency," (2) significantly accelerate the amount and pace at which CO_2 emissions would be decreased, and (3) hire a new Climate Action Plan coordinator charged with developing community partnerships that would lead to net zero CO_2 emissions by 2050. After three work session discussions in mid-summer, the council approved a resolution declaring a "climate crisis," adopted the more demanding 45 percent and 100 percent reduction goals, and directed the staff to recommend within 100 days actions we could take to achieve the 45 percent reduction by 2030. Early in October, we also created a new Climate Action Commission to help us accomplish our climate action goals. In mid-November, the staff presented us with an outstanding report identifying actions the City should consider taking to achieve our new goals (City of Iowa City, 2019). I could not have felt prouder of our staff.

Several of us were influenced by more than the climate strikers' demands. We had had a brutally cold winter in February and March, with lots of snow, ice, and record low temperatures, followed by the third wettest May on record. The amount of rain on top of snow and frozen soils led to massive flooding along the Missouri and Mississippi Rivers, but, luckily for us, flooding along the Iowa River proved not quite so severe. Even so, it was Iowa City's fourth major flood event since 2008. We would have experienced significant flood damage had we not recently completed the Gateway Project and had the City not previously bought out roughly 140 homes in a neighborhood located near the river.

Responding to Unexpected Events

Of course, several unexpected events and pressures disrupted the rhythm of our work, demanded attention, consumed scarce staff time, and, to a degree, made it harder to fulfill the ambitions of our Strategic Plan. These unexpected events included: (1) dealing with a complaint from the Catholic Worker House that the City staff had installed new benches with center arm rests in the Pedestrian Mall as a means of keeping homeless people out of downtown; (2) having a big fire on a very cold and windy March afternoon almost destroy the partially built Hieronymus Square building downtown; (3) finding, in mid-February, that someone had posted hateful anti-immigrant posters on kiosks and signposts downtown and then finding swastikas scribbled on the side of a church in mid-March; (4) having an F1 tornado on May 24 narrowly miss destroying several neighborhoods on the west and north sides of the city; (5) struggling to devise a deer management plan which would meet the conflicting demands of our local constituents and the state's Natural Resources Commission; (6) learning that outside investors were buying up trailer courts in nearby cities, raising rents substantially, and scaring their lower-income tenants; and (7) learning, in early June, that an unidentified entity was very likely to lease property in our industrial park as the site for an "Amazon-type fulfillment center" employing hundreds of people. Near the end of the year, we upset a cluster of non-profit social service agencies by providing (outside of normal funding mechanisms) a small amount of funding to a new non-profit that delivered used furniture to needy households. And, of course, there was always the relentless pressure from land developers to approve their proposed projects.[26] It was my understanding that much of the pressure to approve multi-unit apartment structures came from outside investors who were associated with real estate investment trusts. Confident they could achieve steady returns of 2–3 percent, they had been eagerly investing in the construction of such buildings even though citywide rental vacancy rates had been increasing substantially over the past couple of years.

One of the worst surprises occurred during the public comment period of our May 7 formal meeting, when three evangelical Christian white men affiliated with a church in Davenport, Iowa, told us how much they loved us as neighbors but then roundly condemned us for permitting "abortuaries" to "murder unborn neighbors" in our city.[27] They told us we should do "what is right and just," ignore the U.S. Supreme Court's decision in *Roe vs. Wade*, and end the slaughter of unborn children. "This Council has been appointed by God," one of them said, and "Your job as a governmental official appointed by God … is to make the vile practice of abortion illegal in Iowa City." One of them said we should do what, in his view, we had done with regard to "sanctuary cities" by not enforcing federal law. Apparently traumatized by what they were hearing, at least two women in the audience of 70 or so people fled the room as the men were speaking. As the second man began addressing us, I noticed that two other men were video-recording the event. I thought: Oh, I get it, they are trying to goad us into responding intemperately so that they can capture our responses on video and use them for their own purposes. I responded as calmly and respectfully as I could.

The most exciting surprise occurred early in October when we learned that the inspirational 16-year-old Swedish climate activist Greta Thunberg would be visiting Iowa City to participate in a climate strike on October 4. With only 2 days' notice, our City staff enabled her and other strikers to speak to the public at a prominent intersection downtown. I had the opportunity to introduce her to a crowd of 4,000–5,000 people. Looking at the joyful, excited, and hopeful faces of students, parents, and other adults in the crowd and hearing them react to Greta and what she said, I finally knew that we had a strong constituency for climate action (see Figure 4.3). Fully aware of threats that had been posted online about her, our police officers did a superb job of ensuring she was able to speak safely. I was very pleased to have the opportunity to introduce her. There is something very special about this young woman. Her visit occurred not long after she had sailed across the Atlantic Ocean and spoken to the U.S. Congress. This is the stuff from which myths are made.

Preparing for the November 2019 Council Elections

Inevitably, much thought and many conversations oriented around which of the four original Core Four might seek reelection in November, and who else might offer themselves as candidates. I encouraged the three other members who had been elected in 2015 to seek reelection, while saying I would announce my own intentions after we adopted the budget and CIP in mid-March.

As in 2018, I had been trying, partly for health reasons, to pace myself well and to spend most of my time following through on our prior initiatives, continuing to meet with diverse members of the public, and responding to unexpected events. But I became more fully aware in 2019 of limits on my personal time, ability, energy, and health. I was clearly feeling worn down by the sniping on social media, by the grinding rhythm of preparing for long meetings, by the

FIGURE 4.3 Greta Thunberg inspiring a crowd in downtown Iowa City.
Source: Photo by author, October 4, 2019.

emotional stress of responding to personally negative criticism from political allies, by the lack of big, exhilarating successes, by my deteriorating health and consequent need to meet with doctors, and by other personal matters. After thinking about it long and hard, I concluded that, despite feeling proud of the work we had been doing, and despite wanting to see our new policies and initiatives continued and improved, I needed to step down at the end of my term. With that decision made, I privately informed council members, key City staff, key supporters, and other local officials and then made a public announcement at the end of our council meeting in late April.

In late June, I was surprised to learn that one of the Core Four (Rockne C.) would also not be seeking reelection. Conversely, the other two who had been elected to district seats (Pauline T. and John T.) would be. Three women quickly declared their intentions to seek election to the two at-large positions. I had had lengthy conversations with all of them and felt confident that they were well prepared to become good council members, but I could not yet discern whether they would continue our effort to build a more inclusive, just, and sustainable city, or where they stood on the most controversial development projects. Late in August, we learned that the two incumbents would face no opposition, and that only the three women had filed as candidates for the two at-large positions. On November 5, Laura B. (a young member of former mayor Matt H.'s law firm) and Janice W. (a retired member of the U.S. Foreign Service who also happened to be Jewish) were elected. For the first time in Iowa City's history, the council would consist of five women and two men. They and the five incumbents would decide which of the new council's seven members would become Iowa City's next mayor. Susan M., Bruce T., and Pauline T. let it be known they were interested, but it was not clear at the end of the year whether any of them would be able to obtain the necessary four votes. Mazahir S. indicated she would like to become the next mayor pro tem.

Every End Is a Beginning

On December 17, I chaired my last work session and formal meeting. Those meetings were roughly the 200th set of such meetings I had participated in over 8 years and roughly the 100th I had chaired as mayor. Good words were exchanged all around during the council meetings, during a public reception, and during a private meeting I had with key City staff. It felt like a bittersweet moment, but one that was necessary. It was time to let go and turn things over to younger people. Near the end of the year, I told a friend, "I feel like I am gradually becoming invisible, but that's okay. It's the way it should be." In interviews, news reporters asked me what it had been like to serve as mayor over the past 4 years. I typically told them it had been very hard and stressful, but also very rewarding. I could not claim I had done everything right. Far from it. But I had done the best I could, and I felt very good about that. Inevitably, people would ask, what are you going to do after your term ends? I often responded with cavalier ambivalence, but I knew I first needed to rest and spend more time with my wife, children, and two very young granddaughters. Beyond that, I planned to find ways to share what I had learned with other scholars, with other mayors, with other people who are interested in the quality of city governance, and with people who live in the Iowa City area.

There was no doubt in my mind that much of the stress and exhaustion I had been feeling traced back to the increasing polarization, chaos, and incompetence manifested at the national level. Like many other Americans, I had been feeling in a state of shock ever since the fall of 2016 when it first seemed possible that Donald Trump would be elected president. For me, it felt like experiencing post-traumatic stress disorder day after day for 3.5 years. In my view, the president was acting increasingly like an authoritarian ruler who sought to achieve his ambitions—regardless of how morally corrupt, how unmoored from reality, and how subversive of the U.S. Constitution those ambitions were—solely through presidential emergency powers (Stevenson, 2019). To me, it was clear that he was intentionally hammering a wedge between us in Iowa City and his supporters in the rest of Iowa, not to mention between people like me and his base in other parts of the country. He was treating those of us who were not white, not conservative evangelical Christians, and not his supporters as communists, as people who hate their country, or as people who should, in his words, "go back and help fix the totally broken and crime infested places from which they came" (Rogers and Fandos, 2019). As best I could tell, many of his supporters wanted to transform the United States into a theocratic state dominated by white Christian people of European descent, with a president having near-authoritarian power to do what he pleased (Barr, 2019). If successful, the president's ambitions and actions would make it impossible to govern Iowa City skillfully, inclusively, and compassionately.

Because the 2020 presidential nomination would begin with the Iowa caucuses in January 2020, candidates for the Democratic Party's nomination started flooding the state and our city after the November 2018 elections. As mayor of a Democratic Party stronghold in Iowa, I had ample opportunities to observe, meet, and talk with almost all of the major candidates. Once my term as mayor ended, I expected to do everything I could to ensure the best possible candidate would be nominated and elected.

Notes

1 I understood the council would be adopting this as the guiding purpose of the 2016–2017 Strategic Plan. I understood "inclusive" to mean, first, acknowledging the increasing diversity of Iowa City's population; second, altering City practices to ensure the full range of city residents could participate in developing City policies and programs; and modifying City policies and programs to help the full range of residents thrive in the city.

2 Grooms and Boamah (2018) examine advocacy planning (upon which my use of "the Just City" was partly based) through a lens provided by political-economic urban governance theories, especially Molotch's (1976) "growth machine." My thinking about advocacy planning derived primarily from planning theorist Paul Davidoff (1965).

3 My use of "path dependency" was based on Sorensen (2015) and Pierson (2004). According to Sorensen, "The core idea of 'path dependence' is that, once established, some institutions tend to become increasingly difficult to change over time, and so small choices early on can have significant long-term impacts" (Sorensen, 2015, p. 21). With regard to land development in a city, this means a city's transformation risks being a resultant of the enduring power of prior decisions. According to Sorensen, in the worst case, such a process can produce a "rigidity trap" that inexorably leads to the "predictable surprise" of catastrophe. The practical challenge is, therefore, to figure out how to take advantage of "critical junctures" and turn away from such destructive paths, step-by-step.

4 The housing complex needed renovation, and only about half of the complex's 410 apartments were occupied; however, the 140 or so households required to move were among the most vulnerable households in the city. As a *legal* matter, the tenants were not being evicted; however, they would be required to vacate their apartments not later than the expiration dates of their leases. For details about how severely evictions can harm tenants, see Desmond (2017).

5 In the spring of 2014, I had met with a group of refugee/immigrant kids in a City high school English Language Learner (ELL) class. This visit had made me realize that the number of Congolese refugees had been increasing significantly, and that many of them lived in the South District. I needed to find some way to

connect with them and with the city's growing population of Sudanese immigrants. This realization was reinforced by a report from the Iowa City Community School District (2015) which indicated that, in 2014–2015, the number of ELL students had basically doubled over the previous 2 years to 1,100 students. More than 50 languages were spoken by students, with Spanish, Arabic, Swahili, Chinese, and French being the most predominant. The increase in ELL students contributed to a larger demographic shift: almost 20 percent of the district's K–12 students were African-American, 7 percent were Asian-American, 8 percent were Hispanic, and 0.3 percent were American Indian. The total minority population (slightly over 35 percent) was 3 percent higher than it had been in 2011–2012 and was considerably larger than it was for Iowa as a whole (23 percent).

6 The Iowa City Housing Authority also managed approximately 1,100 Section 8 housing vouchers, but the waiting list for vouchers was long.

7 Opticos's work in the South District derived from an updated South District Plan, which the council adopted in October, 2015. I had pushed pretty hard in 2014 to have that plan updated and to ensure there would be a reasonably diverse mix of students at the new school. To achieve that diverse mix, we would have to do more than listen only to property owners, developers, and the small number of current residents in the area. We would also need to imagine who the future residents/users of the school's neighborhood might be. Consequently, I especially liked the updated plan's references to the possibility of including missing-middle-type housing in the south district. (For insight into "imagined users," see Ivory, 2013.)

8 To the best of my knowledge, there is no precise legal definition of a "sanctuary city." However, the term generally refers to a city that limits its cooperation with federal immigration enforcement agents in order to protect low-priority undocumented immigrants from deportation, while still turning over those who have committed serious crimes. For an exploratory study about ways in which recent narratives have influenced the development of public policy toward sanctuary cities, see McBeth and Lybecker (2018).

9 In late July, the U.S. Senate failed to repeal the Affordable Care Act by a 49:51 vote.

10 For details about their claims and my responses, see Throgmorton (2017d).

11 On August 2, 2017, Charlottesville, Virginia., was the site of a Unite the Right rally by armed white supremacists and neo-Nazis who brandished swastikas, Confederate battle flags, anti-Semitic banners, and "Trump/Pence" signs while chanting "blood and soil." The rally led to fighting in the streets and the death of a young woman and the injury of 19 other people after a gray Dodge Challenger driven by a Nazi sympathizer rammed into a group of counter-protesters. This led me to write a guest opinion condemning hate speech (Throgmorton 2017e).

12 Being located within walking distance of the university, these older (and sometimes historic) neighborhoods face extreme market pressure from students who want to rent units located near the university and from developers and investors who want to meet that demand by converting owner-occupied structures to rental housing. The new ordinance placed a cap on the percentage of single-family and duplex structures for rent in neighborhoods. In neighborhoods that exceeded the cap, no new conversions to rental housing would be permitted. Conversions would be permitted in all other parts of the city until such time as the percentage cap was exceeded.

13 As noted previously, property tax reforms the state legislature adopted in 2013 had many consequences for Iowa City. One key consequence of the reforms was to give owners of multi-family student-oriented housing substantial property tax benefits. I could see no reason to believe those tax reductions would be passed along to students.

14 Benjamin R. Barber (2014) argued that city mayors, singly and jointly, were responding to transnational problems more effectively than nation-states mired in

ideological infighting and sovereign rivalries. However, he understated the extent to which cities, at least in the U.S., are creatures of state governments and have no powers other than ones granted to them by their various states.

15 The MIP meeting in Burlington, Vermont, might have been the best of hundreds of conferences I have attended. It was very intimate and very focused on topics of direct contemporary interest to mayors and cities. The many face-to-face conversations I had with other mayors felt especially fruitful.

16 The city manager's memo can be found at: www.iowa-city.org/WebLink/DocView.aspx?id=1816145&dbid=0&repo=CityofIowaCity

17 John T. was heavily influenced by the work of "Strong Towns" advocate Charles L. Marohn, Jr. See: www.strongtowns.org/

18 Several weeks before the tour began, pursuant to an invitation from Henri H., I made a lengthy invited keynote speech at the Civil Rights Tour fundraising banquet.

19 One of the sites we visited was the recently opened Legacy Museum in Montgomery. A "narrative museum," it tells the history of black Americans from enslavement, through the "Jim Crow" era of lynching and racial segregation, through the heroic actions of the Civil Rights Movement, to the present moment of mass incarceration and retrenchment. Its founder, Bryan Stevenson (2014) is the widely acclaimed public interest lawyer and author of *Just Mercy*.

20 On February 14, 17 students were murdered at Douglas High School in Parkland, Florida. Five days later, City, West, and Southeast Jr. High students marched to the Pentacrest in downtown Iowa City demanding effective gun control. On October 27, a shooter murdered 11 Jewish people at the Tree of Life Synagogue in Pittsburgh because they were Jews and because the president had been inflaming the passions of his base with lies and incitements. I was one of several people who spoke to about 400 people at a vigil held in their memory at the University of Iowa's Iowa Memorial Union.

21 Shortly after receiving the application for rezoning 12 Court Street, we also received a consultant's report concerning historic preservation in the downtown. It recommended that we create a new district that would become part of the National Register of Historic Places.

22 Early in 2019, I read planning scholar Michael Batty's (2018) *Inventing Future Cities*. His work, which is rooted in complexity theory, had a significant effect on my thinking.

23 By this time, the City's planning staff had stabilized considerably. Two or three outstanding new senior planners had been hired and had immediately begun doing excellent work.

24 Early in October, an out-of-state developer of upscale student housing projects proposed a new 400-bed project for a site in the RFC District. Rezoning would enable him to build a four-story structure, but he indicated he would be applying for the maximum permissible height bonus. Much like the 12 Court Street project, and for similar reasons, the same 4:3 majority of the council indicated it favored the requested bonuses.

25 MidAmerican provides almost all of the electric power and natural gas used in Iowa City and accounts for well over half of the city's CO_2 emissions. But it has made a major shift toward generating electric power with renewable energy since the mid-2010s. In 2019, 61.3 percent of the electric energy it generated came from renewable sources, especially wind (www.midamericanenergy.com/nr-2019renewable). The university's power plant accounts for another 15 percent. City government has no authority over either of these entities. Moreover, state government had preempted the ability of local governments to adopt energy efficiency standards stricter than the state's Energy Code.

26 In August, the council's Economic Development Committee received a public briefing about a proposed 11-story building, which would be set back from the Pedestrian Mall downtown. It would be the first major test of the TIF amendments we adopted in 2017 and it would produce the kinds of "exceptional public benefits" on which I had staked so much political capital.

27 The transcript of this meeting can be found at: www.iowa-city.org/WebLink/DocView.aspx?id=1868910&dbid=0&repo=CityofIowaCity

References

Arnold, M. (2017), "Iowa City Council unanimously approves resolution concerning local police, immigration enforcement", *The Gazette* (January 17); available at: www.thegazette.com/subject/news/government/iowa-city-council-unanimously-approves-resolution-concerning-local-police-immigration-enforcement-20170117 (last accessed January 5, 2021).

Barber, B. R. (2014), *If Mayors Ruled the World*, Yale University Press, New Haven (CT).

Barr, W. P. (2019), "Attorney General William P. Barr delivers remarks to the Law School and the de Nicola Center for Ethics and Culture at the University of Notre Dame", (October 11); available at: www.justice.gov/opa/speech/attorney-general-william-p-barr-delivers-remarks-law-school-and-de-nicola-center-ethics20190306 (last accessed January 5, 2021).

Batty, M. (2018), *Inventing Future Cities*, MIT Press, Cambridge (MA).

City of Iowa City (2013), IC2030 Comprehensive Plan Update, Iowa City (IA); available at: www8.iowa-city.org/weblink/0/edoc/1965450/Comprehensive%20Plan%20Updated%2010.2020.pdf (last accessed January 3, 2021).

City of Iowa City (2018), Presentation by Axion Consulting during a public hearing before the City Council on May 29; available at: www.iowa-city.org/WebLink/DocView.aspx?id=1788122&dbid=0&repo=CityofIowaCity (last accessed October 29, 2021).

City of Iowa City (2019), Accelerating Iowa City's climate actions, Iowa City (IA); available at: www8.iowa-city.org/WebLink?0/edoc/1898237/100%20Report-Nov.2019.pdf (last accessed January 5, 2021).

Davidoff, P. (1965), "Advocacy and pluralism in planning", *Journal of the American Institute of Planners*, v. 31, n. 4, pp. 331–338.

Davis, A. (2016), "Council delves into affordable housing action plan", *Des Moines Register* (September 20); available at: www.desmoinesregister.com/story/news/local/2016/09/20/council-delves-into-affordable-housing-action-plan/90742194/20190306 (last accessed December 21, 2020).

Davis, A. and Hines, H. (2016), "Trump protestors shut down I-80 in Iowa City", *Iowa City Press-Citizen*. (November 11); available at: www.press-citizen.com/story/news/2016/11/11/city-high-students-walkout-march-downtown-protest-iowa-city-donald-trump/93661796/ (last accessed December 21, 2020).

Desmond, M. (2017), *Evicted: Poverty and Profit in the American City*, Broadway Books, New York (NY).

Frum, D. (2017), "How to build an autocracy", *The Atlantic* (March); available at: www.theatlantic.com/magazine/archive/2017/03/how-to-build-an-autocracy/513872/ (last accessed December 21, 2020).

Iowa City Community School District (2015), "Enrollment Projections Report for the District", Iowa City (IA).

Iowa City Downtown District Board (2016), "ICDD responds to mayor's memo", *Iowa City Press-Citizen* (October 8), p. 7A.

Ivory, C. (2013), "The role of the imagined user in planning and design narratives", *Planning Theory*, v. 12, n. 4, pp. 425–441.

Gramlich, J. 2020. "What the data says (and doesn't say) about crime in the United States." Pew Research Center (November 20); available at: www.pewresearch.org/fact-tank/2020/11/20/facts-about-crime-in-the-u-s/ (last accessed April 23, 2021).

Grooms, W. and Boamah, E. F. (2018), "Towards a political urban planning: Learning from growth machine theory and advocacy planning to 'plannitize' urban politics", *Planning Theory*, v. 17, n. 2, pp. 213–233.

Hambleton, R. (2014), *Leading the Inclusive City: Place-Based Innovation for a Bounded Planet*, University of Chicago Press, Chicago (IL).

Intergovernmental Panel on Climate Change (2018), "Special report on global warming of 1.5°C"; available at: www.ipcc.ch/sr15/ (last accessed on April 10, 2019).

McBeth, M. K. and Lybecker, D. L. (2018), "The narrative policy framework, agendas, and sanctuary cities: The construction of a public problem", *Policy Studies Journal*, v. 46, n. 4, pp. 868–893.

MacLean, N. (2017), *Democracy in Chains: The Deep History of the Radical Right's Stealth Plan for America*, Viking, New York (NY).

Mims, S. (2018), "The Iowa City council is halting valuable housing projects because they don't like tall buildings", *Little Village* (June 15); available at: https://littlevillagemag.com/letter-to-the-editor-susan-mims-city-council-riverfront-crossings/ (last accessed on December 30, 2020).

Molotch, H. (1976), "The city as a growth machine: Toward a political economy of place", *American Journal of Sociology*, v. 82, n. 2, pp. 309–332.

Petroski, W. and Pfannenstiel B. (2018), "Iowa bill punishing 'sanctuary cities' headed to governor's desk. But will any cities actually be affected?", *Des Moines Register* (April 4); available at: www.desmoinesregister.com/story/news/politics/2018/04/04/sanctuary-cities-iowa-bill-passes-iowa-senate-sent-governor-kim-reynolds-illegal-immigration/484463002/ (last accessed on January 5, 2021).

Pierson, P. (2004), *Politics in Time: History, Institutions, and Social Analysis*, Princeton University Press, Princeton (NJ).

Rogers, K. and Fandos, N. (2019), "In a Twitter rant, Trump goes after rogue Democrats," *New York Times* (July 15), p. 1.

Snyder, T. (2017), *On Tyranny: Twenty Lessons from the Twentieth Century*, Tim Duggan Books, New York (NY).

Sorensen, A. (2015), "Taking path dependence seriously: An historical institutionalist research agenda in planning history", *Planning Perspectives*, v. 30, n. 1, pp. 17–38.

Stevenson, B. (2014), *Just Mercy: A Story of Justice and Redemption*, Spiegel & Grau, New York (NY).

Stevenson, J. (2019), "A different kind of emergency", *The New York Review of Books*, v. 66, n. 9, pp. 24–26.

Throgmorton, J. A. (2015), "2 contending visions for Iowa City's future", *Iowa City Press-Citizen*, (April 8), 11A.

Throgmorton, J. A. (2016a), "Propose changes consistent with voters' values", *The Gazette*, (January 5), 5A.

Throgmorton, J. A. (2016b), "State of the city", speech presented during an Iowa City city council meeting, (February 16).

Throgmorton, J. A. (2016c). "Throgmorton lays out development future in memo", *Iowa City Press-Citizen*, (September 3), p. 7A; available at: www.press-citizen.com/story/opinion/contributors/guest-editorials/2016/09/02/throgmorton-lays-out-development-future-memo/89781674/ (last accessed on January 9, 2021).

Throgmorton, J. A. (2017a), "State of the city", speech presented during an Iowa City city council meeting, (February 21).

Throgmorton, J. A. (2017b), "Local planning and governing in a Trumped up age." Presented at the annual conference of the Association of European Schools of Planning, Lisbon, Portugal (July 10–14).

Throgmorton, J.A. (2017c), "Paradise in the wreckage of war", Iowa City *Press-Citizen* (May 12); available at: www.press-citizen.com/story/opinion/2017/05/12/paradise-wreckage-war/313719001/ (last accessed on December 21, 2020).

Throgmorton, J. A. (2017d), "Iowa City's actions protect public safety", *Des Moines Register* (February 2); available at: www.desmoinesregister.com/story/opinion/contributors/guest-editorials/2017/02/02/iowa-citys-actions-protect-public-safety/97404650/ (last accessed on December 21, 2020).

Throgmorton, J. A. (2017e), "Mayor: We reject hate speech, violence." *Iowa City Press-Citizen* (August 19), p. 7A.

Throgmorton, J. A. (2018a), "State of the city", speech presented during an Iowa City city council meeting, (February 20).

Throgmorton, J. A. (2018b), "Tour brings dark events in American history to life." *Iowa City Press-Citizen* (July 21), p. 6A.

Throgmorton, J A. (2018c), "Memo to council: Proposed conditions for 12 Court Street rezoning", (June 28).

Throgmorton, J. A. (2018d), "Storytelling, city crafting, and place making in a contested age", Invited presentation at Aalto University, Helsinki, Finland (August 15).

Throgmorton, J. A. (2018e), "Memo to council: Height bonuses for Pentacrest Gardens", (November 15).

Throgmorton, J. A. (2019), "State of the city", speech presented during an Iowa City city council meeting, (February 19).

Trump, D. (2016), "Remarks of President Donald J. Trump—As prepared for delivery. Inaugural Address" (January 2).

5
TWO DAYS IN THE LIFE OF A MAYOR

This chapter steps back in time, first to the spring of 2015, when I began my campaign for reelection, and then to two days in May 2019.

Recall that, when announcing my campaign for reelection, I said I wanted to build on what was already great about Iowa City and help lead it toward becoming a more just city. For me, a more just city would be one that is good on the ground for all its residents, both now and in the future. Several months later, after being elected mayor, I joined other council members in adopting a new Strategic Plan for the city which indicated we intended to foster a more inclusive, just, and sustainable city. Based on that Strategic Plan and its priorities, we adopted a budget and a capital improvements plan and started acting on the Strategic Plan's priorities.

As indicated earlier in this book, I gradually began to think that cities unfold with multiple human and non-human actants being part of a never-ending and very complicated process of co-crafting the direction the unfolding will take. Moreover, I thought that mayors can play an important role in co-crafting their cities' unfolding, with persuasive storytelling being one of their primary tools, but that the direction a city will unfold cannot be predicted or formally planned.

With this perspective in mind, I thought that every step I took as mayor should be, as much as it could be, a step toward producing a more inclusive, just, and sustainable city. As I repeatedly told people over my 4 years as mayor, that is my north star. What would this principle mean on a day-to-day basis, and how well would I be able to live it out? I decided to take careful notes on two days early in 2019 to generate partial answers to those questions.

DOI: 10.4324/9781003160991-5

March 6, 2019

It was a rough night of sleep. I awoke around 3:30 a.m. thinking about yesterday's big fire at Hieronymus Square's construction site. The fire occurred around 3 p.m. the previous day, but I didn't learn about it until about a half an hour into it. Strong winds caused the fire to spread rapidly. Happily, our firefighters got there very quickly and, despite encountering strong winds and brutally cold temperatures, efficiently ended the blaze (Arnold, 2019). But the fire caused lots of damage, and it's not yet clear what it means for completion of the $42 million project. While trying to sleep, my mind kept moving back and forth from the big fire to the interpersonal difficulties I'm having with the newest member of our city council, and then to a form pertaining to my University of Iowa retirement account that I needed to sign within the next 3 days or else pay a large penalty. Just couldn't get back to sleep. Every time I turned over, I felt cold. (At nighttime, we set our thermostat at 58 degrees to minimize our use of natural gas.) But eventually I drifted back to sleep.

Six in the morning. Time to get up, have coffee and a bagel with my wife Barbara, clean up, get dressed, and drive to KXIC Radio's studio just north of Interstate 80 for Jerry L.'s morning show. This interview is something each member of our city council does roughly once every 7 or 8 weeks, and I've done 50 or so such interviews over the past 7 years.

Before talking with Jerry, I quickly skimmed my calendar to remind myself of what I've been doing over the past several days. Jerry wouldn't be very interested in hearing about the annual check-up with my urologist, or my efforts to assemble information for a forthcoming meeting with a tax consultant, so I focused on what I had done as mayor. I had met with a city councilman about where parking "cut-outs" should be located near Horace Mann Elementary School, which is currently being renovated and expanded and is located adjacent to North Market Square neighborhood park; met with members of the Refugee Alliance; met with the two University of Iowa undergraduate student liaisons to the city council; and met with an applicant for the Public Library's Board of Trustees. I talked with the city manager about a range of topics, including: making sure the City staff was well prepared to respond to flooding; learning where things currently stood with regard to updating our Affordable Housing Action Plan; and discussing how to respond to bills in the Iowa House and Senate. One of the bills would preempt our ability to use the "rental cap" program we adopted 18 months ago in response to a prior preemption. The city manager and I also reviewed a possible major project downtown. This project would, if pursued by the developer, be the first test of the TIF policy amendments we adopted 1.5 years ago. I also attended a meeting of Solarize Johnson County; met with two likely candidates for city council; attended the local Chamber of Commerce's annual banquet; met with the director of the Downtown District; discussed a variety of issues with another council member; attended the Crisis Center's annual Pancake Breakfast; attended the Black Voices Project's annual Soul Food Dinner; attended a couple of events involving presidential candidate Pete Buttigieg; sat in on a meeting of our Climate Action Advisory Board; co-chaired a meeting of the City–University Partnership for Alcohol Safety; and joined City staff and another council member in a phone conversation with the head of Opticos about a possible FBC for the North Marketplace area.

Guess what Jerry and I discussed first at KXIC. That's right: the big fire. I praised our fire chief and the firefighters who stemmed the blaze, especially one firefighter who climbed a tall construction crane to help the crane operator descend safely. I told listeners what I knew about the fire, its causes, and immediate consequences, but I also expressed my empathy for the owners of the property and the construction firm. Following that, I read aloud a headline from today's *Press-Citizen* and roundly condemned the cowardly or sadly misinformed person or people who had inscribed a swastika and racist sentiments on the exterior of the Church of the Nazarene. The building houses not just the church but also the offices of IC Compassion, which is a non-profit organization trying to help Congolese, Sudanese, and other refugees adjust to life in Iowa City and the United States. I told Jerry and his audience that I was saddened and outraged that some people in our city and state would be scribbling swastikas on a building here after almost 417,000 American soldiers had lost their lives fighting against Nazis and Fascists in World War II. Jerry and I then turned toward a local controversy concerning our plans to convert Mormon Trek Boulevard on the west side of town from four to three lanes, with bike lanes on both sides of the road and with the center lane being reserved for turning vehicles. Jerry expressed the views of many people he talks with on his show. In their view, this four-to-three-lane "road diet" is a very bad idea. The primary purpose, I said, is to enhance public safety by reducing the number and severity of crashes and collisions, most of which are caused by vehicles travelling over the speed limit or turning left from one of the two center lanes. And so on. Jerry wanted to make sure afterwards that I hadn't taken any of his vigorous questioning personally. Nope, I said. It was stimulating, plus the emotional intensity signals how strongly some people feel about the issue. We concluded by briefly discussing bills being "fast-tracked" in the Iowa House and Senate, which would compel us to rescind the rental cap program we had adopted 18 months ago. So much for local control.

After talking with Jerry, I drove to a coffee shop which I like to use when I'm on the east side of town. It seemed as though almost every street was littered with potholes. Owing largely to snow, ice, and extremely cold weather, they are springing up like crocuses. Checked email. The amount of relevant email I receive varies a lot from day to day; I use it mainly to be accessible to constituents and to schedule meetings. Yesterday, I received a completely unexpected invitation from the mayor of Baghdad, Iraq, to attend its annual Festival of Flowers in mid-April. I'm not sure what I want to do in response. I need to talk with the city manager and the director of the University of Iowa's International Writing Program. He and I had an extraordinary visit to Baghdad almost 2 years ago, but I'm not sure I want to try it again. Regardless of how fascinating and rewarding that visit was, it was also very hard on me, both physically and emotionally.

I also put some thought into how to respond to the unique challenge one of our newest city council members (Mazahir S.) poses, at least for me. Just a few days ago, she told the city manager she wanted to amend our proposed budget for Fiscal Year 2020 by transforming 38 hourly/part-time City positions into permanent positions with benefits by increasing the employee benefits levy. The city manager reminded her via email that state law requires us to formally adopt the budget not later than March 15, and that the council had already directed him to analyze the positions and consider how specific changes might affect the organization, current hourly employees, and current permanent employees. He also presented her with a process by which the council could amend the budget after it was adopted. This led Mazahir to claim that specific council members and staff had misled her. After I responded that no one had intentionally been misleading her, she indicated that, as a new council member, she hadn't been given the support required to accomplish her job. Whether this was intentional or not, she added, this kind of thing had been happening all the time. The city manager responded that he had been very clear about the schedule and deadline during our last few public meetings. She did not agree and basically told the city manager that he had not been clear enough, at least not to her, a minority council member who needed support to understand City rules and regulations. She urged the city manager to recognize that she does not understand everything as easily as council members who were born in the U.S. and know a lot about how things work. In her view, the City needed to adopt a new way of dealing with people like her when they have been elected: the Iowa City community was changing, and the City must adapt to include and welcome all the people of Iowa City.

If this email exchange had been the first conflict over process, I wouldn't find it to be so problematic. But similar conflicts have occurred over the 15 months since she came onto the council, and I have not been able to find a mutually satisfactory way to improve the situation. It has caused me to do considerable soul searching.

I see this troublesome situation as being neither her fault nor mine, but a challenge that the two of us face together.[1] As best I can tell, our disagreements over several City-related topics have not been over values or policy, but have instead involved overlapping differences in gender, race, ethnicity, and experience with governing. She is a female, a person of color, a Muslim immigrant from Sudan, a 20-year resident of the city, and a smart and educated person who speaks English well enough but often appears not to track what City staff and other council members write or say to her. She also has very little experience working within governmental bodies and often demands that we do what she advocates and takes personal affront when a majority does not. On the other hand, I have never been a female, a person of color, an immigrant or refugee, or a follower of Islam. But I have learned a lot about how hard it is for immigrants and refugees who have limited command of English to live and work in our city, and I am fully persuaded that we need to alter many City codes and practices to facilitate their participation in city governance. I have also learned through experience how confounding it can feel to be a novice council member. I know what it feels like to advocate actions but have the council majority either ignore me or else make only modest changes in response to them. And, as a person who has had a great deal of training and experience with regard to policy-making in general and local politics and governance in particular, I know how difficult it can be to co-craft a decision that at least a majority of the council can support. She and I need to meet privately and find a mutually agreeable way to proceed. But we can't do that in the short run because she will soon be visiting her family in Sudan.[2]

I couldn't think about that anymore right then. While at the coffee shop, I also thought a bit more about a welcoming speech I will be making next week at the United Nations Association of Johnson County's Night of 1,000 Dinners. The idea is a good one: to celebrate the contributions women from diverse backgrounds have made over the years. I also plan to read a proclamation declaring International Women's Day and Women's History Month at our meeting next Tuesday night, but I've been struggling with a draft the organizers sent me. If I am going to read it, I have to feel comfortable with its language. But this draft feels too nationalistic and essentialized: it focuses too much on what *American* women have done and seems unaware that many women have actively opposed many of the actions the proclamation praises.

Time to leave. I had to drive home to feed my dog and cats, let the dog out and back in, and then drive to City Hall for a regular weekly meeting with the city manager and the mayor pro tem. We had many topics to discuss, including: the big fire and its implications, the possible trip to Baghdad, conflicts with Mazahir, and a bill in the legislature that would dampen the use of solar PV arrays on private homes and businesses to the benefit of electric power utilities such as MidAmerican Energy, which provides most of the electric energy used in Iowa City. I also wanted to learn about a project the city manager has been working on with MidAmerican: to possibly sell or lease 3–5 acres of City-owned land to the utility as a site for a large utility-owned PV array. That led me to express concerns about the University of Iowa's tentative plan to contract with a private firm to manage the university's power plant for the next 50 years. This is a very worrisome idea, I told him, and I think the Climate Action Advisory Board will be telling us why in a forthcoming letter. Shifting to another topic, we discussed a developer's proposal to preserve a historic building at 400 N. Clinton Street if we will approve a higher-density apartment building on property next to it. I agreed with the city manager that we should schedule a March 12 work session discussion about this possibility. We ended the meeting with the city manager walking us through the tentative schedule of future work sessions and then through the formal meeting agenda for the night of March 12. There are many items on that agenda, including adoption of the proposed FY 2020 budget and the CIP for 2019–2023, but, on the whole, it's not too complicated. The work session is likely to be much more difficult, partly because Mazahir S. will almost certainly demand that we amend the budget before we adopt it. (Later, I remembered that she would be in Tunisia that night. Because she is the first Sudanese-American member of a city council in the U.S., Tunisians had invited her to talk with them about her experiences.)

After the meeting, I asked the mayor pro tem to chat briefly. Picking up on a brief conversation she and I had had at the Soul Food Dinner a couple of nights ago, I wanted to respond more forthrightly to her rhetorical question: "You do intend to run for reelection, don't you?" I wanted to tell her that it was highly unlikely that I would seek reelection, primarily because the past 7 years, especially the past 3 years as mayor, have taken a big toll on my physical and emotional health. It's not an easy decision, I said. Enacting the role of mayor can feel tremendously rewarding: I am very proud of the good work we have done and I don't want to see the council slip back to where it was 4 years ago. But it's been very hard on my health, and I don't want to die in office like our friend on the Board of Supervisors did. I also wanted to be clear with her that, yes, I had been speaking with a woman who is likely to be candidate for city council in the fall, but, should that person run against the mayor pro tem for the district she serves, I would not support the other person. The mayor pro tem praised the work I have been doing, and then we talked briefly about the likelihood that some people in her district would vote against her because of their opposition to the four-to-three-lane conversion on Mormon Trek.

Time to go. I had to drop some donated items off at Trinity Episcopal Church for my wife and then drive to the north end of town for an appointment with my eye doctor. I have macular degeneration and have been having medicine injected into my eyes every 6–12 weeks for the past 4 or so years. I'd be blind in both eyes by now were it not for those injections. I always feel down emotionally while having the injections and immediately afterwards. They are part of the physical deterioration I have been experiencing for the past several years. Another part has to do with my feet. I have Reynaud's Syndrome, and chilblains in several of my toes become especially severe during the winter and make it painful to walk. Moreover, I have arthritis in the big joint of the big toe on my left foot. That has made it effectively impossible for me to jog as I had been doing until about a year ago. And then there's the prostate cancer, for which I had an operation 9 years ago. Happily, I have started swimming laps at the City's Robert A. Lee Recreation Center downtown. It's a terrific pool with a wonderfully sunny view looking south out a big array of windows. Swimming is such great whole-body exercise. I love it.

I drove back downtown to have a light lunch at the Bread Garden on the Pedestrian Mall and then a cool drink at Prairie Lights bookstore while letting my eyes recover. Much to my surprise, I ran into a friend who is a professor at Dortmund University in Germany. We had a very pleasing chat about his work and mine, and about how things are going politically in Germany. Not good, he said: things are drifting to the Right.

Checking email again. Thankfully, there were no big surprises. I typed a few notes about the day and then had a couple of beers with my friends Dirk M. and Dan L. at Joe's Place downtown. We try to do this about once every quarter. It feels good to just talk with them about what they have been doing, reading, and writing. Dirk wanted to know whether I would be seeking reelection. I told them not to be surprised if I do not.

To home I drove. Had a light vegetarian dinner with Barbara, watched a lengthy episode of a made-for-TV series titled *Vera*, washed dishes, fed the animals, cleaned up, went to bed, and read a few pages from a novel by Pat Barker titled *Life Class*. It is instructive to see how the outbreak of World War I caught her novel's young characters completely by surprise. They had no idea what was coming or what would happen as a result. In that sense, Barker's novel reminded me of Walter Kempowski's *All for Nothing*. In it, minor Prussian nobility living in the East Prussia part of Nazi Germany denied the threat posed by the oncoming Russian army until it was too late to do anything except flee and, in many cases, die.

Looked at my calendar before going to bed, wanting to make sure I know what I have to do tomorrow and the next few days. Looks like a pretty easy day ahead.

March 7, 2019

Awoke around 1:30 a.m. realizing that I had not yet heard back from my investment advisor about the form he needed to notarize and send to TIAA within 2 days. I went downstairs to download the form from TIAA's website so that it could be signed and notarized in the morning. Back to sleep.

After having a light breakfast, cleaning up, and dressing, I drove to High Ground in the North Marketplace area to meet the local Chamber of Commerce's legislative liaison. We had a fruitful exchange of information and views concerning the proposed set of four 15-story buildings at 12 Court Street, the "net metering/grid interconnection" bill MidAmerican Energy is pushing in the state legislature, the Chamber's effort to promote innovation in K–12 education, and our mutual puzzlement over the School District's recently publicized need to cut spending and perhaps as many as 75 jobs.

Drove home to feed our animals and walk our dog. It felt mighty cold outside, partly because there was more humidity in the air. It's just been such a brutally harsh and long winter, so dispiriting for everyone. We have had so much ice and snow that it appears very likely we will experience another flood. The only real question is, how severe will the flooding be? Drove back downtown to buy bagels for the coming week's breakfasts and then to the northeast part of the city to take care of submitting the form to TIAA. Happily, that was a very brief visit. Drove to Billy's High Hat to check email while having lunch. I've had to drive a lot more frequently over the past day and a half than I usually do. Normally, I walk or, when the weather is warmer and the streets less treacherous, ride my bike. After parking my car near City Hall, I walked to the City's Public Library to read some council-related material and follow up on some phone messages. Talked with the director of the International Writing Program (IWP) about the invitation we had received from the mayor of Baghdad. I told him I was inclined not to go for a range of reasons, whereas he told me he would be in Iraq around that time for a different reason and that he could easily go by himself as a representative of Iowa City and the University of Iowa's IWP. Sounds good to me, so long he conveys my appreciation and regrets to the mayor. Ran into a friend at the library. She has been very actively engaged in an effort to get our minds and spirits in the right place for a good life on this planet, and she praised the work I have been doing. Also had a brief chat with the president of Friends of Historic Preservation. While at the library, I also received a phone message from a reporter for KCRG-TV asking if I could be available for a TV interview about the recent neo-Nazi defacement of the Church of the Nazarene's building.

Drove home to feed the critters again, phoned the TV reporter and arranged to meet him at the library around 4:15 p.m., drove back downtown for a cup of coffee at the Bread Garden on the Ped Mall, and then walked a few feet to the library to meet with the reporter. He wanted to know how I felt about the defacement and what I wanted to tell his viewers about it. The interview lasted for about 3 minutes, but I guessed he'd use only 10–20 seconds of it. Immediately after that interview, the reporter and I both went into another room of the library to attend an open house being conducted by University of Iowa urban planning graduate students about their preliminary efforts to help Iowa City devise an autonomous vehicle plan. Their work built on prior work done by another planning student as part of an internship with the City last summer.

Drove home again and discovered that my wife was waiting for me at Moonrakers, which is a small pizza restaurant located just above the 126 Club downtown. I fed the critters, let the dog out and back in, and then drove downtown to meet her at the restaurant. Looking out the window, I could see much more traffic on Washington Street. It was being rerouted from Burlington Street as a consequence of the big fire. Chatted briefly with Matthew, the owner of both restaurants.

After dinner, Barbara and I drove to the University of Iowa's Hancher Auditorium to hear a discussion involving two famous African-American operatic singers, Lawrence Brownlee and Eric Owens, and a hip-hop moderator. The moderator performed a spectacular hip-hop version of one of his poems and then posed a few questions to the singers. I found both of them to be quite impressive and engaging. The more I listened, the more I heard great (if implicit) understanding of, and advice about, the kinds of choices one must make when inhabiting the role of mayor. It's about being confident—primarily as a result of one's years of practice—in one's technical knowledge and skill, but then letting go of thinking about that and focusing instead on being in the moment, listening to and observing closely what others say and how they say it, and responding authentically in the moment. I wish a video and transcript of their dialogue—which is part of the university's Creative Matters series—were available for viewing and reading.

Barbara and I drove home in the dark, both of us feeling quite moved by what we had just heard. I quickly scanned email and found a withering critique of the climate action part of the State of the City speech I had presented on February 19. Under my leadership, the writer said, the City had taken no real action. I see some truth in her critique, but she also completely ignores what we have done and certain key constraints that limit what we can do. I want to provide her with some specific answers to her questions while also filling in those gaps.

I fed the critters, let the dog out and back in, typed some notes, and looked at my schedule for tomorrow. Barbara and I have to meet with our tax consultant in the morning. I think I've compiled all the relevant information, but I'm not sure I've finished adding up some of my deductions. Plus, I've been reading that people are being surprised this year by having smaller refunds or actually owing money, primarily as a result of the federal tax "reforms" adopted late in 2017. I'm also supposed to meet with a University of Iowa dental school graduate student from Syria about the National TPS (Temporary Protected Status) Alliance. I really don't know anything about the Alliance. At 2:15 p.m. I'm supposed to meet the first candidate for the vacant position of the University of Iowa's Vice-President for Diversity, Equity, and Inclusion. Who (s)he is has not yet been announced, and I haven't had a chance to read anything about her/his background. And, at 4 p.m., I'm meeting with a council member and a former county supervisor to discuss the state legislation that is being pushed by MidAmerican. Both of them have very negative opinions about the proposal. Throughout the day, I'll also have to begin skimming through the material we receive pertaining to next Tuesday night's council work session and formal meeting. I've been reading this kind of material every other week for over 7 years. Sometimes, I feel almost ill the moment I begin diving deeply into it. There typically is a substantial amount of material to read, but sometimes the topics are tremendously complicated and require considerable time and thought. For those kinds of issues, I have to do more than simply digest the complex material and formulate my own ideas. I also have to consider how other council members are likely to respond and, depending on how important the issue is, think about how I want to frame our discussion. Being a council member can be very hard work; I can only imagine how much harder it must be for the newest member on our council.

Went to bed. Don't know if I'll be able to fall asleep easily. As any good artist or craftsman or farmer knows, you have to get up every morning and do the work. Over and over, step by step, day after day.

What Do These Two Days Reveal?

At the outset of this chapter, I indicated that I believe every step I take as a mayor should be, as much as it could be, a step toward producing a more inclusive, just, and sustainable city. I asked, what would this mean on a day-to-day basis, and how well would I be able to live it out?

This "two days" narrative amply conveys the essence of co-crafting as I understand it. It entails communicating with a large number and variety of institutional actors (both public and private), engaging in a great deal of inter-jurisdictional coordination and negotiation, having innumerable face-to-face discussions with a wide range of individuals, and adjusting our actions in response to state preemptions. As is the case with this book as a whole, this "two days" narrative focuses on what I was doing and thinking. But many other people and organizations are playing their parts in the co-crafting process, and all of them have their own purposes and perspectives.

It is not just human actors that participate in this co-crafting process. So too do non-human "actants." Consider the fire at Hieronymus Square with which the "two days" narrative begins. Or the swastikas scribbled on the exterior of the Church of the Nazarene. Or the brutally cold winter and potholes in the streets. Or the medicine being injected into my eyes. Although these actants do not have intentions, they do cause human actors to respond.

It is harder to see the step-by-step unfolding of the city, or even parts of it. To see that, one has to know what came before and after several of the conversations and then infer that the conversations themselves might yield changes on the ground. For example, one would need to know what our TIF policy was prior to the amendment we adopted late in 2017, what the amendment required, and what the developer of the major project downtown was proposing. My KXIC interview discussion about the four-to-three-lane conversion on Mormon Trek provides another example. Still another is the discussion with the city manager about preserving the historic building at 400 N. Clinton St. And what about that fire? Would the developers be able to continue construction?

What is much easier to see is how important relationships are in the co-crafting process. Such relationships have to be established, nurtured, and strengthened, and they require continual attention. The "two days" narrative abounds with examples: attending the Chamber's annual meeting, going to the BVP's annual Soul Food Dinner, meeting with the city manager and mayor pro tem, meeting with members of the Partnership for Alcohol Safety, and many others. If not attended to, relationships will wither and possibly die. For me, establishing and strengthening relationships were almost entirely about having face-to-face conversations with people in places they would feel comfortable. Having such conversations was a way of recognizing the other person as a valued member of the Iowa City community, of paying respect, of building mutual trust, and of creating the possibility of meeting again in the future. I typically would greet people warmly, find some comfortable way of sliding into conversation, and then attend carefully to what they said and how they said it. Dialogue was at the heart of these meetings. I tried to learn from them, make it easy for them to learn from me, and be open to having my views changed. I often promised I would take certain actions, but I tried never to promise what the council or City government as a whole would do. And, whenever possible, I tried to help the person I was talking with see connections between her/his interests and those of other individuals and organizations. In other words, I tried to increase collective capacity for collaborative action and, when appropriate, strengthen coalitions for political action. For a mayor to have these kinds of conversations with the diverse array of people in her or his city is to make governance more inclusive and, hence, more democratic.

The "two days" narrative also highlights ways in which a mayor can tell a consistent, ethically sound, persuasive story about the direction in which the city is and should be unfolding. Here I refer to being interviewed at KXIC Radio, speaking to the United Nations Association of Johnson County, revising the proclamation about Women's History Month, being interviewed by the KCRG-TV reporter about the swastikas, praising and inspiring the urban planning grad students, and conversing with all the other individuals mentioned in the tale.

One feature of the narrative might come as surprise. It never refers to meetings taking place in the mayor's office. The explanation for that is simple: Iowa City's mayor does not have an office. Consequently, as I would tell constituents, my office is wherever I am. The lack of an office symbolizes the limited formal power of the mayor in Iowa City.

As the reference to eye injections exemplifies, the "two days" narrative also amply documents the challenge of juggling work, family, and self as a mayor. The tale alludes to poor sleep, bodily afflictions, and appointments with doctors and financial advisors. It also implies that maintaining a reasonable family life can be very difficult, largely because a mayor can spend so much time speaking with people about city matters. In the end, the tale reinforces the need to build what I have previously characterized as a "sustainable economy of spirit," both for oneself and as part of a larger community (Throgmorton, 2000). In my case, I thrived on the conversations: I loved talking with people about matters they and I cared about and I loved being able to share my values and knowledge with them while being open to hearing about theirs. I especially loved connecting with people who feel disconnected from (or ignored by) the government of the city in which they live. Simply to be present with them was a step toward a more inclusive and just city.

Ultimately, this tale highlights some of the complications associated with trying to build a more inclusive city. The difficulties Mazahir S. and I had vividly reveal how opaque City government's codes and processes can be to anyone who is not involved in its day-to-day operations and, especially, to people who are not fluent in English, who are unfamiliar with democracy as practiced at the local level, who fear they or people they love might be arrested and deported by ICE, who are people of color who live in a world structured and controlled by white people, or who feel threatened by swastikas and hate mail. City policies, codes, and practices must be altered enough for people in such communities to participate in the governance of the city in which they live. And yet, I also think one owes it to oneself to learn how local government works before occupying a position of leadership within it.

Notes

1 For an insightful discussion of the constructive role of passion in democracies, see Mouffe (2016).
2 While Mazahir S. was gone, I read a lengthy and enlightening book about Khartoum, the city from which she came (Mahjoub, 2018). It helped me understand better the history, culture, politics, and diversity of Sudan in a way that enabled us to have more fruitful conversations after she returned.

References

Arnold, M. (2019), "Iowa City fire caused by propane heater, damage estimate at $1 million", *The Gazette*. (March 6); available at: www.thegazette.com/subject/news/public-safety/iowa-city-fire-caused-by-propane-heater-damage-estimate-at-1-million-20190306 (last accessed January 5, 2021).

Mahjoub, J. (2018), *A Line in the River: Khartoum, City of Memory*, Bloomsbury, London (UK).

Mouffe, C. (2016), "Democratic politics and conflict: An agonistic approach", *Política común*, v. 9; available at: https://doi.org/10.3998/pc.12322227.0009.011

Throgmorton, J. A. (2000), "On the virtues of skillful meandering: Acting as a skilled-voice-in-the-flow of persuasive argumentation", *Journal of the American Planning Association*, v. 66, n. 4, pp. 367–383.

6

CONCLUSION

The preceding chapters tell a story about crafting city futures in a contested age. More specifically, they tell a story about how the elected leaders of one city in the U.S. tried to craft their city's future while being immersed in a complex, emotionally challenging, and often politically contentious flow of action. Having narrated that story, I now want to step back and reflect on what can be learned from it.

I had four specific aims in writing this book. First, I wanted to give readers a sense of what democratically elected city council members and mayors in the United States do and what it feels like to occupy and enact those roles. Second, I sought to document what happened when council allies and I tried, during my term as mayor from 2016 through 2019, to lead our relatively small Midwestern city toward becoming a more inclusive, just, and sustainable place. I also sought to provide readers insight into what it feels like to be an urban planning scholar serving as a council member and mayor, and to share lessons I learned which would be of value to other scholars and practitioners. And last, based on the experiences documented in the book, I wanted to stimulate thinking, research, and action by offering a practical set of ideas about how the real flesh-and-blood residents and elected leaders of a city, using democratic processes of governance, can best guide the unfolding of their city while being immersed in the flow of action.

I sought to achieve these aims by narrating a fine-grained story about what the city council of Iowa City, Iowa, did from 2012 through 2019. Narrated from my personal point of view as a council member and later as a council member-mayor, the story orients around three key conflicts, only the first of which I anticipated at the beginning of my term in 2012. Those conflicts were, first, interlocal economic competition between Iowa City and its neighboring

DOI: 10.4324/9781003160991-6

cities, especially Coralville, to attract capital investment and highly educated workers. The preceding chapters rarely address it explicitly, but this conflict provided the foundation for most of the city council's and city manager's key actions from 2012 through 2015. The second conflict was between neoliberal "Boomtown" advocates (a.k.a. the growth machine) and a loose coalition (a.k.a. the Core Four) which sought to turn Iowa City toward becoming a more inclusive, just, and sustainable city. And the third was the extremely sharp conflict between the political preferences of most Iowa City residents and the conservative Christian, ethno-nationalist, free-market fundamentalist regimes that dominated state and federal government. Two key turning points marked the emergence of the second and third conflicts: the surprise election of the Core Four in November 2015, followed 1 year later by the even more surprising election of Donald Trump as president.

What Council Members and the Mayor Do

Being a Council Member Can Be Very Challenging but Rewarding

Being a council member can be very hard work, both intellectually and emotionally; it is far more difficult than the general public imagines. The work often can feel fruitless and frustrating, especially if the council member finds him- or herself on the losing side of too many important votes. But being a council member can also feel quite rewarding. Unlike most people, council members have the opportunity to contribute to democratic governance at its most fundamental level, to help shape key decisions for their cities, and to alter key City policies and practices in ways that reflect the council member's values.

In Iowa City, a council member's work involves a challenging set of tasks, including: (1) reading a steady flow of information and agenda packets from the City staff; (2) listening attentively and participating knowledgeably in a large number of council work sessions and formal meetings; (3) advocating actions which are consistent with the member's values; (4) taking part in periodic meetings with City staff, other council members, and other governmental leaders; (5) attending public meetings and events; (6) routinely communicating with members of the public, many of whom have a strong emotional stake in the topics being discussed; and (7) taking other actions council members believe are necessary to perform their elected jobs well.

New council members have a lot to learn if they want to perform these tasks well. In my experience, most new council members typically campaign for election on the basis of one or just a few issues that matter to them, and they often know their parts of the city but have rarely (if ever) travelled through (or know people in) other parts. Likewise, many incoming council members know little about the annual and biennial rhythms of council activities and, hence, tend to be caught off guard when key elements of those rhythms kick in, such as when the City Conference Board meets, when the council meets in executive sessions, when the council reviews the performance of its appointees, and more. Moreover, prior to taking office, most new council members have typically not met most of the City's department heads, have little detailed knowledge about what those departments do, and have not visited the departments' various facilities.

Once having joined the council, new members rather quickly become inundated by a flood of topics and issues, some of which are very complicated, have their own specialized rhetoric, and often concern matters the new members have never thought about before. Some of the topics they encounter have a continually evolving backstory, which City staff and some sitting members of the council already know and have become skilled at narrating, but which comes as news to incoming council members. New members can feel pressured to act quickly and decisively even though they might actually need more time to understand the topics adequately.

To function effectively in this context, council members must learn how to pay close attention to the flow of action pertaining to each of the topics that come their way. By "flow of action" I mean that each topic has its own starting point, sequence of events, decision points, and outcomes. Moreover, council members soon realize they cannot focus their attention on everything; rather, flooded by issues, they must distinguish the mundane from the important and, as much as possible, focus attention on what really matters to them. This requires knowing or discovering what they value. Moreover, they are typically so immersed in processing the flood of issues that they have very little time to reflect upon how well their decisions are conforming with their values and campaign themes. Nor do they typically have time to reflect upon where their councils' decisions are leading their cities.

As they gain experience, council members are likely to learn that specific topics are often part of a continually evolving and interwoven array of complicated and emotionally challenging topics—that is, are part of a whole that is constantly changing. Chapters 2 and 3 provide ample evidence for this in Iowa City.

Given the difficulties of being a good council member, scholars in urban planning and related disciplines might fruitfully ask themselves, how can we help these elected officials enact their roles better? One answer to this question is to ensure the City's professional staff provides council members with the best possible information and advice. To do this, City staff act as "skilled-voices-in-the-flow": they frame issues for council members, provide members with information, and (normally) recommend actions. The challenging part is that the typical council member's lack of expertise with regard to specific topics initially places council members at a severe disadvantage relative to the City staff. Consequently, council members must learn not to rely exclusively on what the City staff tells them. Instead, councilors must call upon interested members of the attentive public to provide information and highlight values the staff has missed or marginalized, to learn what people outside City government think, to test alternative ideas, and to assess the feasibility of proposals. Once having done that, they will be in a better position to engage constructively with City staff and to negotiate differences with the staff and with other council members. At times, council members might feel a need to reframe issues City staff present to them. They should not feel shy about doing so; it is part of what democracy is all about.

Being a Mayor Is Far More Difficult

If being a council member is difficult, being a mayor is far more so. Moreover, there is a very big difference between mayors who want to keep their cities on their present courses and mayors who, as I did, intentionally seek to alter the direction of their cities' step-by-step unfolding. Turning a city in a new direction, toward a different future, cannot be accomplished by simply identifying the characteristics of a planner's ideal "good city," adopting ambitious new policies, or having the mayor snap her or his fingers and say, "Make it so!" Making that turn also demands hard work on the ground, in the trenches, working with other people, and transforming city policies, plans, budgets, codes, and practices where necessary. In a word, making that turn requires skill at *crafting* roughly analogous to a carpenter's skill at turning a blueprint into an addition on a house. This ability to craft the step-by-step transformation of new priorities into new plans and then into incentives, regulations, and investments requires many diverse skills, each of which can be learned and nurtured. I would emphasize the following eight.

First, *mayors who seek to play their part in crafting this kind of step-by-step unfolding must know their cities: that is, their histories, residents, businesses, and physical/environmental features.* I found it especially enlightening and rewarding to traverse my city regularly in my car, on a City bus, on my bike, or on foot. Mayors also need to have a good understanding of the specific place-based ways their cities are affected by the global economy, by transnational movements of people, by changes in the global climate, and by actions at the national and state levels.

Second, *novice mayors have much to learn.* Regardless of how much they know about their cities, almost all mayors begin their terms without having been taught how to enact the role well. In my case, being a novice mayor meant having to process many difficult and sometimes completely unfamiliar issues while also responding in a timely and effective fashion to an irregular drumbeat of unexpected events, including turnover in key staff and council membership and the election of a president whose polices diametrically opposed ours. Responding effectively to such events had to be accomplished while dealing with the normal rhythm of reading lengthy packets of material every 2 weeks; voting as a member of the council; and facilitating council work sessions, formal meetings, and executive sessions. During the council meetings, I learned how important it is to remain in the moment—that is, to listen carefully to what other people said and how they said it, to attend not just to the speakers' words but also to their affect, and to respond in ways that demonstrated I had heard and felt what they said. This "being-in-the-flow" certainly applies to interactions with council members and City staff, but it is especially important with regard to engaging members of the public. They have a right to be present, to be treated with respect, and to have their ideas treated as valuable gifts.

Preparing for council meetings every 2 weeks can, over time, prove to be a grueling experience for any council member. It is especially difficult for mayors in cities structured like Iowa City because the mayor must enable interested members of the public to express their views, ensure the City's professional staff have an adequate opportunity to bring their professional expertise to bear on agenda items, and be prepared to express the mayor's own views and to vote on agenda items while also facilitating discussion among council members. This means the mayor frequently has to judge how vigorously to foreground her/ his own views while also ensuring that all council members have an adequate opportunity to express their views, learn from one another, and influence the final decision. This can be a delicate balancing act that requires considerable finesse and interpersonal skill. At times, intemperate outbursts from individual speakers have to be dealt with. Whenever I encountered such outbursts, I tried hard to remain focused on the issue at hand and the interests being expressed, rather than let the conflict become personal. Doing all this over 3–6 hours at night can be exhausting.

Third, good mayors must know how to convert aspirations into action. To convert aspirations into action, mayors must be very knowledgeable about the structure, existing legal authority, and standard procedures of their city governments. And, once in office, mayors must be able to skillfully negotiate interpersonal conflicts among council members and to help at least a majority of the council (in our case, four) get to "yes" when decisions are required. And mayors must be able to build strong relationships with City staff based on a sense of mutual respect and trust. The last of these can require a tricky balancing act: while pushing for changes in the staff's behavior and actions where necessary, mayors must also get out of the way and let the staff do its job.

Fourth, being skilled at ethically sound, persuasive storytelling can help. Mayors who seek to change the direction in which their city is unfolding must also convey—through speeches, media interviews, guest opinions in newspapers, formal proclamations, and innumerable face-to-face conversations—an ethically sound, persuasive story about where their cities should be headed. To tell an ethically sound story, mayors and others first need to establish, in the here and now, relationships of mutual respect and trust with diverse residents, business leaders, directors of nongovernmental organizations, and others. Success will not be possible without those relationships. Once such relationships are in place, mayors and other council members should actively listen to the stories those diverse people tell, learn how they are being affected by the City's actions, help them understand how specific policies and actions form parts of a larger effort to turn the city in a better direction, and incorporate the diverse tales back into a steadily evolving story about where the city should be headed.

The experience of being a mayor refined my understanding of the multiple ways in which storytelling affects the co-crafting of a city. In brief, once one thinks in terms of co-crafting a city's unfolding and acknowledges the potential ability of elected officials to provide leadership for that unfolding, then the presumption that planning and politics can be kept separate disappears. It also means that storytelling should be treated as a key component of the co-crafting process. One key example was my own effort to tell and enact an ethically sound, persuasive story about the merits of building a more "Just City" and then to forge a political majority that could put that vision into action. A second example can be seen in the ways in which the city council and staff told continually evolving stories about what they had been doing with regard to particular issues. Whenever we would be criticized for "doing nothing" about affordable housing, racial equity, and climate action, I and others in City government wanted people to *acknowledge what we had done* and then push us to do more. Being told we were "doing nothing" while we knew what we had done, often with great effort, only made us feel defensive. A third example would be the diverse ways in which multiple actors routinely told Iowa City's locally grounded versions of "common urban narratives." These narratives focused on (1) preserving the historic character of the city, (2) marketing and growing "the creative corridor," (3) "driving while black" and experiencing other conflicts related to race and racism, and (4) adjusting to life in the city as a refugee or immigrant, as well as (5) stories uniquely found in small university cities. A fourth and extremely important example concerned the efforts by the president and his core supporters to tell intentionally manipulative stories, especially with regard to the alleged dangers of "illegal aliens" and "sanctuary cities."

Fifth, with each step, mayors should use the discretion they have to ensure that their cities' actions are bending in the preferred direction. Looking back over my mayoral term, I see a nearly endless array of moments when I chose how to act (within constraints established by existing laws and ordinances). The major choices included: (1) entering the loose coalition called the Core Four; (2) supporting Kingsley B. and then Pauline T., rather than Susan M., as mayor pro tem; (3) striving to be the "strongest weak mayor" I could be; (4) occupying the mayoral role as a "pragmatic visionary" making incremental changes rather than pushing for large-scale, immediate transformations; (5) advocating appointment of the assistant city manager as permanent manager; (6) focusing City government's attention on making Iowa City a more inclusive, just, and sustainable place and giving priority attention to affordable housing, racial justice, and climate action; (7) leading the City toward producing an ambitious climate action plan that had strong political support; (8) pushing hard to formulate new standards pertaining to development on the expanding edges of the city; (9) advocating an effective synthesis of preservation and redevelopment downtown, especially by amending our TIF policy; (10) trying to alter the 12 Court Street project; (11) using policy memoranda, op-eds in newspapers, and presentations to diverse organizations as ways to frame important issues and influence public opinion; (12) living out my commitment to inclusivity by meeting with diverse groups all over the city; and (13) standing with immigrants and refugees, especially during the sanctuary city controversy.

If I were to express disappointments about my own choices, highest on the list would be not working hard enough at the start of 2018 to have our 2018–2019 Strategic Plan call for the City government and the larger community to produce a racial equity plan which would address the fundamental causes of race-related inequities. Other than that, the biggest mistake I made occurred in 2014 when I voted for the Riverfront Crossings District Form-Based Code despite believing its height bonuses were excessive.

Conducting research into how mayors use their discretion would provide planning theorists and other urban scholars with an opportunity to ask a range of "what if?" questions about actual mayors' key discretionary actions, such as: were these wise decisions? Will they keep the city going in the preferred direction? What might have happened if the mayor had made different choices? What political values should mayors and other elected officials use to guide a continually unfolding "good city" today, and what combination of political action and good technical analysis/planning is required to bring such a good city to life *in particular places at particular times*?

Sixth, good mayors have to be part of a strong electoral coalition. Ultimately, this means mayors must also help form and maintain electoral coalitions that are strong enough to put new policies in place and convert those policies into effective action (Stone, 1993).[1] Much as one might wish it were otherwise, political conflict does not simply disappear after elections. It continues at a very fine-grained level with each step the change-oriented mayor and council take to commission new plans, alter policies, change the city's budget and CIP, appoint new members to boards and commissions, diversify the City staff, and so on. Consequently, members of the electoral coalition need to be present and active all the way down, both inside and outside government. And they need to keep doing that for many years—4 years is not enough time.

Seventh, good mayors must strengthen and improve existing interjurisdictional relationships. Being a good mayor requires communicating with a very large number and variety of institutional actors (both public and private), a great deal of interjurisdictional coordination and negotiation, and innumerable face-to-face discussions with a wide range of individuals. For me, these actors included the School Board leadership, the county supervisors, the mayors of Coralville and North Liberty, the president of the University of Iowa, the directors of key economic-development organizations and non-profit organizations, the leaders of public-interest groups, reporters affiliated with local news media, and many others.

And eighth, mayors must expect the unexpected. They must be capable of rather deft footwork and be able to respond skillfully to unexpected events (e.g., floods, tornados, fires, derechos, corporate relocations) which are likely to have originated outside the city's region. At times, a mayor might have to display moral courage in the face of actions taken by others and, in the end, will learn there are limits to what she or he controls and can accomplish. No mayor can be perfect.

Being a Mayor Can Also Feel Immensely Rewarding

Regardless of how difficult and stressful it can be to occupy the role of council member or mayor, having the opportunity to co-craft the unfolding of one's city can also feel tremendously rewarding. It certainly has for me. I can see on the ground (and hear residents speak about) the beneficial effects our actions have produced. While I tried to provide leadership, producing those beneficial effects required determined efforts by my fellow council members, our City staff, a very large number of residents who volunteered their time and energy toward improving life in the city, and all the other actors involved in co-crafting our city's future.

As a retired professor of urban planning, I was especially pleased to see many graduates of Iowa's School of Planning and Public Affairs doing excellent work in prominent positions, not just for our city but also for adjacent jurisdictions, and to know that formal planning by City staff and consultants contributed greatly to our accomplishments over the 4-year period. But it is extremely important to note that many of these plans would not have been commissioned had the Core Four not been elected in 2015, and had the new council not focused the City's Strategic Plan on forging a more inclusive, just, and sustainable city.

I have also been thrilled to have so many opportunities to meet and learn from other mayors, especially through the Mayors Innovation Project and the Mayors Institute on City Design, and to speak to a wide variety of audiences about major topics of mutual interest. These conversations enriched my understanding of the range of discretion mayors have about how (within legal bounds) to enact their roles. Where the rules authorized me to exercise my own judgment and discretion, I consistently made choices that I thought would lead to a more inclusive, just, and sustainable city. This included trying, often successfully, to resolve conflicts behind the scenes.

In addition to having the opportunity to serve the people of Iowa City, the greatest joys for me have been having the opportunity to attend Baghdad's Festival of Flowers; to participate in a Civil Rights Tour with young black residents; to meet a large number of visitors from other parts of the world; and to stand with our city's immigrants, women, African-Americans, lower-income Whites, Hispanics, Muslims, refugees from Congo and Sudan, gays and lesbians, students, scholars, and others who have felt endangered by the tidal wave of executive orders, policies, and laws emanating from the national and state administrations. I like to think that their mayor's willingness to stand by their side has made a difference in their lives.

What kept me going was finding solidarity and support every day by meeting my fellow residents face to face and by talking with them at various places throughout the city. The conversations rejuvenated me, reminded me how important it was to do my job well, and helped me know I was not running alone into a very strong wind. I was running with a beloved community at my side.

What Happened When We Tried to Lead Iowa City toward Becoming a More Just City

With the help of other council members, City staff, and members of the local community, our effort to lead Iowa City toward becoming a more inclusive, just, and sustainable city has borne considerable fruit. As documented in Chapter 4, from 2016 through 2019, we made significant strides toward increasing the supply of affordable housing, decreasing race-related disproportionality in traffic stops and arrests, improving police–community relations, appointing a more diverse mix of residents to our boards and commissions, and supporting plans to build a new Behavioral Health Access Center. We also adopted an ambitious climate change and adaptation plan, and we greatly reduced possible damage from future floods by completing the Gateway Project and moving a wastewater treatment facility out of the floodplain. We supported the School District's construction of two new elementary schools and renovation of older ones in Iowa City. In addition, we improved many neighborhood parks significantly, built a new Riverfront Crossings Park where the treatment facility used to be, significantly renovated parts of downtown, and greatly expanded the range of community groups with which City government routinely engages. And we accomplished all this in a fiscally sound manner. Consequently, Iowa City is thriving, and more people are benefiting from their city's prosperity.

And yet, as the preceding chapters document, the mayor of a city cannot simply snap her or his fingers and expect the City staff to respond immediately. If a mayor and council majority want to change the direction their city is headed, they have to transform their priorities into new plans and then into incentives, regulations, and investments. In my case, this proved especially difficult with regard to land development and climate action. As our city attorney often reminded us, city staffs have standard ways of doing their work and are committed to following the City's existing codes, plans, and policies. The standard practices are based on the City staff's professional training and

FIGURE 6.1   Looking north along Dubuque Road at the completed Gateway Project.
Source: Photo by author, April 29, 2021.

FIGURE 6.2   Renovated Horace Mann Elementary School in Iowa City's Northside
neighborhood.
Source: Photo by author, April 30, 2021.

FIGURE 6.3 The 15-story Chauncey as viewed from the southwest.
Source: Photo by author, June 25, 2019.

FIGURE 6.4 Looking south into the Riverfront Crossings District past Hieronymus
Square and the Hilton Garden Inn.
Source: Photo by author, April 29, 2021.

FIGURE 6.5 Iowa City's Sudanese community learning about the democratic revolution in Sudan.

Source: Photo by author, October 6, 2019.

experience and, at least in the case of planners, might at times conflict with professional planners' code of ethics (Johnson, Peck, and Preston, 2017). The existing codes, plans, and policies can be crucial contributors to "path dependency" (Sorensen, 2015, 2018) and, hence, can generate conflict (or at least tension) between change-oriented mayors/councils and their professional staff. Resolving such conflicts takes considerable time and skill.

Inevitably, mayors are likely to be disappointed by the slow pace at which the staff converts some of the mayor's and council's priorities into action. Four years is simply not enough time to fully embed a turn toward a more Just City into the basic codes and practices of a city government.[2]

Beyond the basic challenge of getting things done, our accomplishments required working through the three key types of conflict mentioned at the start of this book. One recurring type of conflict involved Iowa City's interlocal economic competition with neighboring cities, especially Coralville. This conflict oriented around that city's aggressive use of tax increment financing as a way of attracting investment and, in the judgment of Iowa City officials, luring key businesses out of Iowa City. Failure of the local option sales tax referendum in 2014 can be attributed primarily to that conflict. As mayor, I worked hard to improve relationships with Coralville's elected leaders, and our city manager successfully negotiated a communication protocol with Coralville and one other city pertaining to the recruitment of businesses. Regrettably, we had very little success with regard to altering land development and transportation policies/actions at the regional scale. Likewise, we had very little success in encouraging the two largest contiguous cities to take effective action pertaining to the affordability of housing and the reduction of carbon emissions. They were their own entities, and their leaders governed as they thought they should. That said, there have been non-trivial changes in the leadership of those cities, and I like to think that our actions in Iowa City influenced those changes.

Another recurring conflict was between the Core Four (and allied groups) and the council members and organizations which comprised the growth machine. This conflict was intense during the first year of my mayoral term, but it waned somewhat as we demonstrated that we could govern effectively and after we approved several major new development projects. In part, my strategy for managing this conflict was, within reasonable time constraints, to conduct all of our council meetings as a form of deliberative democracy—that is, as an opportunity for all interested and affected parties to express their views, engage in dialogue about the decisions at hand, and influence the outcomes while treating everyone with respect. I also thought it would be wise to have an experienced and knowledgeable advocate for the growth machine occupy prominent positions on our council and, therefore, asked council member Susan M. to chair the council's Economic Development Committee, to join me as liaisons to the School Board, and to serve as the City's representative on the Behavioral Health Access Center's advisory board. Outside the council, I consistently reached out to leaders of the local economic development organizations, engaged in continuing dialogue with them, and looked for opportunities to act in concert with them.

Ultimately, however, I think my strategy for managing this conflict was insufficient. Although we were able to make important incremental changes in City policies, my sense is that a political majority based on a loose coalition, as was the case in Iowa City when I was mayor, lacks the political legitimacy required to pose a fundamental challenge to the growth coalition. At a minimum, a political majority on the city council needs to be supplemented by a long-game effort to strengthen a durable "justice coalition" based on a well-informed and inclusive democracy. One step in this direction would be deepen discursive democracy outside City government by organizing a continuing public forum which would enable members of the public to discuss key city issues, to explore the interconnections among them, and to consider possible actions pertaining to them.

Although we received important assistance from various state agencies for flood recovery and other projects, we had no success in tempering conflicts with the governing regimes at the state and national level. What normally happened was that our council or the county supervisors would adopt an ordinance or policy state legislators did not like, and the legislators would preempt local governments' powers pertaining to it. Moreover, the fact that Iowa City was a "blue" city in an increasingly "red" state meant that "red" legislators were increasingly inclined to impose their will on the larger cities of the state without engaging leaders of those cities in dialogue based on mutual trust and a desire to work through differences. The conflict over our "sanctuary cities" action perfectly exemplifies the point. State government—which was closely allied with President Trump—had the power and imposed its will. Not once in my 4 years as mayor did the governor, the two Republican senators representing Iowans, or Republican legislators in other parts of the state reach out to me or our council and say, let's talk. When Iowa's current governor first assumed office, I asked to meet with her so that I could congratulate her and talk about matters of mutual interest. Her staff told me she was not available to meet, and nothing came from that effort. Likewise, I reached out more than once to a Republican state representative whose district includes a small portion of Iowa City, but he never responded. Increasingly, I felt as though many national and state leaders were treating Iowa Citians as enemies to be destroyed, rather than as political adversaries with whom one disagrees.[3]

I could have done more, and I wish I had. One cannot negotiate differences without understanding the other entities with whom one is in conflict, and such understanding requires face-to-face conversations and active listening.

What a Planning Scholar Learned and Contributed by Serving as Council Member/Mayor

As Chapter 1 documents, I had spent most of my career focusing on environmental issues, on the history of cities and urban planning, and on theories about planning within democracies. Although I had read a great deal about architecture, urban design, and physical planning for cities, I did not consider myself an expert on those topics. Likewise, I did not consider myself an expert on city management, financing, and budgeting. In the end, therefore, my background as a planning scholar prepared me for much but not all of the work I did as a council member/mayor.

My urban planning background influenced my actions on the council and as mayor in at least four ways. First, as a planning scholar, I was usually better prepared than most other council members to analyze issues in detail, to see interconnections among them, and subsequently to express my views in memos and guest opinions. This does necessarily mean I was right, for judgments about what is right and wrong, good and bad, are normative judgments that cannot be made simply through analysis.

Second, as a planning theorist, I recognized diverse theories of planning when they were being used. Neoliberal planning, which treats citizens as consumers and local governments as public entrepreneurs in competition with one another, dominated the City government's efforts during the first 4 years of this tale. The City's public works staff clearly applied a "rational decision-making" model when making recommendations to the council about Idyllwild and the Gateway Project. Step-by-step change is consistent with incrementalism. The work of the Affordable Housing Coalition nicely exemplifies what planning theorists call "advocacy planning." Efforts by the Center for Worker Justice and the student climate strikers were consistent with "insurgent planning," in which people situated outside government (and usually in opposition to it) seek to empower marginalized and oppressed groups. Opticos's form-based code work in the South District was an instance of New Urbanism, as was the City planning staff's master plan for the Riverfront Crossings District. And various aspects of "interactive-communicative planning" can be found throughout the tale. All of these theories contributed to the action documented in this book, but none of them, by themselves, explain how actions and the city itself unfolded from 2012 through 2019. To understand how and why they unfolded as they did, and to make sense of the emotional resonance their unfolding had on the people of Iowa City, one needs to have those actions woven together and placed into narrative form. Hence, this book.

   Third, my scholarly and public work pertaining to conflict resolution, environmental issues, and electric power planning enabled me to be a better council member/mayor. Having taught conflict resolution courses, I often thought in terms of "getting to yes." I tried to make sure that other key City actors understood our BATNAs and usually looked for opportunities to negotiate or mediate conflicts, but I eventually concluded that the best way to do this was to live out the principles in action rather than talk about them. I think this skill served me well, especially when managing contentious council meetings. Likewise, having spent many years of my life focusing on environmental issues and electric power planning, I was able to speak authoritatively about the need for climate action and for building a strong local constituency supporting it. What served me best, however, was my scholarly work rooted in the importance of telling stories persuasively, of framing issues and defining problems, of listening actively, of building strong relationships based on mutual trust, and of engaging in dialogue oriented toward mutual understanding whenever possible.

   I rarely sensed during my first 4 years in office that, by itself, my scholarly background carried much weight with other key City actors on spatial-planning issues. My background had greater influence after the Core Four were elected, but I don't think it ever dominated; other actors (e.g., the landscape architect, the financial planner, and the lawyers on the council; the city manager; and the City's planning and public works staffs) had their own professional sources of credibility. Consequently, my ability to affect the City's spatial-planning actions was often limited to being one council member out of seven. My sense is that I did not possess sufficient spatial planning/urban design expertise to back up my advocacy for high-quality urban design and for mid-rise rather than high-rise density. The absence of a strong external political constituency for high-quality urban design did not help. Even if there had been such a constituency, it would have had to articulate how high-quality design would contribute to the creation of a more inclusive, just, and sustainable city. "Missing-middle" housing was a step in the right direction.

And fourth, my urban planning background enabled me to discern important limits to the City staff's advice. Consider the planning staff's advice in particular. Good planning by skilled technical staff is a necessary part of guiding a city's unfolding in a preferred, arguably better, direction. In fact, from 2012 through 2015, the city council commissioned several important plans, including one for the Gateway Project, another for the downtown streetscape, and, most important, a third for the Downtown and Riverfront Crossings District. In the next 4 years, when I was mayor, the council commissioned an affordable housing action plan, a climate action and adaptation plan, a bicycle master plan, a master parks plan, a transit system study, as well as development of a new form-based code for an emerging neighborhood near a new elementary school on the city's southern edge, and more.

But good planning is not sufficient. There are multiple reasons for this, but the key one is that the values elected officials communicate largely determine which plans will be commissioned; whether those plans will be approved and used to guide action; and how, and for what reasons, the approved plans will be amended over time. And the current council members' values might not coincide with the values that previous councils had when adopting ordinances, policies, and plans. To perform their role in co-crafting the unfolding of a city in a good (or at least better) direction, city planners need good elected officials.[4] This raises another important question for theorists: how can planning scholars help improve the quality of elected officials and the quality of those officials' two-way interactions with city planners and other professional staff members?

A second reason why city planning is not sufficient is that the unfolding of a city is affected by more factors than the ones normally addressed in the city planners' plans and recommendations. Mayors and city council members routinely must address particular topics and issues that affect the direction in which their city will change—for example, police–community relations—but that fall well outside the professional planners' purview.

And a third reason is that city planners are not fully autonomous agents. In my experience at least, the information and recommendations city planners provide must first be filtered through the city manager's office. *Here I want to emphasize how crucial it is for elected officials to feel they are receiving trustworthy information from both the city planners and the city manager.* If that sense of trust breaks down, then difficulties will ensue. If the city manager exerts strong control over the planners' recommendations, then council members will be unable to discern whether they are receiving the planners' best professional advice or the city manager's politically inflected transformation of that advice: the advice emerges from a "black box" into which council members cannot see. During my years as a council member, from 2012 through 2015, my trust in the city manager and two members of our planning staff waned, and it did so largely because of how they had framed council discussions about a few politically controversial development projects. My sense was they were enacting a particular kind of politics—that is, a neoliberal/entrepreneurial form of planning.

After being elected mayor in 2015, I told our newly appointed city manager that I thought our planners' recommendations should represent *their* best professional judgment. If he disagreed with their judgment, he should articulate why he disagreed and then express his own view. Put differently, I wanted to know precisely where the planners and the city manager were exercising their own judgment and discretion.

As a planning scholar, I would say the central question for professional planners is, how can they help democratically elected leaders lead their cities in the best possible direction? How, in other words, can planners act as "skilled-voices-in-the-flow" in a city which is a "problem in organized complexity" while also engaging in democratic governance?

My profession's original answer to this question was that professional planners should plan the physical development of the city; however, experience has revealed that things are not that simple, at least not in viable democracies. My background and my deep immersion in our city's political life have transformed my understanding of the planners' role in guiding the transformation of cities. I no longer focus on planning as an autonomous effort to plan the city's future. As this book has shown, I gradually began forming a set of ideas, or a tentative theory, that might help.

Thinking in Terms of Co-crafting Might Help

By the end of my first full term as a council member, I had begun to assemble a set of ideas into a tentative theory that would guide much of my subsequent work as mayor. This "theory" began with a simple presumption: to get to the future city, one has to continually start from the here and now. From that present condition, *cities unfold*, with multiple human and non-human *actants* being part of a never-ending and very complicated process of co-crafting the *direction* that step-by-step unfolding will take.[5] My sense was that professional planners play an important role in this process of co-crafting, but they do not act autonomously: someone must commission them to prepare plans. Consequently, elected officials and city managers (that is, the ones who do the commissioning) play critical but not exclusive roles in this process of co-crafting. Mayors can play an especially important role, with persuasive storytelling being a key means by which they can signal the direction in which the city's unfolding should go.

So, what did my 4 years as mayor reveal about the merits and viability of these ideas about co-crafting? In brief, my experiences persuade me that my tentative ideas have considerable merit but, by themselves, are not sufficient. Actions did unfold step-by-step, as was exemplified by the linkage between our 2016 Strategic Plan and the subsequent steps pertaining to affordable housing. The city did unfold step-by-step, as was amply demonstrated by the Riverfront Crossings District's transformation. Mayors and other elected officials did play important roles in crafting each step, as exemplified by the process by which we ultimately adopted a modified climate action plan late in 2019. Multiple other local organizations and governmental entities did contribute to the co-crafting of the step-by-step change. The School Board's construction or renovation of schools in Iowa City provides one good example, as does the county's diligent pursuit of a new Behavioral Health Access Center. Actions taken by more distant governmental entities, especially the Iowa legislature, also shaped or constrained what we could do in Iowa City, as did executive orders and budgets adopted by the president and Congress at the national level. Distant corporations (for example, investors in the Rise at Linn and Court, the "Amazon-type" entity, and Procter & Gamble) had a hand in co-crafting the city as well. Non-human actants such as the emerald ash borer, deer, a tornado that narrowly missed Iowa City, and a river which is increasingly prone to flooding owing to climate change also loomed large.

Although my 4 years as mayor persuade me that my ideas about co-crafting the step-by-step unfolding of cities have merit, I am much less confident that a mayor, city council, or city government as a whole can fully control the *direction* in which their city will unfold. And I have learned how much I did not know when I was mayor about the published scholarly literature pertaining to urban theory, urban governance, and complexity.

As I close this book, therefore, I will briefly state what I learned about the challenges co-crafting presents, and then connect what I learned to urban theory and governance.[6]

First, co-crafting the direction in which a city unfolds can be very hard. It is very hard precisely because cities are, as Jane Jacobs wrote, problems in organized complexity. It takes a substantial amount of time, experience, and knowledge to begin grasping what this entails. And yet, as was revealed quite clearly in our council's debates about the Forest View project, 12 Court Street, "the Kinnick House," and the realtors' response to our rental cap, most people and organizations are strongly inclined to focus on single interests and display little awareness of, or concern about, the connections between their preferred actions and other aspects of the city's unfolding. Consequently, co-crafting a city requires communicating with a very large number and variety of institutional actors (both public and private), a great deal of interjurisdictional coordination and negotiation, and innumerable face-to-face discussions with a wide range of individuals. At the scale of Iowa City, this is difficult but manageable; at much larger scales, it would be far more challenging, if not impossible. The demands of interjurisdictional coordination might be the most challenging aspect of co-crafting.

Moreover, the complexity to which Jacobs refers extends far beyond the city's geographical limits. Urban scholar Michael Batty's *Inventing Future Cities* (2018), which I read in 2019, is particularly instructive on this point. In it, Batty, who builds upon his intricate knowledge of "complexity theory," claims the futures of cities cannot be predicted and will not unerringly follow formally planned trajectories; rather, they will evolve from the present. He buttresses this broad claim with several more specific ones: (1) several decades from now, virtually the entire global population will be living in cities; (2) cities will vary in size from very small to conurbations containing 65 million or so people; (3) cities will be so interconnected globally that the kinds of face-to-face relationships that once defined urban life will be global in scale owing to a great transition roughly equivalent to the industrial revolution and the "death of distance" associated with internet-based technologies; (4) this great transition will have significant effects on the physical form of cities; (5) flows, networks, and connections make cities more like organisms than machines; and (6) cities continually renew themselves from within through a process economist Joseph Schumpeter (1942) termed "creative destruction."

Another key factor that makes co-crafting so difficult has to do with limitations on a city's and its mayor's legal authority (Frug, 1999; Frug and Barron, 2008; Schragger, 2018). In the United States, cities are creatures of the individual states, and the extent of a city's authority depends on what its state's legislature gives or takes away. In our case, the Iowa legislature took several new steps to constrain further the power of local governments. These steps included reforming property tax laws and preempting our authority to become a "sanctuary city," to adopt a rental cap ordinance, to establish stricter energy efficiency regulations for new buildings, to ban plastic bags, and much more.

Constraints imposed by Iowa City's Charter also made co-crafting by our city's elected officials more difficult. Roughly equivalent to a local constitution, our Charter establishes a "council–manager" form of government. Unlike the "strong mayor" form of government, the council–manager structure sharply limits the formal powers of the mayor, allocates considerable power to the city manager, and requires a mayor to be elected every 2 years by the seven council members, rather than by registered voters for a longer term. The Charter also implicitly presumes that the mayor and other council members will serve on a part-time basis while typically being employed full time outside of City government, financially supported by someone else, or retired. These factors greatly weaken Iowa City's mayor and council members relative to other elected officials, especially those who serve at the county or state levels.

No two cities are entirely alike. But readers who live in cities other than mine might benefit from considering the following recommendations. For democratic governance to thrive in Iowa City, the City Charter needs to be amended. In my judgment, amendments should increase the authority of the mayor, have the mayor be elected to a full-time position directly by the people, extend the mayor's term to 4 years (with term limits), and increase the mayor's salary substantially from its current $15,000 or so per year. The revised charter should also require the mayor to make her or his State of the City speech at a public venue away from City Hall and to include sufficient time for questioning by the public. Being elected by the people would give the mayor much greater credibility and legitimacy, would enable voters to choose between competing visions for the city's future, and would enhance Iowa City's influence relative to other governmental entities in the county and state. To become engaged democratically, the public needs conflict and drama, and having candidates compete for a stronger mayoral position would enhance that kind of engagement.

Co-crafting can also be very stressful. In my case, it has proven quite stressful partly because the Just City vision and our Strategic Plan's emphasis on forging a more inclusive, just, and sustainable city conflicted in important ways with the local growth machine's and the state regime's commitment to growing the local/regional economy without adequately considering the relationship between that growth, social justice, and the long-term sustainability of the city and region. The conflicts proved to be quite sharp at times, especially over the Chauncey, the three cottages, 12 Court Street, and redevelopment versus historic preservation in the downtown area.

In some cases, I sensed that our city manager was recommending actions that were consistent with the local growth machine's agenda. But I was also fully aware that the City staff cannot be expected to do *my* bidding. In Iowa City's form of government, the city manager must always be assessing what a majority of the council wants him to do. And he was fully aware that the policy preferences of our council majority might not continue past the November 2019 council election. Moreover, key City staff cannot do everything at once, and they felt stressed by local political struggles, by the pressure to respond effectively to our policy initiatives, and by the federal government's "shock and awe" form of governance after 2016. In fact, they did extraordinarily well under very trying circumstances. This leads me to emphasize how important it is to have a good city staff, delegate authority to them, trust they will do the best they can under stressful circumstances, monitor their progress in achieving goals, hold them accountable when warranted, and collaborate with them when responding to unexpected events.

Unilateral rule by one political party—a party that had come under the control of Christian fundamentalists, ethno-nationalists, and radical libertarians who displayed no interest in collaboration or negotiation—at the national and state levels after the November 2016 elections also dramatically increased the difficulty and stress of trying to influence Iowa City's unfolding. Feeling treated as an enemy by the president, some state legislators, and trolls on social media—most notably over debates about Iowa City's "sanctuary city" status—was no fun.

Additional stress comes from the emotional intensity of governing a city democratically in a contested age. In our case, there were several instances in which members of various groups came to our council meetings and loudly berated us for doing nothing about the issues they cared about, demanded that we fire the city manager or other city staff members, shouted that council members and I should quit, or called me a "fucking coward" who should "burn in hell." Regrettably, this kind of thing is a normal part of contemporary city politics. What proved especially stressful for me was to find myself engaged in emotionally charged disputes with council members and residents who represented communities I was most determined to assist.[7]

The constraints of the role, the complexity of co-crafting, and the stress just described would complicate things for anyone occupying the role of mayor. In my case, being 74 and having my share of chronic ailments added to the challenge. Had I been younger and felt healthier, and had certain important aspects of my personal life not changed, I would have run for reelection.

After completing my term in office, I had time to explore recent theory pertaining to urban politics, economics, and law. In brief, I learned that our efforts to turn Iowa City toward becoming a more inclusive, just, and sustainable city ran counter to conventional urban theory. Ever since political scientist Paul Peterson published *City Limits* back in 1981, the dominant reasoning in the U.S. has been that cities inevitably must compete with one another to attract private investment and highly educated residents and, hence, must adopt business- and development-friendly policies. This reasoning limits democratic engagement within cities to relatively inconsequential matters, makes city politics mostly irrelevant, and goes a long way toward explaining why residents of Iowa City typically know more about national than local politics and why such a small percentage of registered voters vote in city council elections.

Interestingly, however, legal scholar Richard Schragger (2016) recently published a sophisticated and detailed counter-argument. Expressed succinctly, he basically argues that the subservience of cities to global markets and the federal government is not inevitable, that there is more room for an expansive municipal politics, and that cities might be able to adopt policies that are responsive to values other than economic growth. Not only did I find theoretical justification in his book for much of what we did in Iowa City, but my sense is that our work provides empirical evidence supporting his counter-argument. Schragger also argues that conventional urban theory essentially depoliticizes crucial aspects of what cities do and, hence, undermines democratic governance at the local scale. My sense is that, by making the controversial decision to assemble a loose coalition back in 2015, we brought meaningful politics into Iowa City and, hence, enabled residents to see that they could, through democratic engagement, actually influence key decisions their city's government would make.

But Iowa law circumscribes what local governments can do in the state. Urban theory offers at least two possible solutions to this problem while also enabling the direction of a city's unfolding to be co-crafted more effectively.

In *The New Localism*, Katz and Nowak (2017) characterize cities as "networks of public, private, and civic institutions that coproduce the economy and cogovern critical aspects of city life" (p. 230). But they also argue that leadership is required to activate the problem-solving capacity of these multisectoral networks and to create the institutional vehicles required to get things done. They claim that local leaders display a high degree of "network intelligence" when trying to solve hard problems (pp. 229–239). First, leaders must learn to cultivate collaboration, connection, and trust among people who rarely interact and often have vastly different missions and organizational cultures. Second, leadership comes from the deployment of soft rather than hard power. Third, leadership is often exercised by people who act as connectors who bridge the gap between major stakeholders, forge consensus solutions and initiatives, and then execute with firm backing. Fourth, leadership depends on the power of affirmative vision, and such a vision enables a common narrative that can be repeated and customized to different audiences. Fifth, leadership depends on grounding affirmative visions in affirmative evidence. And last, leadership depends on being active rather than passive. While I agree with Katz and Nowak that networks of public, private, and civic institutions contribute significantly to the co-crafting of a city's unfolding, my sense is that what Katz and Nowak advocate might tie the hands of democratically elected officials and undermine their freedom to guide their own cities. Katz and Nowak also pay too little attention to the ways in which the federal and, especially, state governments can constrain cities and compel them to take actions that run counter to the will of city residents.[8]

In *City Bound*, Frug and Barron (2008) argue the task is "to build city power in a way that can help direct it toward a sensible version of the city's future" (p. xii) and they claim "[d]esigning a decision-making structure is part of the process of designing America's urban future" (p. xiii). They investigated the "city structures" (the legal frameworks within which cities operate) that govern seven major American cities and they sought to identify key ways in which city structures mattered, especially with regard to cities' power and capacity to solve the pressing problems they face. This led them to focus on three specific ways (regulations, laws, and financing) by which states shape city structures. They concluded that, by limiting or prohibiting more proactive or innovative ideas, the states' efforts to shape city structures strongly influenced the actions cities ultimately decided to pursue. Using a simplified framework of four possible city futures (global city, tourist city, middle-class city, and regional city), Frug and Barron illustrate how existing laws make it easiest for cities to pursue the global and tourist city agendas while making the other two agendas more difficult and often impossible. After describing why cities are unable to pursue the regional city agenda, Frug and Barron propose an alternative regional legal framework which would enable cities to pursue it. Through their book, Frug and Barron emphasize the need for a "regularized local voice in state decision making about local government law." My sense is that Frug and Barron are precisely right in focusing attention on how states shape what cities like Iowa City can and cannot do. For Iowa's cities to thrive, the state of Iowa needs a thoughtfully crafted urban agenda. With help from legal scholars and advice from amenable state legislators, members of the Metro Coalition (the ten largest cities in the state) could co-draft such an agenda.

Both of these perspectives have merit, and perhaps they can be synthesized. Regardless of which of them one prefers, it is not really possible to know or fully control how one's city will unfold over time. A city is co-crafted step-by-step, and the best council members and a mayor can do is use the discretionary power they have to keep their city moving in the direction they value.

Coda

Little did I know when I stepped down as mayor at the end of 2019 that the following year would be marked by a Senate impeachment trial; a global pandemic; a massive economic downturn; huge street demonstrations and protests following the death of another black man (George Floyd) at the hands of the police;[9] record-setting fires all along the West Coast of the U.S.; the death of a Supreme Court Justice and a rushed effort to install a replacement for her just weeks before the November elections; a victory by Joe Biden over President Trump by 7 million votes and a 51:47 percent margin; frantic efforts by the president and his supporters to undermine the legitimacy of the election; and a resurgence of the pandemic, resulting in over 485,000 deaths from the virus as of mid-February 2021.

Nor did I know that, on January 6, 2021, a few thousand white nationalists, evangelical Christians, violent extremists, conspiracy theorists, and ordinary Republican supporters would storm the U.S. Capitol building in an effort to stop the U.S. Congress from certifying Joe Biden's election and perhaps also to physically harm senators, representatives, and the vice president. So, there was no way I could know that the assault on Congress would lead to the second impeachment of now former President Trump and a second Senate vote not to convict him.

To my surprise, therefore, the events of 2020 and early 2021 have expanded the meaning of this book. Initially intending to report how people in one relatively small city in the middle of the U.S. tried, from 2012 through 2019, to craft their city's future, I now find that the events of the past year have undermined the quality of life in Iowa City and throughout the country and have demonstrated that democratic governance is very much at risk in the United States.

Notes

1 DeLeon (1992) describes how planners' texts figured in efforts to turn San Francisco in a direction preferred by the city's pro-growth regime. In an earlier work (Throgmorton, 2005), I characterized those texts as *tropes* (persuasive figures of argument) in the pro-growth regime's story. Achieving the regime's vision required physical redevelopment, but, more deeply, it required construction of a political

coalition that would supply the strategic leadership, mobilize the resources, and coordinate actors in such a way as to guide and empower the city's transformation.

2 One might counter that politicians come and go and are focused on single issues rather than the city's organized complexity, whereas administrators and bureaucrats provide expertise and stability. So, one might argue, if Iowa City reverted back to a council controlled by the growth machine, the same bureaucrats would also be slow to dismantle all the council had achieved during my 4 years as mayor. Maybe their slow pace and reluctance to change too fast too soon protect us from crazy politicians who might come to power, ignore existing laws, appoint their preferred officials, and try to bypass the City's version of "the Deep State." This is a good topic for debate.

3 With regard to this conflict, I am very influenced by Chantal Mouffe (2016). She claims that confrontation between adversaries constitutes the essence of a vibrant democracy. In her view, "A well-functioning democracy calls for a confrontation of democratic political positions. If this is missing, there is always the danger that this democratic confrontation will be replaced by a confrontation between non-negotiable moral values or essentialist forms of identification" (p. 4). She stresses the importance of having alternatives presented to people, with passions being mobilized in the service of constructing a "people" and forging a progressive "collective will."

4 This echoes a point planning scholar Pierre Clavel (1986) emphasized 35 years ago.

5 Planning scholar Ernest Alexander (2017) makes many claims that are quite compatible with my conception of co-crafting, especially when he stresses the importance of design, complexity, uncertainty, contingency, reciprocal interdependence, and multiple types of planning practice.

6 For a very recent exploration of key concepts, trends, and approaches in contemporary urban governance research, see da Cruz, Rode, and McQuarrie (2019).

7 From a planning theory point of view, this conflict can be interpreted as a conflict between planning "from above" by bureaucratic actors who "see like a state" (Scott, 1998) and social mobilization "from below" by elements of civil society. According to Sanyal's (2018) insightful review of John Friedmann's work, the two types of planning differ in terms of their ways of framing problems, their preferences for technical vs. experiential knowledge, and their willingness to engage in political action to achieve their ends. For insight into insurgent planning, see Sandercock (2003), Miraftab (2009), and Marcuse (2009).

8 There are strong similarities between the kind of mobilized networks Katz and Nowak advocate and collaborative planning as advocated by urban planning scholars Innes and Booher (2010) and others. According to Innes and Booher (2010, p. 8), "A process is collaboratively rational to the extent that all the affected interests jointly engage in face to face dialogue, bringing their various perspectives to the table to deliberate on the problems they face together."

9 Just a few months after I had retired and Bruce T. had replaced me as mayor, large multi-ethnic crowds of protestors led by Iowa Freedom Riders (IFR) peacefully but loudly marched for weeks through different Iowa City neighborhoods every night (at times to city council members' homes) while chanting, "Say their names! George Floyd," carrying signs, and tagging buildings and streets with markers such as "BLM" and "Fu_k 12."

References

Alexander, E. (2017), "Chance and design: From architecture to institutional design", *Journal of the American Planning Association*, v. 83, n. 1, pp. 93–102.

Batty, M. (2018), *Inventing Future Cities*, MIT Press, Cambridge (MA).

Clavel, P. (1986), *The Progressive City: Planning and Participation, 1969–1984*, Rutgers University Press, New Brunswick (NJ).

da Cruz, N. F., Rode, P. and McQuarrie, M. (2019), "New urban governance: A review of current themes and future priorities", *Journal of Urban Affairs*, v. 41, n. 1, pp. 1–19.

DeLeon, R. E. (1992), *Left Coast City: Progressive Politics in San Francisco, 1975–1991*, Lawrence, KS: University Press of Kansas, Lawrence (KS).

Frug, G. E. (1999), *City Making: Building Communities without Building Walls*, Princeton University Press, Princeton (NJ).

Frug, G. E. and Barron, D. J. (2008), *City Bound: How States Stifle Urban Innovation*, Cornell University Press, Ithaca (NY).

Innes, J. E. and Booher, D. E. (2010), *Planning with Complexity: An Introduction to Collaborative Rationality for Public Policy*, Routledge, London (UK).

Katz, B. and Nowak J. (2017), *The New Localism: How Cities Can Thrive in the Age of Populism*, Bookings Institution Press, Washington (DC).

Johnson, B. J., Peck, M. K., and Preston, S. A. (2017), "City managers have ethics too? Comparing planning and city management codes of ethics", *Journal of the American Planning Association*, v. 83, n. 2, pp. 183–201.

Marcuse, P. (2009), "From critical urban theory to the right to the city", *City*, v. 13, n. 2–3, pp. 185–197.

Miraftab, F. (2009), "Insurgent planning: Situating radical planning in the global south", *Planning Theory*, v. 8, n. 1, pp. 32–50.

Mouffe, C. (2016), "Democratic politics and conflict: An agonistic approach", *Política común*, v. 9; available at: https://doi.org/10.3998/pc.12322227.0009.011

Peterson, P. E. (1981), *City Limits*, University of Chicago Press, Chicago (IL).

Sandercock, L. (2003), *Cosmopolis II: Mongrel Cities in the 21ˢᵗ Century*, Continuum, New York (NY).

Sanyal, B. (2018), "A planner's planner: John Friedmann's quest for a general theory of planning", *Journal of the American Planning Association*, v. 84, n. 2, pp. 179–191.

Schragger, R. (2016), *City Power: Urban Governance in a Global Age*, Oxford University Press, New York (NY).

Schumpeter, J. A. (1942), *Capitalism, Socialism and Democracy*, Harper & Row, New York (NY).

Scott, J. C. (1998), *Seeing Like a State: How Certain Schemes to Improve the Human Condition Have Failed*, Yale University Press, New Haven (CT).

Sorensen, A. (2015), "Taking path dependence seriously: An historical institutionalist research agenda in planning history", *Planning Perspectives*, v. 30, n. 1, pp. 17–38.

Sorensen, A. (2018), "Institutions and urban space: Land, infrastructure, and governance in the production of urban property", *Planning Theory & Practice*, v. 19, n. 1, pp. 21–38.

Stone, C. N. (1993), "Urban regimes and the capacity to govern: A political economy approach", *Journal of Urban Affairs*, v. 15, n. 1, pp. 1–28.

Throgmorton, J. A. (2005), "Planning as persuasive storytelling in the context of 'the network society'", in L. Albrecht and S. J. Mandelbaum (eds.), *The Network Society: A New Context for Planning?* Routledge, London, pp. 125–145.

INDEX

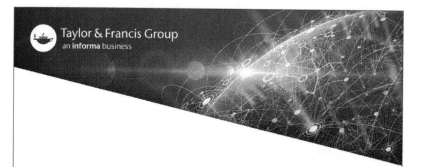